CONTRACT LAW

To gain a deep understanding of contract law, one needs to master not only the rules and principles of the field but also its underlying theory and justification, and its long and intricate history. This book offers an accessible introduction to all aspects of American contract law, useful to both first-year law students and advanced contract scholars. The book is grounded on up-to-date scholarship and contains detailed references to cases, statutes, *Restatements*, and international legal principles. The book takes the reader from contract formation through interpretation and remedies, considering both the practical and the theoretical aspects throughout. Each chapter also includes helpful lists of suggested further reading.

Brian H. Bix is the Frederick W. Thomas Professor of Law and Philosophy at the University of Minnesota. Before teaching at the University of Minnesota, Professor Bix had full-time appointments at King's College London and Quinnipiac Law School, and he has had visiting positions at Georgetown University Law Center, George Washington Law School, University of Haifa, and Interdisciplinary Center Herzliya. He is a member of the American Law Institute and a Reporter for the Uniform Law Commission. He has published widely in contract law, jurisprudence, and family law. He has written, edited, or coedited fourteen books and more than a hundred articles. Bix's work has been translated into seven languages, and he has given invited lectures in countries all over the world.

CAMBRIDGE INTRODUCTIONS TO PHILOSOPHY AND LAW

Series Editors

Brian H. Bix
University of Minnesota

William A. Edmundson
Georgia State University

This introductory series of books provides concise studies of the philosophical foundations of law, of perennial topics in the philosophy of law, and of important and opposing schools of thought. The series is aimed principally at students in philosophy, law, and political science.

Matthew Kramer, *Objectivity and the Rule of Law*

Larry Alexander and Emily Sherwin, *Demystifying Legal Reasoning*

Larry Alexander, Kimberly Kessler Ferzan, and Stephen J. Morse, *Crime and Culpability*

William A. Edmundson, *An Introduction to Rights,* 2nd edition

Robin West, *Normative Jurisprudence*

Gregory S. Alexander and Eduardo S. Peñalver, *An Introduction to Property Theory*

Contract Law

RULES, THEORY, AND CONTEXT

BRIAN H. BIX

University of Minnesota

CAMBRIDGE
UNIVERSITY PRESS

CAMBRIDGE UNIVERSITY PRESS
Cambridge, New York, Melbourne, Madrid, Cape Town,
Singapore, São Paulo, Delhi, Mexico City

Cambridge University Press
32 Avenue of the Americas, New York, NY 10013-2473, USA

www.cambridge.org
Information on this title: www.cambridge.org/9780521615532

First published 2012

Printed in the United States of America

A catalog record for this publication is available from the British Library.

Library of Congress Cataloging in Publication Data

Bix, Brian H.
Contract law : rules, theory, and context / Brian H. Bix.
p. cm. – (Cambridge introductions to philosophy and law)
Includes bibliographical references and index.
ISBN 978-0-521-85046-9 (hardback)
1. Contracts – United States.   I. Title.
KF801.B55   2012
346.7302–dc23   2012012299

ISBN 978-0-521-85046-9 Hardback
ISBN 978-0-521-61553-2 Paperback

Contents

Preface

The series in which this book appears is Cambridge Introductions to Philosophy and Law. There is a special challenge to philosophical introductions to law – in particular, when the topic to be introduced "philosophically" is a doctrinal area of law. It is difficult to speak knowledgeably about the theoretical aspects of contract law in general, or about particular subcategories (doctrinal rules and principles, or transaction types), without a strong grounding in the specific rules and cases.[1] For that reason, this book offers an introduction to philosophy and contract law that is grounded on the detailed rules and principles of American contract law; the book then offers theoretical claims that can be made regarding those rules and principles. As will be seen, such claims can be made at different levels: the individual rules, "doctrine," transaction types, and American contract law more generally. It will be part of the theoretical argument of Chapters 8 and 9 that particular claims about the nature of (American) contract law, and claims one level of abstraction up, about the nature of contract theorizing, are weakened or refuted by the details of existing contract law rules. The theoretical discussions in this book are most present in Chapters 1, 8, and 9, and in end sections of other chapters; the historical discussions are primarily in Chapter 2 and one section of Chapter 3; there are doctrinal discussions throughout.

It is also part of the view underlying this text that theories of an area of law need to be supported by, or at least informed by, history. Understanding contract law is in part a process of understanding why we have the rules and principles we have. Too often in law schools, law journals, and elsewhere, discussions of the purpose of contract doctrine (and doctrine from other areas of law) are a strange form of "just so" story known as "rational reconstruction" – what justification could be offered for the rules we actually have, regardless of whether that justification

---

[1] This assumption is generally shared. One can find a comparable level of detail in other, better-known discussions of contract theory (e.g., C. Fried 1981).

has any connection to the actual reasons for why the rule was introduced or why it persisted.[2]

I do not mean to dismiss rational reconstruction; it is valuable to legal reasoning in the United States (and many other countries) because courts actually use it, so practitioners should be adept at it as well. However, there is a type of understanding of doctrine that can come only from familiarity with the actual origins and purposes of rules, even beyond the current reworkings we can imagine for those rules and principles.

What does it mean to have a contract law theory? A theory is an explanation of the subject of the theory,[3] but what does it mean to explain contract law? If someone asks you to explain the game of baseball or a legislative process, one's initial response would be to detail the rules under which the activity occurs. However, those seeking an explanation of contract law are looking for something more than a recitation of doctrinal rules. The questioner would likely want a deeper explanation, one that discussed how the rules and practices got to be the way they are (and this is the role history plays in theories of doctrinal areas) and why they have been maintained rather than radically revised (and here is the place for justification of some sort).

However, the process of explanation is complicated by the dynamic nature of law (in particular – though not exclusively – common law areas of law), where it is the case not only that the law changes regularly and significantly but also that explanations, justifications, and recharacterizations play a role in those changes.[4] This is the sort of feedback that Dworkin captured in his idea of "constructive interpretation."[5] And as Michael Moore has pointed out, theory – at least, theorizing of a sort – plays a role within legal reasoning and legal practice, as much as being about legal reasoning and legal practice.[6]

In Chapter 7, and again in Chapter 9, I express skepticism about the idea of "contract law" as a simple category, or as an area that is likely to be helpfully explained or justified by a single universal theory. However, given that attitude toward the subject, a reader might wonder on what basis I have selected the topics to

---

[2] Of course, to the extent that a rule serves a present purpose, even if it were not its original purpose, this may help explain why the rule has persisted. (I am grateful to Daniel Schwarcz for this point.)

[3] Barnett (1986: 269) asserts (in the context of presenting and defending his own theory of contract law) that "[t]heories are problem-solving devices" and that "[w]e assess the merits of a particular theory by its ability to solve the problems that give rise for a need for a theory." As is indicated in the coming chapters, I think this view of theory in general, and contract theory in particular, is too focused on the perspective of the judge or advocate, and not sufficiently on the observer who may not have an immediate stake in doctrinal disputes.

[4] In discussing alternative objectives for theories, Moore (2000: 732; 1990: 120–121) distinguishes explanation (in terms of historical-causal discussions) from description (a discovery of patterns that may be distant from either historical discussion or justification and rational reconstruction). The distinction is useful, but I prefer to use "explanation" broadly, because I think that the idea of explanation ranges over a number of different objectives and that it is important to emphasize that scope.

[5] Dworkin 1986: 49–53.

[6] Moore 1990: 118–129.

be covered in a book called *Contract Law*. The simple response is that I have picked the topics that are most often covered in American law school courses under this name (although there is sufficient variation in coverage that for any given course there may be some topics I do not touch on). These courses generally deal with the rules for enforcement of promises and exchanges in our society. The way this book tracks the conventional law school course also means that, although Article 2 of the Uniform Commercial Code is regularly mentioned throughout the book, the text follows the conventional practice of these courses in giving only sporadic coverage to the special rules for the sale of goods and related commercial law topics. (One technical matter relating to sources and citations: all references to the Uniform Commercial Code (UCC) are, unless otherwise indicated, to the prior Articles 1 and 2 of the Code, not to the revised UCC.[7])

Additionally, American contract law is primarily a matter of state (not federal or local) law. Therefore, there are potentially fifty-one different rules of American contract law for any given issue.[8] Although in practice there is significant convergence in different states' approaches, different approaches among the states remain on many issues. I have tried to note the variation in the text, but students and practitioners are well advised to check their own state's law before assuming that the present text accurately reflects the contract law of their jurisdiction on any particular point of law.

I have tried to write this book so that it could be of use to a variety of audiences for different purposes: to give a concise overview of basic doctrine while also offering some more detailed arguments about the rules and underlying policies; and offering theoretical and historical arguments for scholars more interested in those aspects of contract law. With luck, this book might thus be beneficial to first-year students, new to contract law; to academics already well established in the field; and to those in between, simply curious about the fascinating issues raised in and about contract law.

I am grateful for the comments and suggestions of Matthew D. Adler, Peter A. Alces, Larry A. Alexander, Curtis Bridgeman, Sean Coyle, William A. Edmundson, Daniel A. Farber, Bruce W. Frier, Daniel J. Gifford, Andrew S. Gold, Robert W. Gordon, Oren Gross, Robert A. Hillman, Peter Huang, Matthew H. Kramer, Jody S. Kraus, Jeff Lipshaw, David McGowan, Alexander M. Meiklejohn, Dennis M. Patterson, Margaret Jane Radin, Beatrice Rehl, Mark D. Rosen, Keith A. Rowley, Hanoch Sheinman, Stephen A. Smith, Jane K. Winn, an anonymous reader for Cambridge University Press, and participants at faculty workshops at the Georgetown University

---

[7] Revised Article 1 was promulgated in 2001; revised Article 2 was promulgated in 2003. Generally, the section numbering was not changed by the revisions; where it was I often offer both the pre-revision and the revised section numbers. Revised Article 1 has been adopted by thirty-seven states; no states have adopted revised Article 2, and in May 2011, the American Law Institute withdrew the 2003 Amendments to UCC Article 2 (and the Amendments to Article 2A).

[8] That is, the fifty states and the District of Columbia.

Law Center, University of Illinois Law School, the University of Minnesota Law School, the William S. Boyd School of Law at the University of Nevada–Las Vegas, and the Analytical Legal Philosophy Conference. I am especially grateful to William A. Edmundson, Joshua Gitelson, Brett H. McDonnell, Daniel Schwarcz, Jason Steck, and William Whitford for reading (at various stages) the entire manuscript. I also want to pass along my special thanks to the series editor at the time this book was commissioned, William A. Edmundson, and to the Cambridge University Press editors in charge of the series, Beatrice Rehl and John Berger, for their support throughout this process.[9]

---

[9] On a related point, I should note that I recognize the dubious appearance of being an author in a Cambridge series in which I am a coeditor. By way of explanation, I want to report that I was commissioned to write this text (and had a proposal approved by readers and by the Cambridge University Press Board) long before I had been asked to coedit the series, and long before I even had any thought of doing so. It may have been an error to have me write this text (I leave that to others to judge), but it was not self-dealing.

1

Philosophical Problems of Contract Law

Contract law is a category within legal practice (and legal education), although there are many occasions in which contract law has significant overlaps with other categories, or where the borderline is not especially clear. (For example, some commentators have argued that contract law should be seen as a mere subcategory of tort law;[1] and, in different ways, the boundary lines between contract law and areas such as restitution and property are fluid and uncertain much of the time.)

Contract law is a category of particular rules and decisions, but (as elsewhere in law) it is a mistake to focus too narrowly on the "facts" of the actual decisions and the "black-letter rules" of treatises. Law is, and likely has always been, a reflective exercise, in which there is a natural tendency (among practitioners and observers both) to seek more general principles, to explain and justify past decisions and give guidance for future decisions.

One of the problems facing those who wish to reflect on contract law – or on any other area of law – is the appropriate level of generality or abstraction. There is an obvious attraction to finding the essence of contract law (perhaps of contract law everywhere, and in all possible legal systems). Part of the argument of this book (particularly, Chapters 8 and 9) is that this is not the right – or at least not the best – focus. In short (the longer argument is detailed in those chapters), the claim is that approaches to promises and agreements vary too greatly (both in substantive rules and in procedural constraints and remedial options) from one jurisdiction to another, and over time, for any universal theory to be justifiable (for such a theory to create more benefits and insights than costs and distortions). This book emphasizes a narrower focus: on this particular legal system, at this time, and more topic by topic than grand narrative. However, the hope is that this book has things of value

---

[1] *E.g.,* Gilmore 1974.

to offer even to those who disagree about the best direction for contract theory and about the ultimate conclusions.

This book offers an overview of the major doctrines and principles of American contract law while also looking at the themes and theories that ground them. Additionally, the book gives a summary of the major theoretical debates that surround the various topics and rules of contract law.

This text is primarily an exploration of American contract law as it currently is. At different points, the analysis may indicate possible criticisms of the current law, with implications for what government (whether legislatures, courts, or administrative agencies) might do to improve the law, although law reform is not the primary task of the text.

A persistent theme in this text – and it is certainly not distinctive to contract law – is that government regulation (and, here, both legislation and common law judicial legislation are understood as regulation of individual contracting) is hampered to some extent by its need to be general and predictable. The need for generality is most obviously true in legislation and administrative regulation, but it is also true for judicial action – which, although it decides particular cases, sets precedent for an indefinite number of future cases.[2] Parties are differently situated in their levels of knowledge, rationality, sophistication, bargaining power, vulnerability, resources, and so on. Similarly, agreements can be viewed as quite various, whether considering the kinds of parties (e.g., business to business, consumer contracts, informal agreements among friends and family members) or the subject matter of the agreement (e.g., sales of goods, employment agreements, residential leases, commercial leases, franchise agreements, premarital agreements).

The extent to which it would be better to have quite general rules and principles, applied to all agreements, or better to have rules and principles responsive to the context of individual agreements remains a matter of dispute among theorists, with the different views reflected in (rather than resolved by) the doctrines and case law.

As is discussed in greater detail here, it is not the view of this book that there is a single theory of contract law (although the text summarizes the views of theorists who take that approach). The philosophical aspects of contract law considered here partly are reflections on that question but, to a greater extent, are the theoretical disputes reflected in particular doctrines and lines of judicial decisions.

Among the persistent issues and themes that we will see are the extent to which the contracting parties' subjective understandings should prevail when they differ from the "objective" meaning of the terms used or the actions undertaken; what role, if any, the fairness of the contractual terms should play in determining whether agreements are enforced; the extent to which law should impose and enforce formal requirements for the enforcement of transactions; and what the appropriate remedy is for a breach of contract.

---

[2] E.g., Schauer 1987.

At the end of Chapters 2–7, there are brief discussions of the theoretical implications of the chapter's discussions. Chapters 8 and 9 offer more extended considerations of larger contract law theory topics.

SUGGESTED FURTHER READING

Peter Benson (ed.), *The Theory of Contract Law: New Essays* (Cambridge: Cambridge University Press, 2001).

Charles Fried, *Contract as Promise: A Theory of Contractual Obligation* (Cambridge, MA: Harvard University Press, 1981).

2

History and Sources

Whether one thinks of law primarily as a kind of social practice or social institution or as an integral part of practical reasoning – developing reasons for action – law is a purposive human enterprise. As such, it is useful to consider legal history: the original context in which legal rules and practices were developed and the circumstances and concerns that prompted their development. This chapter attempts to give an overview – necessarily a brief and somewhat sketchy overview – of the history of American contract law.

Along with the general context value of history, there is sometimes a specific need for historical explanation – where moral or consequentialist reconstructions of rules and practices fail, a reference to the historical reasons for a certain rule may be the only valid explanation.[1] This becomes an explanation in the minimal terms of showing why we have the rules we have, not any more robust sense of offering a moral or policy justification for keeping (or obeying) those rules.[2] (Of course, one justification for keeping a rule might be that, although it would not be sensible to adopt the rule if starting from scratch, it would be too costly – and insufficiently beneficial – to change the rule at this point.[3])

Historical origin, as a simple causal narrative, may explain why or how a rule originated, but something further may need to be said about why the rule has

---

[1] Cf. Holmes 1897: 468–473; Calabresi 1998. I want to be clear that in advocating the occasional importance of history in explaining contract law (and perhaps other areas of law), I am not thereby endorsing the rather ambitious claims about the relationship of society, law, and history associated with the school of historical jurisprudence (a school associated with the works of Sir Henry Maine and Friedrich Carl von Savigny, and sympathetically discussed in Berman 2005).

[2] As Holmes famously wrote: "It is revolting to have no better reason for a rule of law than that so it was laid down in the time of Henry IV. It is still more revolting if the grounds upon which it was laid down have vanished long since, and the rule simply persists from blind imitation of the past." Holmes 1897: 469.

[3] I am grateful to Daniel Schwarcz for this point.

persisted.[4] Although there are some strange rules from the seventeenth century that persist in Anglo-American contract law to this day, there are, of course, many, many more strange rules from that time that justifiably fell by the wayside long ago. One might suppose that rules that have persisted have done so for some reason: that the rule has some benefits, or at least no burdens on practice that are too significant.

If one wants to trace the history of American contract law, one would focus on two distinct sources: ancient Roman law and the English common law. These will be discussed in turn;[5] there follow sections here on the sources of contract law and international rules and principles. An additional historical survey connected with the doctrine of consideration appears in Section B of Chapter 3.

A. ROMAN LAW

Early Roman law is interesting for the study of contract law, as it is one of the first systematic attempts to regulate promises and transactions, as well as the first documented example of enforcing consensual contracts without the requirement of formalities.[6] In addition, Roman law is the source of the civil law tradition, an approach distinct from the common law tradition, and an approach that displays interesting alternative ideas about whether, when, and how to enforce promises and transactions (as we will see, in passing, at various points in this book).

At least one Roman jurist, Gaius, offered the beginning of a general view of (if not a general theory of) contract law, when he introduced the term *contractus* (and distinguished it from *delictus*, which corresponds to our tort law).[7] Contract here meant, roughly, any lawful conduct that gave rise to liability (again, the contrast with tort).[8] However, most commentators seem to think that "in fact the Romans had no abstract concept of 'contract.'"[9]

Roman law in this area was not a matter of general principles but a series of more scattered functional forms.[10] There were set rules for loans, deposits, pledges, leases, sales, and partnerships.[11] The result seemed, from a modern perspective, "uneven"; for example, the state "enforced an agreement to exchange goods for money, but not an agreement to exchange goods for services."[12] If an agreement did not fall

---

4 I am grateful to Brett McDonnell for this point.
5 The history of American commercial law is a distinct topic, mostly beyond the scope of this text, but is well summarized in Rogers 1995.
6 Watson 1984: 8.
7 Gaius, *Institutes* 3.88, as cited and discussed in Gordley 2002: 11–12.
8 Kaser 1980: 197.
9 Watson 1984: 2.
10 "It is often said that the Romans never developed a system of contract but only of individual contracts" (Watson 1984: 3 (footnote omitted)), and even these developed separately, over the course of centuries. Watson 1984: 2–3.
11 Kaser 1980: 202–232.
12 Watson 1984: 1.

under one of the set forms, it might nonetheless be binding if the parties had used specified language (*stipulatio*).[13] However, the *stipulatio* failed as a general form of contract, as it required the parties to be in one another's presence, and therefore precluded enforceable transactions in many cases where the parties were merchants living some distance apart.[14]

The influence of Roman law of contracts on the English writ system (discussed in the following section), and subsequently on modern American law, has been largely sporadic and indirect.[15] One can see aspects of the Roman law view of contracts in the treatise writers of Continental Europe, and in the civil law codes that developed in those countries, and those sources in turn had occasional effects on the development of English law. There is also Roman law influence on the ecclesiastical law, which seems to have affected the way English contract law developed. The extent to which the English common law "received" or was influenced by Roman law remains a matter of some controversy,[16] but the resolution of that dispute need not concern us. It is sufficient to note the significant evidence that the civil law tradition influenced the development of English and American contract law at a crucial time – the nineteenth century – when many significant doctrinal concepts were developed or solidified.[17]

B. ENGLISH WRIT SYSTEM

In medieval times, European societies generally did not treat what we now call contract as a separate category. In some Continental European communities, one might have distinguished between different kinds of claims and wrongs, but these categories would cut across the boundary lines of what we now call contract, property, and tort.[18]

English contract law – or the earliest even rough approximation of contract law (or, indeed, private law generally) – begins in the thirteenth century.[19] Both before that

---

[13] Kaser 1980: 206–209. Paradoxically, it appears that the general form and procedure for enforcing agreements, *stipulatio*, appeared in Roman law first, and the narrower forms of enforceable contracts followed later. Watson 1984: 4–5. The difference between the narrow specified agreements and all other enforceable agreements is sometimes characterized in terms of "nominate" and "innominate" agreements.

[14] Watson 1984: 16–17.

[15] J. H. Baker 2003: 3–13. For a view expressing a somewhat stronger influence, see Ibbetson 1999: 1: "The Common law of obligations grew out of the intermingling of native ideas and sophisticated Roman learning. The friction between them was a prime force for legal change, and has remained so right up to the present day."

[16] E.g., Zimmermann 1996: xi.

[17] See Simpson 1975b. This influence apparently occurred primarily from the earliest English treatise writers, who, it seemed, borrowed significantly from existing civil law treatises. Simpson 1975b: 254–257.

[18] Ibbetson 1999: 1–6.

[19] Ibbetson 1999: 13–23. "The twelfth-century royal courts seem to have been little concerned with personal obligations." Ibbetson 1999: 13. For the state of the civil law prior to the thirteenth century, see Glanvill 1965.

time, and for generations afterward, disputes regarding private agreements could be brought to local (non–common law) courts and other tribunals (including church courts).[20] However, private law doctrines were developed not in those courts but rather in the King's Court. Over time, the common law King's Court gained greater and greater jurisdiction over private disputes, and it is in those courts that contract law doctrine and principles, as we know them, were primarily developed.[21]

In medieval English law, if an action was brought before the King's Court, the plaintiff had to plead a series of facts to make a case fit within certain accepted "writs" (causes of action): a series of facts needed to be alleged, and, if proved, the court would provide a set remedy.[22] Those writs closest to the modern understanding of (breach of) contract were covenant and debt. For covenant, the agreement would have had to have been made with a "specialty" – a formal document affixed with a wax seal – and the plaintiff would have had to claim that the defendant had not complied with the terms of that document.[23] For debt, one had to claim an agreement under which one was owed a fixed sum.[24] Those who performed a service and had not been paid, or had lent money and not had it returned, could obviously use the writ of debt; the use of a bond allowed buyers of service and products also to use the writ. Under the bond, the person providing the product or service promised to pay a large sum of money, with that obligation becoming void if the service was done or the product delivered by a particular date.[25]

The limitation of covenant was that most agreements were not made with the formality required to bring this action.[26] With debt, the limitation was that the plaintiff might be complaining of something other than the failure to pay a fixed

---

[20] E.g., Simpson 1975a: 3–5; J. H. Baker 2002: 12–27, 318–320, 327; Helmholz 1975, 1990. As discussed here, for the church courts, plaintiffs had to allege that the agreement had been made under formal oath; the action in the church court "existed . . . because it was a sin to violate one's oath." Helmholz 1975: 423.

[21] However, there are indications that the slow development of the writ of assumpsit in the central courts might reflect the availability of "an analogous remedy in many local courts." J. H. Baker 2003: 813. For the role of the canon law in developing the idea of general contractual liability and also a number of its doctrines, see Berman 2008.

[22] There is evidence that these writs developed from orders by the king to transfer property based on wrongdoing; the writs were modifications of such orders, allowing the subjects of the order to defend against the accusation in court. Simpson 1975a: 54–55.

[23] There is some evidence that the writ was not so narrowly applied in its earliest years, but the requirement of a sealed deed was firmly entrenched by 1321. J. H. Baker 2002: 318–319; *see also* Ibbetson 1999: 24–28

[24] E.g., Simpson 1975a: 73. More precisely, debt was a demand that the defendant yield up some amount of an undifferentiated matter – either money or fungible goods (unspecified goods of some generic description) – that belonged to the plaintiff. J. H. Baker 2002: 321 & n.25. For the retrieval of identifiable goods (whether owed under a purchase agreement or left as a bailment), the appropriate writ was detinue. J. H. Baker 2002: 321, 391–394.

[25] J. H. Baker 2002: 323–324.

[26] See, e.g., Simpson 1975a: 43. Even where the requisite formality was present in the agreement, parties rarely used the writ of covenant. Simpson suggests that the reason for the rarity of use might have been that most agreements were under seal, and the party seeking enforcement of an agreement under seal also had the option of enforcing a penal bond (under a writ of debt), where the recovery would likely

sum, for example, damage caused by an inadequate performance. In addition, a defendant to an action of debt could resist the claim simply by "compurgation" ("wager of law"): having a sufficient number of (usually, eleven) other people claim under oath that the defendant was not in fact indebted to the plaintiff.[27] Even without considering this defense, the writs of covenant and debt left the vast majority of parties complaining of breach of their informal contract with no recourse at common law.[28]

In part in response to the limitations of covenant and debt, the common law courts developed – slowly (over centuries) – an alternative avenue of relief. The existing writ of trespass, which had been available for public harms, was slowly extended to private wrongs (under the label "trespass on the case"). Where the claim was a private wrong based on a duty the defendant had voluntarily assumed (as in a commercial exchange), the writ became known as "assumpsit."[29] Assumpsit had no requirement of a specialty and no defense by wager of law. By 1602, it was held that plaintiffs could elect to use assumpsit, even in cases that would normally have fallen clearly under debt.[30]

Modern contract law thus developed (in a sense) out of tort law: assumpsit was a reworked action on the case.[31] Ibbetson writes: "From its inception, the emergent

have been much greater than the damages available under a claimed breach of covenant. Simpson 1975a: 117.

[27] Simpson 1975a: 137–138; McGovern 1968. The idea being that most people in those times thought that perjury under oath would cause them to be damned (the vast majority of defendants chose trial by jury over wager of law (Simpson 1975a: 138–139)), so having eleven other people swear under oath to one's position was an impressive showing. Simpson 1975a: 139–140; Milsom 2003: 9. For whatever the combination of reasons, only a small percentage of defendants (in one calculation, only 10 percent of cases in 1535) avoided liability through wager of law. J. H. Baker 2003: 836.

There is some evidence that the chancellor would sometimes allow creditors to invoke equitable jurisdiction to prevent a debtor from avoiding a debt through compurgation. Barbour 1914: 99–100. It should be noted that although lying under oath was perceived as endangering the soul of the perjurer, he or she was apparently not in danger of criminal prosecution. Simpson 1975a: 138.

There were certain categories of actions in which wager of law was not allowed (including debt on a bond and debt for rent), and the Court of Common Pleas "showed no hostility to the procedure," whereas the King's Bench began in the sixteenth century to resist the use of the procedure. J. H. Baker 2003: 835–837, 871–874.

[28] Simpson 1975a: 47. However, there may have been limited recourse in other courts: it appeared that the chancellor sometimes enforced oral contracts. Barbour 1914: 160–168. Also, as noted herein, until the late sixteenth century, promises could also be enforced in the ecclesiastical courts if the promise was made under oath, and there are indications that such actions constituted a significant portion of church court business. Helmholz 1975, 1990: 50–59.

[29] Simpson states that assumpsit had the sense of an undertaking, something stronger than mere agreement, with connotations that the defendant had done something or said something that gave sufficient assurance that the defendant might be strictly responsible for ensuring that some matter occurred. Simpson 1975a: 215–218.

[30] Slade's Case (1602) 4 Coke Rep. 91a, 76 Eng. Rep. 1074 (Q.B.).

[31] Helmholz (1975: 422) writes: "It is well known that when assumpsit began to be used in cases of nonfeasance in the sixteenth century, the allegations of deceit and tortuous damage used in medieval assumpsit and appropriate in cases of misfeasance, did not drop out of the pleadings. . . . Most assumpsit actions also included the allegation of lost reputation and profits" (footnote omitted).

action on the case for breach of contract was held in tension between its trespassory and contractual aspects. This tension was not to be fully resolved until the first half of the seventeenth century, and the developed form of the action was never to lose the scars of its passage through the thicket of tort."[32] Among the doctrines that show a tort law origin is the focus both in breach of contract and in "quasi-contract" (restitutionary) claims on the harm caused rather than on the promise made.[33]

A separate influence on the development of the writ of assumpsit was the suit in the English Church courts of *fidei laesio* (breach of faith),[34] by which parties could enforce promises made under oath. (Although the ecclesiastical courts had been directed as early as the twelfth century not to hear cases involving agreements,[35] they continued to do so well through the sixteenth century, under the rubric of enforcing oaths made to God, which in the case of merchants might include oaths about the performance in a commercial exchange. Only when the common law courts developed the writ of assumpsit did the church courts stop having a significant role in enforcing commercial contracts.[36])

As Richard Helmholz has argued, there is significant indirect evidence that *fidei laesio* was phased out by the church courts at the same time assumpsit was being developed, which strongly affected the course that writ took. Especially in the early years of assumpsit (when it remained largely distinct from the writ of debt), the elements that needed to be pled and the obligations that could be enforced tracked those of *fidei laesio*.[37]

The initial resistance to the expansion of the writ of assumpsit was understandable: where the process of proof by evidence was at a rudimentary stage, there was a fear that allowing plaintiffs to go forward without having presented a formal deed, and without allowing defendants to resort to wager of law, would create a great danger of fraud. Initially, this fear led the courts to allow assumpsit only in cases of misfeasance, something done poorly (as contrasted with allegations of nonfeasance, something that was not done at all), where the partial performance would give evidence of the agreement.[38] At that time, cases of nonfeasance, allegations of something not

---

[32] Ibbetson 1999: 130.

[33] Helmholz 1990: 64–65.

[34] More precisely, the suit was *"causa fidei laesionis seu perjurii."* Helmholz 1975: 406. The church courts could hear these cases because of their "general jurisdiction over the sins of laymen," here, the sin "to violate one's sworn promise." Helmholz 1975: 406 (footnote omitted). As Remus Valsan has pointed out, the ecclesiastical courts would often focus more on what needed to be done to remove the spiritual dangers to the defendant's soul (who had broken an oath made to God, thus putting that person's salvation at risk) than on redressing the wrong done to the plaintiff. Valsan 2009. Canon law developed remedies to the wronged parties only gradually over time. Berman 2008: 130–131.

[35] Helmholz 1975: 407–408.

[36] Farnsworth 2002: 701–702. "Both here [England] and on the mainland the secular courts were put on their mettle, so to speak, by the competition of the spiritual power." Pollock 1893: 390.

[37] Helmholz 1975: 408–428.

[38] Simpson 1975a: 222–227.

being done at all, were shunted to covenant, or to no recovery at all (in the High Court) if there were no deed. However, this requirement fell away over the course of the fifteenth and early sixteenth centuries, and the writ was extended to cover nonfeasance as well.[39]

Many of the distinctive doctrines of American contract law doctrine can be traced to nineteenth-century England – what is significant here, of course, is not the tracing of American law to England (most of American law was brought over with the British colonists and was maintained even after independence) but the fact that so many doctrines developed relatively recently. These include the doctrines of offer and acceptance,[40] the requirement of an intention to create legal relations, frustration, mistake, and foreseeability of damages.[41] Many of these doctrines were in turn adapted by English jurists from civil law, or from earlier Roman law sources.[42]

Part of the reason for the recent development of much of contract law doctrine is the distinctive nature of law and procedure under the writ system: where all the focus was on detailed rules of pleading, and there was little attention to substantive rules of proof. As Simpson states:

> Under the medieval system of common law, attention concentrated upon the pleadings, and the intricate body of rules as to what must be pleaded, and what must not, gave expression to principles of substantive law. But once the case passed the pleading stage, and an issue was submitted to a jury, we enter an area of no-law. There existed at this time no law of evidence.... Indeed many attempts to trace back rules of law into medieval times are futile because of a failure to appreciate the fact that on many questions there were then no legal rules.[43]

The historical origins of many of the doctrines of contract law are discussed in passing in the coming chapters, as those doctrines are analyzed. One topic, however, warrants separate discussion here – the history of the doctrine of consideration, which is considered in Chapter 3, Section B.

C. THE RANGE AND LIMITS OF CONTRACT LAW

Sir Frederick Pollock and Frederic William Maitland, in their famous history of early English law, wrote the following:

> We have been laying stress on the late growth of a law of contract, so for one moment we must glance at another side of the picture. The master who taught us that "the

---

[39] Simpson 1975a: 248–273; Ibbetson 1999: 126–230.
[40] As Simpson (1975b: 260) points out, the doctrine of consideration predates offer and acceptance by 300 years.
[41] Simpson 1975b: 258–277.
[42] *See, e.g.,* Simpson 1975b: 259–261, 266–268, 274–276.
[43] Simpson 1975a: 245–246 (footnote omitted). The context of this discussion was the question of what was needed (in the fifteenth century) to show that a warranty had been given. Simpson 1975a: 245–246.

movement of progressive societies has hitherto been a movement from Status to Contract," was quick to add that feudal society was governed by the law of contract. There is no paradox here. In the really feudal centuries men could do by a contract, by the formal contract of vassalage or commendation, many things that they can not do now-a-days. They could contract to stand by each other in warfare "against all men who can live and die"; they could (as Domesday Book says) "go with their land" to any lord whom they pleased; they could make the relation between king and subject look like the outcome of an agreement; the law of contract threatened to swallow up all public law. Those were the golden days of "free," if "formal," contract. When first the idea that men by their promises can fix their rights and duties is emerging, it is an unruly, anarchical idea. If there is to be any law at all, contract must be taught to know its place.[44]

There is much talk among commentators and judges about "freedom of contract," and this book refers to that concept and ideal as well. The notion is that parties (at least those who are legally competent adults) should have an unhindered right to enter legally binding arrangements, without regard as to whether the terms of the agreement seem to others to be wise or fair. However, among modern commentators, even the most ardent supporters of freedom of contract assume that there are certain agreements that are not and should not be enforceable, such as an agreement that would create even the possibility of becoming another party's slave.[45] Pollock and Maitland remind us of these constraints, in part by pointing out that some of them were once absent, that once one could agree to become someone's vassal or serf. Contract law's domain was once far greater than it is now, dominating much of tort law (as many tort duties were frequently thought to be restricted by "privity of contract"[46]) and large sections of public law as well.

D. SOURCES OF CONTRACT LAW

1. *Domestic Law*

Much of this chapter has tried to offer a sense of the rich history behind current doctrines of American law. On the whole, American law came from English law, and both English and American law regarding contracts was, until quite recently, primarily developed by the courts through case-by-case decision making. One prominent exception is the Statute of Frauds (discussed in Chapter 3, Section C), which started as a single statute in England and is the general name for a large number

---

[44] Pollock & Maitland 1895: vol. 2, 230. The reference to "from Status to Contract" is to the famous quotation by Sir Henry Maine (Maine 1986: 165).

[45] *E.g.*, Craswell 2012.

[46] *See, e.g., Donoghue v. Stevenson* [1932] A.C. 562 (H.L.) (extending tort liability beyond privity of contract).

of provisions in most state legislative codes requiring written evidence for a wide variety of agreements.

A group of prominent academics, under the auspices of the American Law Institute, have produced two *"Restatements"* of the law of contracts, the most recent in 1979. The *Restatement* volumes sought to summarize the case law and legal principles in the area, at times choosing among the conflicting rules in different states according to the approach the commentators thought best and at times promoting rules that might not yet have had the support of many, or even any, court decisions. The *Restatements* are very influential, and many courts have considered it sufficient to note that an approach was approved by the *Restatement* to justify adopting it. However, the *Restatements* are not themselves law, and they have no legal force unless and until courts adopt their recommended rules. This text frequently cites *Restatement* sections as support for propositions of contract law, but with the understanding that, by itself, *Restatement* support gives no guarantee by itself that all, or even most, states follow the view in question.

The first significant dent in the domination of American contract law by judge-made rules came in the middle of the twentieth century, with the drafting of the Uniform Commercial Code (UCC), Article 2 of which deals with the sale of goods.[47] The UCC was adopted to try to support commerce by creating greater uniformity and predictability across different states.[48] Article 2 of the UCC[49] has been adopted by all American states except Louisiana. (The special contract and commercial law rules of Louisiana are not discussed in this text.) However, for agreements other than the sales of goods, most of the applicable law remains judge made. For better or for worse, contract law has escaped the large-scale codification that has supplanted judge-made law in other areas.

There are a number of state and federal statutes and administrative regulations that touch on different sorts of agreements, often relating to the protection of consumers, tenants, and small businesses. Some of these are discussed in Chapter 7, which deals with particular types of transactions. A few, such as the federal antitrust laws, are

[47] In addition, a small number of states, for example, California and Georgia, have codified significant portions of the common law principles of contract law. The extent to which this codification has limited or altered the judicial development of contract doctrine in those states is not clear.

[48] As mentioned in the preface, unless otherwise indicated, references to the UCC will be to prior UCC Articles 1 and 2, not to the revised versions of Article 1 (promulgated in 2001) or Article 2 (promulgated in 2003). Generally, the section numbering was not changed by the revisions; where it was, I usually offer both the pre-revision and the revised section numbers. (Revised Article 1 has been adopted by thirty-seven states at the time of writing; no states have adopted revised Article 2, and the American Law Institute in 2011 officially withdrew the 2003 amendments to Article 2.)

[49] Future references to UCC Article 2 may go by just "UCC," for simplicity's sake. The other articles of the UCC have great importance in commercial and real estate transactions, but it is usually only Article 2 (and the definitions of Article 1) that is covered in contract law courses, books, and discussions. In any event, the citation of UCC provisions indicates which article they come from, by the first number in the citation (e.g., § 2-207 and § 2-313 are both from Article 2).

sufficiently complex that they require whole books and courses unto themselves, and they are far beyond the scope of the present project.

2. *International Sources*

In recent years, developments of contract law within particular jurisdictions have been both influenced and augmented by the development of rules and principles promulgated by transnational organizations, with the intention either to regulate international transactions or to create some convergence in the rules of different nations.

The most important such source is the UN Convention on Contracts for the International Sale of Goods (known generally as "CISG," or sometimes as "the Vienna Convention"). The CISG was the product of a 1980 diplomatic conference sponsored by the UN Commission on International Trade Law, but it did not go into effect until 1988.[50] As of May 2012, seventy-eight countries were party to the CISG, including nine of the ten top trading countries (the United Kingdom is the sole exception; Japan is the most recent signature among the group, in 2009).[51] The provisions of the CISG apply to international transactions, where the transactors come from nations that are both signatories to the CISG, although the agreement does not apply to consumer agreements.[52]

Where contracts are entered between merchants from different countries, each of which is a signatory to the CISG, then the CISG applies as a matter of law.[53] Like Article 2 of the Uniform Commercial Code, the CISG applies only to the sale of movable goods. As noted, unlike UCC Article 2, it does not apply to the sale of goods to consumers.[54] (There are some other small exclusions, such as relating to auctions, stocks, and electricity.) As with what is probably the majority interpretation of the UCC, where there are transactions involving both goods and services, the CISG applies where goods are "the predominant part" of the transaction.[55]

---

[50] Lookofsky 2008. The United States ratified the CISG in late 1986, effective January 1, 1988.

[51] The list of ratifiers is given at http://www.uncitral.org/uncitral/en/uncitral_texts/sale_goods/1980CISG_status.html.

[52] CISG art. 2(a). Although the CISG, where it applies, preempts state contract law, there is at least one case that holds that it would not preempt a state promissory estoppel (*Restatement* § 90) claim. *Geneva Pharmaceuticals Technology Corp. v. Barr Laboratories*, 201 F. Supp. 2d 236 (S.D.N.Y. 2002), *rev'd on other grounds*, 386 F.3d 485 (2d Cir. 2004).

[53] Under special circumstances, the CISG can sometimes apply to agreements between parties of different countries when only one of those countries is party to the CISG. CISG art. 1(1)(b). However, the CISG allows countries to choose not to be bound by that provision, CISG art. 95, and the United States has so chosen. Therefore, its merchants will only be subject to the CISG when dealing with merchants from other CISG countries. In addition, even if the CISG would otherwise apply, the parties may, by express agreement, "opt out" of having their agreement governed by the CISG. CISG art. 6.

[54] CISG art. 2(a).

[55] CISG art. 3(2); *cf. Princess Cruises, Inc. v. General Electric Co.*, 143 F.3d 828 (4th Cir. 1998) (UCC art. 2 does not apply to mixed transaction of goods and services, where services predominate).

Among the important differences between the CISG and domestic American contract law are the following:

1. Under the CISG, a contract is not enforceable without a price term, or some means of determining the price objectively; this is contrary to the American common law, but UCC Article 2 does allow for enforcement without a price term if the parties understood themselves as bound.[56]

2. Offers are irrevocable either if so designated, or even if not so designated, if the offeree reasonably understood the offer to be irrevocable and relied on it; this last goes beyond the relevant UCC provision,[57] which in turn goes further than the American common law.[58]

3. Acceptance is valid upon receipt by the offeror.[59] There is no "mailbox rule" in the CISG, under which acceptance might be valid upon sending.[60]

4. There is no consideration requirement for modification or termination of agreements.[61] This is largely consistent with UCC law but is a sharp departure from traditional (non-UCC) law.

5. There are no restrictions on the consideration of parol evidence.[62] The UCC's parol evidence rule[63] adds some additional exceptions to the traditional parol evidence rule (e.g., greater admissibility of trade usage, course of dealing and course of performance), but it stops far short of the CISG approach.

6. Like UCC Article 2 and, to some extent, the *Restatement* approach to non-UCC law, the CISG gives priority to course of performance and course of dealing (i.e., how parties actually act in the course of the agreement) in interpreting a contract, when this conflicts with custom or trade usage.[64]

7. Like non-UCC law, but distinctly unlike UCC Article 2 law,[65] the CISG applies a "mirror image ("last shot") approach to the "battle of the forms."[66]

---

[56] *Compare* CISG art. 14(1) *with* UCC § 2–305.

[57] *Compare* CISG art. 16(2) *with* UCC § 2–205. Under the UCC provision, an offer is "firm" if so designated by a merchant offeror in writing. Under the UCC, an offer cannot become irrevocable simply on the basis of the offeree's understanding, however reasonable.

[58] Under which even a promise that an offer will be kept open is not enforced unless there is consideration for that promise (as in an option contract). The offeree's reliance on the promise to keep an offer open has been held sufficient to enforce that promise only in the context of construction bids (the subcontractor's implied promise that its offer will remain open until, and shortly after, the general contractor is informed whether it has won the bid).

[59] CISG art. 18(2).

[60] On the mailbox rule, see Chapter 3, Section A.

[61] CISG art. 29. On the rules for modification in American law, see Chapter 5, Section B.

[62] CISG art. 8.

[63] UCC § 2–202.

[64] *Treibacher Industrie, A.G. v. Allegheny Technologies, Inc.*, 464 F.3d 1235 (11th Cir. 2006). On these principles of interpretation within American law, see Chapter 4.

[65] UCC § 2–207. *See* Chapter 3, Section A.

[66] CISG art. 19.

8. While the UCC contains a writing requirement ("Statute of Frauds") for sales of goods worth more than five hundred dollars,[67] the CISG contains no writing requirement. That noted, the CISG expressly allows a country to opt out of that provision, thereby requiring agreements to be in writing.[68]

There are also other international instruments that might affect the validity or interpretation of contracts. The same UN organization that promulgated the CISG also approved (in July 2005) the Convention on the Use of Electronic Communications in International Contracts.[69] To date, only a handful of countries (including China, but excluding the United States, Canada, Japan, and the European countries) have signed the convention.

The International Institute for the Unification of Private Law (UNIDROIT), an independent intergovernmental organization (founded in 1926 under the auspices of the League of Nations), promulgated the "Principles of International Commercial Contracts" in 1994 and revised them in 2004.[70] The UNIDROIT principles are meant to fill in gaps left by the CISG, or generally to guide contract interpretation where other laws do not govern. They do not have the status of law, applying mandatorily on their own, but parties can choose, through a choice-of-law provision in their contracts, for their agreements to be governed by the UNIDROIT principles. In addition, courts sometimes apply the principles when it is highly uncertain which country's rules should apply to a transaction.[71]

One might also mention the efforts to create a general contract law for Europe, primarily through the *Principles of European Contract Law*, prepared by the Commission on European Contract Law,[72] and the more recent *Draft Common Frame of Reference*.[73]

E. THEORETICAL IMPLICATIONS

In answering the question, for any legal system, why we have the (contract law) rules we do, a significant part of the answer has to refer to history (a point that is

---

[67] UCC § 2–201. See Chapter 3, Section C.

[68] The writing requirement is CISG art. 11. The opt-out provisions are CISG arts. 12 & 96. Among the countries that have opted out in this way are Argentina and China. This leads to cases in which parties thought they had enforceable agreements, only to find out later that their agreements were not enforceable, because they were not in writing. E.g., *Forestal Guarani, S.A. v. Daros International, Inc.*, No. 03–4821, 2008 WL 4560701 (D.N.J. 2008) (Argentine seller), vacated and remanded by 613 F.3d 395 (3d Cir. 2010); *Zhejiang Shaoxing Yongli Printing & Dyeing Co., Ltd. v. Microflock Textile Group Corp.*, No. 06–22608-CIV, 2008 WL 2098062 (S.D. Fla. 2008) (Chinese seller; alleged oral modification).

[69] Martin 2005, Boss & Kilian 2008.

[70] Farnsworth 1987a.

[71] Farnsworth 1987a: 3.

[72] Lando & Beale 2000; Lando, Clive, Prüm & Zimmermann 2003.

[73] Hesselink 2009.

discussed at greater length in Chapter 9). Some of the doctrinal rules reflect the particular path the law took (developing out of a certain writ or Roman law action), whereas others may reflect the evidence and procedural rules of a certain time (e.g., whether the parties could serve as witnesses, the role of and constraints on the jury). The historical accidents underlying large numbers of rules creates a challenge both for judges and advocates seeking a rational reconstruction of an area of law and for theorists proposing theories of those areas. Historical work about the law, like comparative work about the law, reminds us that there is little natural or inevitable about the way our current law is; it could easily be otherwise (and it has been otherwise).[74]

At the same time, given the fact that some rules developed hundreds of years ago, in different circumstances and to serve purposes and concerns distinctive of that period, the fact that these rules persist may indicate something significant. It may be that the old rules now serve different purposes, that strong reliance interests have built up around those rules, or simply that change would bring more costs than benefits.

In summary, theories that purport to explain contract law as a whole, or particular areas of contract law, need to make room for the distinctive role of history.

SUGGESTED FURTHER READING

Roman Law

Andrew Borkowski & Paul du Plessis, *Textbook on Roman Law*, 3d ed. Oxford: Oxford University Press, 2005.

Richard Hyland, "*Pacta Sunt Servanda*: A Meditation," *Virginia Journal of International Law*, vol. 34, pp. 405–433 (1994).

David Johnston, *Roman Law in Context*. Cambridge: Cambridge University Press, 1999.

English History

J. H. Baker, *An Introduction to English Legal History*, 4th ed. London: Butterworths, 2002.

David J. Ibbetson, *A Historical Introduction to the Law of Obligations*. Oxford: Oxford University Press, 1999.

A. W. B. Simpson, *A History of the Common Law of Contract*. Oxford, UK: Clarendon Press, 1975.

Reinhard Zimmermann, *The Law of Obligations: Roman Foundations of the Civilian Tradition*. Oxford: Oxford University Press, 1996.

International Law

Martijn Hesselink, "The Common Frame of Reference as a Source of European Private Law," *Tulane Law Review*, vol. 83, pp. 919–971 (2009).

Stefan Kröll, Loukas Mistelis & Pilar Perales Viscasillas (eds.), *UN Convention on Contracts for the International Sales of Goods (CISG)*. Oxford, UK: Hart Publishing, 2011.

---

[74] *See, e.g.*, Gordon 1984.

Joseph Lookofsky, *Understanding the CISG*, 3d ed. Alphen aan den Rijn, Netherlands: Wolters Kluwer, 2008.

Stefan Vogenauer & Jan Kleinheisterkamp, eds., *Commentary on the UNIDROIT Principles of International Commercial Contracts (PICC)*. Oxford: Oxford University Press, 2009.

Bruno Zeller, *Damages Under the Convention on Contracts for the International Sale of Goods*, 2d ed. Oxford: Oxford University Press, 2009.

Reinhard Zimmermann, "The UNIDROIT Principles of International Commercial Contracts 2004 in Comparative Perspective," *Tulane European & Civil Law Forum*, vol. 21, pp. 1–33 (2006).

3

Formation

Many people find it easiest to organize thinking about contracts and contract law in a sort of chronological fashion – focusing first on formation, then interpretation and performance, then remedies – and that is how most casebooks in the area are organized. Formation is the question of how and when contracts "come into being," become valid and enforceable in court.

In any litigation for a breach of contract the plaintiff will first have to prove that there was a valid and enforceable contract. The elements the plaintiff will have to prove are offer, acceptance, and consideration. These are the basic requirements for a valid contract and the focus of the beginning sections of this chapter. Later sections touch on other legal issues relating to formation: rules relating to the written or nonwritten character of the (alleged) agreement and defenses available in a breach of contract relating to how the (alleged) agreement was formed.

A. OFFER AND ACCEPTANCE

As is discussed in Chapter 9, one might offer a functional definition of contract law: whatever rules there are to regulate the enforcement of promises or exchanges.[1] It would be impractical for all promises to be legally enforceable, and no legal system of which I am aware even attempts to do so (in part, this is a function of not wanting to overload the legal system with trivial matters, and in part this reflects the general intuition that certain informal promises, especially among friends and family, should be left for extralegal enforcement only). The question that legal

---

[1] Even here, one would need to be more precise. Current gifts and contemporaneous exchanges are usually considered, in the United States and in other common law jurisdictions, to be matters of property law, not contract law. When part of the transaction involves future performance (or the promise of future performance), then the matter is usually thought to fall under contract law.

systems must then face is how to distinguish the legally enforceable from the legally unenforceable.[2]

In American contract law (and in most other common law jurisdictions), the primary criteria for the enforceability of a promise or exchange is the presence of offer, acceptance, and consideration.[3] (There are exceptions to these requirements, which are discussed in due course.) These requirements indicate the basic dividing line for enforcement: promises that are part of exchanges (bargains) are enforceable; other sorts of promises generally are not. This section gives an overview of offer and acceptance; consideration is discussed in the next section.

1. *The Nature of Offers*

The *Restatement*'s definition of an offer verges on the circular: "An offer is the manifestation of willingness to enter into a bargain, so made as to justify another person in understanding that his assent to that bargain is invited and will conclude it."[4] The basic message is something is an offer if it would be so understood by an objective or reasonable-person standard.

To qualify as an offer, the proposal must be sufficiently definite (the *"sufficiently"* indicates that here, as elsewhere with the criteria for something being an offer, we are dealing with a rough standard, and an all-things-considered judgment rather than with a bright-line rule). On the one hand, a proposal that was quite vague would leave a reasonable recipient believing that the party making the proposal was inviting further negotiations rather than inviting a final acceptance. On the other hand, where a proposal remains vague, even if the other party agrees, the resulting agreement will not allow a court to determine when the agreement has been breached or to fashion a remedy if there has been a breach.[5] For example, if the buyer promised only to pay "a good price" for the seller's car, and if there is no further way to make that term precise (e.g., a court might read "good price" to mean the market price as determined by a source like the *Blue Book* for used

---

[2] Of course, even when promises and bargains cannot be enforced legally, the parties may still feel significant social pressure to keep the promise or bargain as written, and there are many contexts in which the social pressure may be more important than any legal recourse.

[3] As mentioned in passing in Chapter 2, Section C, canon law (*see* Helmholz 1990: 51), and a number of civil law jurisdictions, use a different approach: distinguishing among promises those that had *"causa"* (which means, quite roughly, a good legal reason) and those that do not. Historically, it appears that *"causa"* did not significantly limit the enforcement of promises; it was understood to mean that either an exchange or a gift (promises that partake in commutative justice or those that partake in the virtue of liberality) might be worthy of enforcement. Gordley 1990: 382–383. Additionally, although a number of other legal systems require proof that the parties intended to contract, in American contract law, such intention will usually be presumed, and no proof is required (though if it is proved that the parties had a manifest intention not to be bound, that will negate enforceability). Klass 2009; *Restatement (Second) of Contracts* § 21.

[4] *Restatement (Second) of Contracts* § 24.

[5] *Restatement (Second) of Contracts* § 33(2).

cars), then the court will not be able to determine what the monetary difference is between the contract price and the market price at time of breach, or the difference between the market price and what the seller was able to get when the car was sold to a third party (two common ways to measure damages, as is discussed in Chapter 6).

The "black-letter law" for a long time was that advertisements were not offers, but only "invitations for offers" (a suggestion that the other party make an offer, also known as "invitations to treat"). That is, they had no legal status at all, at least as far as the common law was concerned. The existence of an advertisement did not change the legal rights, duties, or powers of the parties (the way an offer does change legal status, as it gives offerees the power to bind the offeror to a contractual relationship and makes the offeror vulnerable to being legally bound).

The *Restatement* offers the following:

> Advertisements of goods . . . are not ordinarily intended or understood as offers to sell. . . . It is of course possible to make an offer by an advertisement directed to the general public . . . but there must ordinarily be some language or commitment or some invitation to take action without further communication.[6]

One practical concern is that where the seller has a single item to sell, or a relatively small quantity of items to sell, treating an advertisement as an offer would subject the seller to the potential of many more acceptances than there were objects for sale. There are exceptions in which courts treat an advertisement as an offer. These tend to be occasions when the advertisement is interpreted in such a way that there cannot be more acceptances than items to be sold (e.g., "I will sell the book to the highest bid received by 5:00 p.m. Friday").[7] Additionally, a few commentators have argued that courts' treatment of advertisements as offers has become the rule rather than the exception.[8] In any event, in many cases, the common law treatment of advertisements may be of little importance, given that state and federal consumer protection statutes may impose liability for false or misleading advertisements, even if state contract law does not.

A note about the relationship between offer and promise: although contract law is often said to be essentially about the enforcement of promises,[9] not all promises are offers, and offers entail much more than a (mere) promise. As will be seen here, American contract law (and the contract law of many other countries) is more about the enforcement of exchanges or bargains than about the enforcement of (mere or "naked") promises. As is discussed further in Section D, modern contract law

---

[6] *Restatement (Second) of Contracts* § 26, Comment b.
[7] Some courts have also held that an intentionally deceptive advertisement could be treated as an offer – as a kind of punishment for the fraud. *See, e.g., Izadi v. Machado (Gus) Ford, Inc.*, 550 So.2d 1135 (Fla. Ct. App. 1989).
[8] *E.g.*, Feinman & Brill 2006.
[9] *E.g.*, C. Fried 1981.

does include equitable resources for enforcing promises where the parties have not otherwise entered an enforceable contract, but these tend to be exceptional cases, and courts are usually reluctant to use these doctrines.

There are still important reasons to focus on promise – if a party's statement is not in some sense a promise, it will also likely fail to be an offer. It is often a difficult judgment call as to whether a party was making a promise – offering a strong assurance – or whether that party was merely (say) offering an opinion, making a prediction, or expressing a current intention.[10]

2. Timing of Offers and Acceptances

Offers to enter a binding legal contract have life spans. It is important to know when an offer exists (comes into being), a topic already touched on, but it is also important to know that offers terminate and that this can happen in a number of different ways. An offer terminates (is no longer capable of being accepted):

1. On its expiration time (e.g., "this offer is open until Friday at 5:00 p.m."); if the offer does not expressly state an expiration time, the offer will be held to expire "after a reasonable time"[11]
2. If the offeree expressly rejects the offer[12]
3. If the offeree responds with a counteroffer (a proposed agreement covering the same subject as the offer but stating differing terms and conditions)[13]
4. If the offer is effectively revoked prior to its acceptance[14] (it is important here to understand that an offer can be revoked prior to an express termination time – or, where no express date is stated, prior to the passage of "a reasonable time" – except where the offeror and offeree have entered a valid option contract, where the offeree pays some consideration in return for an agreement to keep an offer open for some set period of time[15])
5. With the death or incapacity of the offeror (or offeree)[16]

---

[10] Among the many well-known (because frequently taught) cases that turn on such distinctions is *Hawkins v. McGee*, 84 N.H. 114 (1929) (deciding whether statements about length of hospital stay after surgery, ability to go back to work, and appearance of surgically repaired hand could be treated as promise and part of contract).

[11] *Restatement (Second) of Contracts* § 41(1).

[12] *Restatement (Second) of Contracts* § 38.

[13] It is possible to make a counteroffer that does not negate the original offer, but this needs to be done with specific language. *Restatement (Second) of Contracts* § 39(2).

[14] *Restatement (Second) of Contracts* § 42.

[15] This is the standard rule in Anglo-American contract law, but other contract law systems have declined to follow it. For example, CISG art. 16(2) makes an offer irrevocable if the offer states that it is irrevocable or states a fixed period for acceptance or if the offeree relies on an offer that it reasonably thought to be irrevocable.

[16] *See Restatement (Second) of Contracts* § 48; *see generally* Ricks 2004.

As indicated, promises to keep an offer open are generally not binding on the promisor; he or she can change her mind, withdrawing an offer prior to the earlier-promised deadline. Two points need to be noted here. First, while a promisor can withdraw an offer before its "expiration time" (if there is no consideration given for keeping the offer open), if the offeree accepts the offer within the stated period and prior to the offer's being withdrawn, there is a valid contract. Second, the rule is different for sales of goods, where a merchant's[17] written promise to keep an offer open (what the UCC calls a "firm offer") is legally binding, even without consideration.[18]

Back when contractual communications were commonly by methods that took significant periods of time (e.g., postal delivery), problems arose when a communication accepting an offer "crossed" a communication withdrawing the offer. The response of English and American contract law to this problem was known as "the mailbox rule" (and formerly was given extended attention in many first-year law school courses, back in the days when significant communication was done by mail). As an acceptance was usually valid when posted,[19] and a withdrawal of an offer only effective when communicated, when the two crossed in the mail (both the acceptance and the withdrawal having been sent before the other had been received), the acceptance was held to take priority. However, modern commercial dealings with the instantaneous (or nearly so) communications of e-mail, text, telephone, fax, and so on, mean that the mailbox rule has greatly receded in practical importance (and is now excluded from many courses).

A few more words on acceptances and counteroffers: a response to an offer that purports to be an acceptance but in fact changes the terms is not an acceptance but a counteroffer. In basic principle, this is how it should be: one party should not be able unilaterally to bind the other to different terms than what was on offer. However, courts have sometimes gone to extremes, finding small, likely inadvertent, differences in a response and declaring that it must be a counteroffer rather than an acceptance.[20]

For sales of goods, which fall under the UCC, there is less concern with showing a precise offer and acceptance: a "contract for sale of goods may be made in any

---

[17] The UCC defines a "merchant" as "a person who deals in goods of the kind or otherwise by his occupation holds himself out as having knowledge or skill peculiar to the practices or goods involved in the transaction or to whom such knowledge or skill may be attributed." UCC § 2–104.

[18] UCC § 2–205.

[19] The important exception to this rule was that it was subordinate to the general principle that offerors are "masters of their offers," and thus an offeror could expressly state that an acceptance would be valid only when communicated. In such a case, if acceptance and withdrawal crossed, priority would be given to the first to be received. *See Restatement (Second) of Contracts* § 63 & Comment b & Illustration 3.

[20] *See, e.g., Nebraska Seed Co. v. Harsh*, 152 N.W. 310 (Neb. 1915) (offer of "1800 bu. or thereabouts"; response of "1800 bushels" with no inclusion of hedging term, "*about*," held to be a counteroffer).

manner sufficient to show agreement, including conduct by both parties which recognizes the existence of such a contract."[21]

3. *Offers for Unilateral Contracts*

Law school classes and old contract law textbooks are full of long discussions of dares to cross bridges called off midjourney, rewards withdrawn, and auctions stopped just before the gavel fell. These are all examples of unilateral contracts. The basic idea was that there is a category of transactions in which an offer can be accepted only by a performance (in contrast to the conventional situation, in which a mere verbal assent would be sufficient).

One problem with the topic of unilateral contracts is that once students are introduced to the concept, they tend to see them everywhere (there is a similar problem with promissory estoppel – a topic discussed in Section D). The *Restatement* wisely tries to sidestep the whole discussion, by simply distinguishing offers that (by their terms) could be accepted by either a promise or by performance and those that (by their terms) could be accepted only by performance; the second corresponds to unilateral agreements.[22]

It is one thing to allow an offer to be accepted by performance. This happens all the time, such as when one accepts the gasoline station's offer to sell gas at a posted price by pumping that gas into one's car. It is another matter to say that an offer can *only* be accepted by performance, and a "mere" promise of future performance would be insufficient. If the offeror is uninterested in a promise of performance, it is most likely because the offeror considers performance unlikely or especially difficult. Only such offers, where by express language or context it is clear that only performance is requested in response to the offer (as occurs, for example, with rewards and dares), will be treated as one for a unilateral contract.[23]

One reason contract law discouraged treating offers as being for unilateral agreements is that when an agreement could be accepted only by performance, the "logic" of offer and acceptance seemed to indicate that the offeree could have put significant time and resources into performance, but the offeror would have the power to withdraw its offer at any point as long as the performance was not yet complete (i.e., before the offer had been accepted by full performance). There were some cases that held just that, that an offeror could withdraw their offers even when the offeree was on the verge of completing its performance.[24]

---

[21] UCC § 2–204(1); *see also* UCC §§ 2–206(1); 2–207(3).

[22] *Restatement (Second) of Contracts* §§ 30, 32, 54.

[23] The *Restatement* creates a presumption that, when in doubt, offers will be treated as capable of being accepted by either promise or performance – that is, a presumption against treating an offer as being for a unilateral contract. *Restatement (Second) of Contracts* § 32.

[24] *E.g.*, *Petterson v. Pattberg*, 161 N.E. 428 (N.Y. 1928).

In response, case law, eventually affirmed and solidified by the *Restatement*, established that with unilateral contracts, once the offeree has begun performance, the offeror cannot withdraw its offer.[25] The offeror is still not obligated to perform its part of the agreement until the offeree completes the requested performance, but it does not have the power to withdraw an offer in the middle of the requested performance.

4. *Objective and Subjective*

In determining whether negotiations have resulted in an accepted offer, and thus a valid contract, one needs to know whether the parties have agreed on the terms. The question of agreement can itself be approached in an objective or subjective way. "Objective" here means what would be understood from the perspective of an external (and unbiased) observer, using evidence available to such an observer. "Subjective" is focusing on the actual perceptions and understandings of the parties, even when those deviate from a "reasonable person's" understanding of the terms and actions.

The subjective approach is associated with the classic English case *Raffles v. Wichelhaus*,[26] in which the parties agreed to pay for cotton being sent from Bombay on a ship called *Peerless*. However, unknown to the parties, there were two ships called *Peerless* carrying cotton from Bombay, and one contracting party intended the earlier ship, and the other the later ship. The court held that there was no contract because the parties' minds did not meet.[27]

Although this subjective approach to contract formation seems to give due regard to freedom of contract and the importance of a kind of informed consent to contractual terms, the suggested legal standard would lead to too much uncertainty in the enforceability of agreements. Toward the end of the nineteenth century and beginning of the twentieth an objective approach to contract law prevailed for formation issues.[28] An objective approach focuses on the reasonable understanding of public

---

[25] *Restatement (Second) of Contracts* § 45. It is only performance that suspends the offeror's ability to withdraw an offer. Mere preparation for performance does not do so. Thus, if A's offer is to pay $5,000 should B walk across the Brooklyn Bridge, B's buying new tennis shoes or beginning a training regime will not stop A from being able to withdraw its offer, but B's beginning to walk across the bridge will.

[26] (1864) 159 Eng. Rep. 375, 2 Hurlstone & Coltman 906 (Ct. Exch.).

[27] The standard reading of *Raffles v. Wichelhaus* is, as discussed, as a paradigm case of the subjective approach. *E.g.*, Gilmore 1974: 35–42. A few commentators, including, prominently, Justice Oliver Wendell Holmes Jr., have tried to construe the case as consistent with an objective approach (e.g., Birmingham 1985). In any event, it is not crucial that this particular case be read in this way, as there seem to be numerous other cases in which the subjective approach is exemplified. Gilmore 1974: 39–40.

[28] Gilmore 1974. The extent to which the subjective approach dominated earlier contract law and the reasons for its decline are both contested among commentators. Friedman 1965, Gilmore 1974, and Horwitz 1977 generally treat the subjective approach as dominant for a significant period of time, and the transition to an objective approach as largely motivated by commercial interests. Perillo 2000b

acts or the words spoken and written rather than on the parties' (sometimes idiosyncratic) understanding of those acts and words. If one party signs another party's proposed contract, there will be a valid contract, even if the two parties understood the terms differently.[29]

Among the well-known elaborations of the objective approach during that period is Judge Learned Hand's quotation from a 1911 contract case:

> A contract has, strictly speaking, nothing to do with the personal, or individual, intent of the parties. A contract is an obligation attached by the mere force of law to certain acts of the parties, usually words, which ordinarily accompany and represent a known intent. If, however, it were proved by twenty bishops that either party, when he used the words, intended something else than the usual meaning which the law imposes upon them, he would still be held, unless there were some mutual mistake, or something else of that sort.[30]

Oliver Wendell Holmes Jr., discussing the *Raffles v. Wichelhaus* case, wrote: "The law has nothing to do with the actual state of the parties' minds. In contract, as elsewhere, it must go by externals, and judge parties by their conduct."[31]

The objective approach is displayed by the well-known case of *Lucy v. Zehmer*.[32] In that case Zehmer claimed that he had been joking when he offered to sell his farm to Lucy for $50,000, whereas Lucy argued that he had not been aware that Zehmer was only joking and had no reason to suspect it. The court held Zehmer to the contract, noting that "[a]t no time prior to the execution of the contract had Zehmer indicated to Lucy by word or act that he was not in earnest about selling the farm."[33] It was actions and outward appearances that counted, not secret intentions.

5. *Battle of the Forms*

It has become common for businesses to use standardized forms in their commercial transactions. Buyers send out purchase orders on standard forms, which include detailed "boiler-plate" provisions favorable to buyers. Sellers send invoices confirming purchase orders on their own standard forms, whose detailed provisions, unsurprisingly, are more favorable to sellers.

---

argues that the objective approach had always been the dominant approach, that the subjective approach had only a brief period of interest that did not much affect outcomes, and that it disappeared as an indirect response to a change in evidence rules, allowing parties to testify on their own behalves.

[29] It is important to note that even when the courts purported to use a subjective approach – such as the parties' understanding of the transaction's terms – this standard was generally put forward during a period when the parties were not allowed to testify, so that their subjective understandings had to be proved through objective evidence. E.g., Perillo 2000b: 435–436, 443–444, 455.

[30] *Hotchkiss v. National City Bank of New York*, 200 F. 287, 293 (S.D.N.Y. 1911).

[31] Holmes 1963: 242.

[32] 84 S.E.2d 516 (Va. 1954). For more on that case, see Richman & Schmelzer 2011.

[33] *Lucy v. Zehmer*, 84 S.E.2d at 521.

What happens when a buyer orders some good or service using its standard form, and the seller responds on its standard form with what purports to be an acceptance or confirmation? The problem is that while both forms may agree on most of the important details of the transactions (e.g., good or service to be purchased, price, delivery), the terms preprinted on each party's standardized forms will almost certainly not match up. And these terms can include potentially quite significant matters, such as whether disputes regarding the transaction must be brought to arbitration, whether damages for breach of contract will be limited, and whether warranties apply to the transaction.

Under traditional contract law analysis (which still applies to transactions other than the sale of goods[34]), because the two parties' standardized forms do not match, neither can work as an acceptance of an offer from the other, even if the language on the form expressly states that it is an acceptance. Rather, after an initial offer, any subsequent form sent by the other party would constitute a counteroffer, because it has different or additional terms. Whichever form was sent last is the (counter)offer on the table. Whenever the other party (likely thinking itself already in a binding agreement) acts, by sending or accepting a payment, delivering or accepting goods, or performing or accepting the performance of a service, that action will be deemed to be an implied acceptance of the offer on the table. And if the question was litigated before any payment or other performance occurred, then the courts would hold that there was no contract between the parties.[35] This is the so-called "battle of the forms," under the "mirror-image rule" (response is a valid acceptance only when its terms exactly mirror those of the offer) established by classical contract law. It is often called "the last shot" rule, as the last form on the table becomes the contract once the other party performs.[36]

One of the most significant (or, at least, most noted) changes Article 2 of the Uniform Commercial Code made to the existing common law principles was in the treatment of these sorts of "battle of the forms" cases. Under UCC Section 2–207, the Code attempted to create a system in which (a) parties who thought that they were bound would be treated as bound, and (b) one-sided terms could not generally become part of the contract without the other party's express agreement.

There are well-known gaps between the aspiration of Section 2–207 and the actual text, although sometimes when the text varied from the ideal, as will be seen, some courts have applied the ideal rather than the text.[37] Briefly (as Section 2–207 is a

---

[34] E.g., *Princess Cruises, Inc. v. General Electric, Co.*, 143 F.3d 828 (4th Cir. 1998).

[35] *Poel v. Brunswick-Balke-Collender Co.*, 216 N.Y. 310, 110 N.E. 619 (1915), is the standard example, although how common such cases were in practice is disputed.

[36] The mirror-image and last shot principles are followed also by the CISG (art. 19) and by English law. On English law, see *Butler Machine Tool Company v. Ex-Cell-O Corporation*, [1979] 1 W.L.R. 401 (A.C.); *Tekdata Interconnection Ltd v. Amphenol*, [2009] EWCA Civ 1209, [2010] 1 Lloyd's Rep. 357.

[37] Although this may arguably be true to the UCC's text, as Section 1–103 instructs courts that the UCC "must be liberally construed and applied to promote its underlying purposes and policies."

morass that we do not have the time to be properly lost in): Subsection (1) is intended to avoid the problem of parties not being contractually bound, even though they think they are contractually bound, just because their forms have different boilerplate language. Subsection (1) states: "A definite and seasonable expression of acceptance or a written confirmation which is sent within a reasonable time operates as an acceptance even though it states terms additional to or different from those offered or agreed upon."[38] The idea that parties should be treated as contractually bound if they see themselves as bound, legal "technicalities" aside, is reinforced by Subsection (3) (and by a number of other UCC provisions[39]): "Conduct by both parties which recognizes the existence of a contract is sufficient to establish a contract for sale although the writings of the parties do not otherwise establish a contract."[40] In such circumstances, the agreement is constructed from the terms on which the parties have agreed, supplemented by default provisions that the UCC provides.[41]

Many of the problems of Section 2–207 comes from its second subsection. It holds that the additional terms of a purported acceptance are to be treated as proposals for additions to the contract. Between merchants only, such provisions automatically become part of the agreement, unless objected to in advance (e.g., in the boilerplate language of the offeror's form) or after the fact, or if the additional provisions "materially alter" the agreement.[42]

This approach may work adequately when the one-sided provisions are hidden in the offeree's form, but what about one-sided provisions hidden in the offeror's form? As Section 2–207 is written, they would seem to be part of any agreement, as there is nothing in the section's express language that affects their validity or force. In effect, Section 2–207 seems to have changed the law from being a "last shot" rule (favoring the last form on the table prior to performance) to being a "first shot" rule (favoring the initial offer). Courts have gotten around this problem by going to Subsection (3), treating each form as "knocking out" the different terms of the other form and constructing the agreement from the terms on which the parties agreed, combined with UCC default terms.[43] Whether this move is justified by the wording of Section 2–207

---

[38] UCC § 2–207(1). The text continues: "unless acceptance is expressly made conditional on assent to the additional or different terms." The UCC text needed to allow parties a way to make counteroffers, if accepting their additional or different terms was in fact important to the offerees. Consistent with the purpose of Section 2–207, case law has emphasized that such an intention will not be lightly inferred (especially from boilerplate language that was not highlighted or in some other way brought to the other party's attention). *E.g., Ionics, Inc. v. Elmwood Sensors, Inc.*, 110 F.3d 184 (1st Cir. 1997).

[39] *E.g.*, UCC §§ 2–204 (on formation in general), 2–305 (open price terms).

[40] UCC § 2–207(3).

[41] *Id.*

[42] UCC § 2–207(2). Comments 4 and 5 to UCC § 2–207 offer some guidance as to which sort of provisions should be considered "material alterations" and which should not. Additionally, many courts follow a "surprise or hardship" test to determine what counts as a "material alteration." *E.g., Dale R. Horning v. Falconer Glass Industries, Inc.*, 730 F. Supp. 962 (S.D. Ind. 1990).

[43] *E.g., Reilly Foam Corp. v. Rubbermaid Corp.*, 206 F. Supp.2d 643 (E.D. Pa. 2002) (describing this approach as the "majority" approach of courts).

is, at best, arguable, but it does seem to be more consistent with the spirit of the section.

One complaint offered by some companies (and their representatives) about Section 2–207 parallels one made about electronic contracting (the topic of the next section): certain interpretations of the rules (e.g., one that creates a sort of 2–207(3) "knock-out" rule, invalidating any provision that does not appear on both parties' forms) make it difficult, for example, for sellers to get the limitation of damages and disclaimer of warranty provisions they believe necessary. The alternative to allowing sellers to impose such restrictions in a unilateral way, they argue, would be either much more expensive products (where the "insurance" against extensive litigation damages and costs must be incorporated into the price of each product) or wasteful efforts to get each buyer to indicate express assent to such terms (wasteful, not least, it is alleged, because the vast majority of buyers would prefer the lower prices with the restrictive terms to avoiding the restrictive terms by paying much higher prices).

6. *Electronic Contracting and Rolling Contracts*

Modern contracting practices regarding computer software and hardware and Internet purchasing have significantly changed the way contracting scholars (and perhaps contracting parties as well) think about assent. When obtaining software on the Internet, contractual terms are often provided online, with the consumer required to click a box expressing assent to the terms prior to obtaining the software. This is known as "click-ware"; with "browse-ware," the consumer is told there are terms available elsewhere and that the consumer will be bound by them, but no action on the consumer's part is required prior to obtaining the software. "Terms in a box" or "shrink-wrap" terms occur when a computer or software is paid for, and the consumer learns of terms only when opening the box in which the computer was shipped or opening the wrapping around the device on which the software is stored. These terms often involved limitations on or disclaimers of warranties, limitations on consequential damages, mandatory arbitration of disputes, and similar provisions. As is discussed in greater detail herein, such ways of forming contracts are generally as valid and binding as more traditional ways of forming contracts.

These forms of presenting terms, sometimes collectively labeled "electronic contracting" (because of their association with the sale of computer hardware and software, but the same doctrines would apply when such processes are used with other sorts of goods), build on ideas and practices of "rolling contracts" – where some of the terms were provided after an initial agreement on basic terms. Often one purchases an insurance policy on the basis of the general type of policy and price, only to have the policy, with all its definitions and exclusions being sent later. Also, when one buys a ticket to a concert, sporting event, or cruise, the ticket that arrives often contains detailed terms and disclaimers attached to or on the back of the ticket.[44] Although "rolling contracts" had once been peripheral, they are becoming increasingly common.

The inclination of many, perhaps most, consumers, and quite a few law professors, to electronic contracting (e.g., the "terms in a box") would be to say that the contractual agreement was completed when the boxed goods were purchased in the store. However, were this true, the terms "in the box" could not become part of the transaction. (The act of purchasing could not bind me to terms hidden in a box I have not been able to read and may not even have been aware were present. Otherwise, endless mischief could be done by those who hid terms in objects – such as books, clothing, food – we had innocently purchased.)

Existing law gave mixed signals. At least if the transaction were understood as a sale of goods, UCC Section 2–207 seems to apply, under which (as discussed in the prior section) provisions that are introduced after an oral agreement had been reached are, at best, proposals for a new agreement or proposals for a modification of the existing agreement, which would not become effective without assent of the other party. A similar outcome could be reached under non-UCC law, based on the central assumption that an initial agreement had been reached prior to the buyer's exposure to the extra terms.[45]

One standard argument for allowing the enforcement of terms in electronic contracting, despite issues with the timing of the terms' presentation and despite doubts about the likelihood of the terms having been read, is that more stringent requirements would create an unworkable situation, or at least a situation significantly less attractive for consumers and providers alike.[46] Additionally, although recent empirical work has found that software license agreements tend, almost universally, to have pro-seller provisions (relative to default rules), there appears to be little evidence that the agreements were any more pro-seller in dealings with consumers than they were with larger business and corporate buyers.[47]

---

44 *See Carnival Cruise Lines, Inc. v. Shute*, 499 U.S. 585 (1990) (enforcing forum selection clause that was sent with cruise ticket).

45 Judge Easterbrook's analysis in *ProCD, Inc. v. Zeidenberg*, 86 F.3d 1447 (7th Cir. 1996) and *Hill v. Gateway 2000, Inc.*, 105 F.3d 1147 (7th Cir. 1997), depends on the controversial claim that it was the vendors of the software who made the offer, by shipping the product, rather than the more conventional view that the purchaser is the offeror, at the point when he or she ordered the item. *See Klocek v. Gateway, Inc.*, 104 F. Supp. 2d 1322, 1340 (D. Kan. 2000). When the vendor is the offeror, then it is an easier doctrinal argument to make that the offer was made conditional of acceptance of terms still to come. It is much harder doctrinally to include the terms-to-come if the vendor is the offeree rather than the offeror.

46 *See, e.g., ProCD, Inc.*, 86 F.3d at 1452 (Zeidenberg's position, if accepted, "would drive prices through the ceiling or return transactions to the horse-and-buggy age"); *Gateway 2000*, 105 F.3d at 1149 (requiring disclosure of full terms prior to purchase would be impractical and would serve little purpose); *see also* Easterbrook 2005: 965–970.

47 Marotta-Wurgler 2007, 2009.

The American Law Institute recently adopted *Principles of the Law: Software Contracts*[48] in an effort to clarify the legal principles that do – and should – apply to electronic contracting, though to date there is little evidence of the *Principles* affecting the rules adopted and applied by legislatures or courts. The main emphasis of the ALI *Principles* had been to propose greater precontract disclosure of terms. This approach has supporters across ideological lines, as its purpose is to discourage one-sided terms indirectly without using the more direct but more controversial path of mandatory and prohibited terms. However, there is empirical evidence that mandatory disclosure would not even lead to significantly greater reading of terms by consumers, and therefore is unlikely to have a significant effect on what terms vendors offer.[49]

7. Open Terms and Agreements to Agree

There are a series of related problems of formation that arise when the parties might see themselves as bound in some way, but have left terms out, foresee further negotiation, or await the writing of a more formal document.

The common law tends to treat such agreements as unenforceable (as regards the term(s) "to be agreed"; the remainder of the contract may still be enforceable).[50] The justification is straightforward: where the parties have not set the terms, it becomes difficult for a court to determine whether a breach has occurred or to measure damages assuming a breach has occurred. The UCC is more receptive to enforcing sale of goods agreements with open terms, even open price terms, as long as the parties saw themselves as bound.[51]

A related set of issues arises when parties have reached agreement (or an "agreement in principle") on the major issues but await a formal written contract, often with the understanding that a number of minor issues still need to be worked out. Some courts treat such agreements as fully enforceable, if the parties thought of themselves as bound, even if the expected written contract is never produced.[52] When the preliminary agreement is made to encourage investment duties between the parties, in the process of determining the optimal structure for a joint project, it makes sense to impose liability on parties that do not meet their investment obligations (perhaps for strategic reasons).[53] Other courts will not enforce such agreements, especially if the writing to be produced would have involved many provisions not included in

---

[48] American Law Institute 2010; Hillman & O'Rourke 2010.
[49] Marotta-Wurgler 2011; *see also* Ben-Shahar & Schneider 2011.
[50] *See, e.g., Walker v. Keith*, 382 S.W.2d 198 (Ky. App. 1964).
[51] *See* UCC §§ 2–204(3); 2–305.
[52] The multi-billion-dollar judgment in the *Pennzoil v. Texaco* case arose out of such an "agreement in principle" between Pennzoil and Getty Oil. *See Pennzoil Co. v. Texaco, Inc.*, 481 U.S. 1 (1987).
[53] This justification is persuasively described in Schwartz & Scott 2007, where it is also shown that the analysis fits much of the case law in the area.

the "agreement in principle." A few commentators have advocated, and a handful of courts have used, a middle option between the parties being fully bound and the parties not being legally bound at all: that the parties are bound to negotiate in good faith.[54]

One other variation: in business, for example, it is common for banks and other businesses to produce "letters of intent." Such letters create problems for courts, and therefore also for parties, because their whole purpose is to have it both ways: to make a sufficient commitment – usually to assure a third party – without actually being (legally) bound. Although there may be a place in business and other social contexts for half commitments, law opts for a binary system: breach or no breach, liable or not liable, contract or no contract. Ambiguous commitment works for business, but it risks legal liability when things go badly.[55]

8. *Construction Bid Contracts*

In large construction contracts, it is common to have the work organized and over-seen by a general contractor, who in turn delegates many of the tasks to subcon-tractors. Additionally, it is very common for the construction contract to be awarded on a competitive-bid basis. The owner or government agency in charge of the con-struction job sets out specifications for the work; the interested general contractors then collect bids from interested subcontractors before submitting their own bids for the project. The contract to do the job is usually then given to the general con-tractor with the lowest bid.[56] What happens, though, if after a general contractor is awarded the contract, one of the subcontractors who had promised to work on the project with this general contractor either now refuses to do the work or refuses to do the work without being paid much more than it originally bid? Should it make a difference if the subcontractor withdrew its bid before the contract was awarded, if this occurs after the general contractor's bid has been submitted? Such a withdrawal of a subcontractor's bid would most often occur because the subcontractor discov-ered that it had based its bid on an error,[57] but there are other circumstances as well.

Two well-known cases offer alternative approaches to this area. In *Baird Co. v. Gimbel Bros., Inc.*,[58] Judge Learned Hand argued that the subcontractor's bid was merely an offer, and although the parties could have made the offer

---

[54] *See, e.g.* Farnsworth 1987b; Knapp 1969; *Brown v. Cara*, 420 F.3d 148 (2d Cir. 2005) (parties bound by memorandum of understanding to negotiate open terms in good faith); *Channel Home Centers v. Grossman*, 795 F.2d 291 (3d Cir. 1986) (letter of intent to negotiate in good faith was binding).

[55] *See, e.g., Quake Construction, Inc. v. American Airlines, Inc.*, 565 N.E.2d 990 (Ill. 1990).

[56] For public works, giving the job to the lowest bidder may be required by statute.

[57] In such circumstances, even if the subcontractor would otherwise be legally held to its bid, there may be a claim based on the doctrine of unilateral mistake, which is discussed in Chapter 3, Section A.

[58] 64 F.2d 344 (2d Cir. 1933).

nonrevocable (e.g., by agreeing that the use of the bid in the general contractor's submission would be the consideration for keeping the offer open), that is not a reasonable interpretation of what the parties had done or what their documents said. Judge Hand dismissed lightly the possibility of binding the offeror through promissory estoppel (discussed in Chapter 3, Section D), arguing that reliance was appropriate for situations like charitable promises,[59] where the promisor could not expect any return on its promise, but not in a commercial context, where an offeror does not expect to be legally bound unless and until its offer is met by an acceptance.

The opposite approach was given by Judge Roger Traynor in *Drennan v. Star Paving Co.*,[60] in which the court held that the subcontractor had encouraged the general contractor to rely on its (the subcontractor's) bid, and that this reliance justified keeping the offer open, until a reasonable time after the contract is awarded. Judge Traynor grounded the conclusion on the analogy of promissory estoppel and the estoppel element in unilateral contracts (where an offer cannot be validly rescinded after the offeree has relied on it by beginning performance).[61]

Although the *Restatement* expressed the general proposition that promises could be kept open by reliance,[62] courts have rarely kept offers open on the basis of reliance, except in construction bid contracts.[63] However, in that context, the *Drennan* rule has been followed almost universally.[64]

B. CONSIDERATION

1. *Historical Origins*

The doctrine of consideration is distinctive to the English common law approach to contract law (a doctrine and approach that has been adopted by most legal systems that derive from English roots, including American law); it is also a doctrine that both students and commentators find puzzling (and perhaps unjustifiable). Therefore, it is not surprising that significant attention has been given to the questions of when

---

[59] As is discussed in Chapter 3, Section D, promissory estoppel grew out of cases involving charitable promises, family promises, and promises of pensions – all categories of cases in which there is usually no expectation of a direct return on or exchange for one's promise. Boyer 1952. However, the doctrine has become generalized, so that it is no longer confined to those categories of cases.

[60] 333 P.2d 757 (Cal. 1958).

[61] *See Restatement (Second) of Contracts* §§ 45, 90. On unilateral contracts, *see* Chapter 3, Section A; on promissory estoppel, *see* Chapter 3, Section D.

[62] *See Restatement (Second) of Contracts* § 87(2).

[63] For an example of a court rejecting reliance as a basis for keeping an offer open outside the construction bidding context, see *Berryman v. Kmoch*, 559 P.2d 790 (Kan. 1977).

[64] For more on the narrow application of the rule (including the fact that it tends to be used primarily in public construction cases rather than in private construction cases), see Goldberg 2011.

and why the doctrine developed.[65] This subsection offers a brief overview of the doctrine's history.

Although the general idea – that there had to be some level of reciprocity and reasonable reliance for a promise or set of promises to be enforceable – had deep roots in English law,[66] the modern doctrine took firm shape[67] only in the sixteenth century.[68] Both in case law and in commentary, the development of the doctrine of consideration seems to have been guided by the canon law notion of "*causa*." While all promises were morally binding, only promises made "seriously and upon good cause"[69] were legally binding; other promises were "*nudum pactum*," naked pacts, legally unenforceable.[70] In the sixteenth-century cases when the doctrine was being firmed up, *causa* and "consideration" were used interchangeably.[71] Eventually, it became an established part of the pleading for the writ of assumpsit that the plaintiff declare "in consideration of . . ." what the promise had been made, with a requirement that "good" consideration be pled (what counts as good consideration and what does not is examined in the next subsection).[72]

Contractual obligation changed in the later seventeenth and eighteenth centuries, perhaps under the influence of the Puritans, and the view of consideration changed in ways that reflected that transformation. Contract law became less grounded on the idea of punishing the wrong of a broken promise and more focused on remedying the disappointed expectations arising from a breached bargain.[73] And consideration changed from "purpose, or motive or justification for a promise" to "the price paid by the promisee for the promise of the promisor."[74]

From the divergent strands of the history of consideration came its two distinct if overlapping modern tests. The first is the benefit-detriment test, such that something can be consideration if it is of benefit to the promisee or detriment to the promisor. These can be seen as connected to the *quid pro quo* aspect of the writ of debt and the reliance aspect of the older or "special" form of assumpsit.[75] However, Anglo-American contract law came to define *detriment* for these purposes very broadly, as any diminishment of one's legal freedom. Thus, in the famous case of *Hamer v.*

---

[65] Simpson (1975a: 193–196) is persuasive on the argument that the doctrine did not develop from a similar sounding argument, "quid pro quo," which had not been used to determine when an agreement was binding, but rather the question of whether and when a party could bring an action under the writ of debt (*see also* Simpson 1975a: 153–169).

[66] On reciprocity, see, e.g., Ibbetson 1999: 80–83.

[67] What J. H. Baker nicely calls "the conversion of loose words into jargon." J. H. Baker 1981: 358.

[68] J. H. Baker 1981.

[69] J. H. Baker 2002: 339 (footnote omitted).

[70] *Id.*, 339–340

[71] *Id.*, 340 & n. 68.

[72] *Id.*, 340–341.

[73] Berman 2008: 134–139.

[74] *Id.*, 136.

[75] Farnsworth 2004: § 1.6, at 17–18.

Sidway,[76] the court refused to inquire whether a youth's promise not to smoke, drink, or gamble until the age of twenty-one was objectively to his benefit, and therefore not consideration. It was sufficient to show that the youth had a legal right to do these actions.

Where the benefit-detriment test has some bite is with situations in which what is being promised is something the promisor already had a duty (by contract or statute) to perform. This becomes an issue, for example, when parties attempt to modify an existing contract (e.g., paying more money for the same construction job, accepting a smaller payment than the original loan amount).[77] Issues relating to modification are discussed in Chapter 5, Section B.

The second test, of bargained-for consideration, also reflects the basic history of the writ of assumpsit, that each party have given something (of detriment to itself or benefit to the other) in exchange for the promise.[78] In the terms of the *Second Restatement*, a "performance or return promise is bargained for if it is sought by the promisor in exchange for his promise and is given by the promisee in exchange for that promise."[79]

Most commentators (and almost all teachers) view the move from the various writs to assumpsit and consideration as a progress narrative, but not everyone agrees. Milsom wrote: "[I]f the rules of proof governing early contract actions did not always work well, they were clearer in purpose and effect than the main product of these twists, namely the 'doctrine' of consideration."[80]

2. *Current Doctrine*

As has been discussed, consideration is a doctrine, or set of doctrines, that, roughly speaking, separates bargains (i.e., I will do X for you, if you will give Y to me) from other sorts of promises and interactions.[81] One must prove the existence of consideration for there to be an enforceable contract.[82]

On the one hand, the doctrine of consideration does not involve any judgment about the equivalency or adequacy of the exchange (although a particularly one-sided exchange might be evidence of mistake, duress, or undue influence (discussed

---

[76] 124 N.Y. 538, 27 N.E. 256 (1891).

[77] *Foakes v. Beer*, L.R. 9 A.C. 605 (H.L. 1883–84).

[78] Farnsworth 2004: § 2.2, at 47.

[79] *Restatement (Second) of Contracts* § 71(2).

[80] Milsom 2003: 45.

[81] As discussed earlier, civil law traditions have a slightly different requirement, "*cause*" (e.g., French *Code Civil*, art. 1108) or "*causa*" (from canon law), which divides enforceable from unenforceable promises and/or bargains in a distinct but comparable way.

[82] Of course, legislators may codify specific exceptions to the general requirement of consideration. One of the broadest is the Pennsylvania statute that makes releases or promises binding, even without consideration, if they are in writing, signed, and expressly state an intention to be legally bound. 33 *Pa. Cons. Stat. Ann.* § 6.

in Section E) or part of the showing needed for unconscionability (discussed in Chapter 5, Section A)). On the other hand, the court will inquire whether there had been a real exchange, and not just a gift made to look like an exchange (what is sometimes called "sham consideration").[83]

The requirement of consideration leaves whole categories of agreements on potentially shaky legal ground, despite the fact that the parties in such agreements often have a clear intention to be legally bound (as well as the mistaken perception that the promises they are making are legally binding) and the significant economic or social interest in having such agreements enforceable. The promises that the consideration requirement may make unenforceable include: promises to keep offers open, promises to pay for (or give gifts in recognition of) past benefits, promises to release or modify debts, charitable pledges, and promises to take on the debts of another.[84]

The rule of consideration makes almost all promises of gifts[85] unenforceable (in special circumstances, such donative promises may fall within one of the alternative grounds of recovery discussed in Section D). Various justifications have been offered for the nonenforcement of gift promises, such as that making such promises enforceable undermines their value as altruistic actions,[86] or that conventional thinking would want the promisor to have the power to renege on the promise in circumstances that would not ground a defense to contractual enforcement (e.g., if the promisee has acted badly to the promisor, if the promisor has suffered a significant financial setback).[87] (Whether it is a good policy to make promises of gifts unenforceable is, of course, another question.[88])

There are a number of things that are similar to consideration for contract law purposes but do not in fact qualify – e.g., past consideration,[89] illusory promises, conditions on gifts, and preexisting duties. An illusory promise is where one party states something that may have the form of a benefit or detriment but on closer

---

[83] *See* Farnsworth 2004: § 2.11, at 70–72. Other commentators have noted the obvious tensions between the refusal to test the adequacy of the exchange and the hostility to a fake exchange. *E.g.*, C. Fried 1981: 29–30.

[84] *See* Barnett 1986: 288–289; C. Fried 1981: 28.

[85] Completed gifts are another matter, and are, in any event, governed by the law of property, not the law of contract.

[86] However, as Shiffrin points out (2007: 736–737), legal enforcement would still leave the making of the gift promise as an altruistic act; it would only be the ultimate performance of the promise that would become legally required.

[87] Eisenberg 1997.

[88] On this issue, see, e.g., Eisenberg 1979, 1997 (against enforcement); Gordley 2001a: 298–307 (in favor of enforcement); R. Posner 1977 (same).

[89] Promissory restitution, discussed in Section D, Subsection (2) below, allows recovery for a kind of past consideration, but it is not a breach of contract action (there is no valid contract). Additionally, New York has express legislation authorizing enforcement for signed, written contracts where the "consideration for the promise is past or executed . . . and would be valid consideration but for the time when it was given or performed." *New York General Obligations Law* § 5–1105.

examination does not in fact restrain: "I will either buy your wheat at $100 per bushel, or I will not," or "I will buy that painting tomorrow for $500 if I feel like it." However, sometimes courts will imply "good faith" limits on what otherwise would be complete discretion, thereby turning an illusory promise into valid consideration.

Courts in earlier times sometimes questioned whether requirements contracts (agreements to take all one requires in some good from one seller) or output contracts (agreements to sell all of one's production in some good to one buyer) involved illusory promises, as the agreements did not foreclose the possibility that one might have no requirements and thus buy nothing, or have no output and thus sell nothing. However, courts came to conclude that these agreements were not illusory and did include consideration, for the party was constraining itself in a significant way (e.g., for a requirements contract, that if it bought that good at all, it was obligated to buy it from *this* seller).[90]

As for a condition on a gift, if I tell you that if you come over to my apartment, I will give you my old computer, your coming over is not something I seek for its own sake but is simply a way of making my giving you a gift a little easier. Sometimes, the same facts, with a slight change, can support different stories: when the old wealthy man offers $100 per week to be picked up at his house, this could easily be just a condition on a gift, but one could also tell a story of a lonely man for whom even modest social interaction was worth much more than $100 per visit.

As already noted, when one promises to do what one already has a preexisting contractual or statutory duty to perform, then there is no valid consideration. One example of a preexisting duty is a police officer who tries to collect an offered reward for recovering stolen property, when such work solving crimes is already part of the officer's existing duties under her employment contract or under statute. The more common example of preexisting duty, however, is the contractor who asks for more money than the contract authorizes.[91] Under classical common law principles, even if the other party agrees, such modification agreements would be unenforceable. The modern approach, under which modifications are at least presumptively enforceable, despite the absence of new consideration, is discussed at greater length in Chapter 5, Section B.

The doctrine of consideration has never lacked for critics. In the previous subsection, the historian S. F. C. Milsom was quoted to the effect that even the old writ system would be preferable to the doctrine of consideration; a 1936 *Harvard*

---

[90] *See* Farnsworth 2004: § 2.15, at 82.
[91] Another example is the when a creditor agrees to accept less than the amount due on (certain) debt. This modification of the underlying agreement has been held, under English law and most American jurisdictions, to be unenforceable for lack of consideration. *See Foakes v. Beer*, L.R., 9 A.C. 605 (H.L. 1884); *see* Farnsworth 2004: §4.23, at 274–275. If there is a dispute about the amount owed, then there is no consideration issue (on the related topic of accord and satisfaction, see Chapter 5, Section B, Subsection 3).

Law Review article thought the case for abolishing the doctrine was clear; and in 1958 the contract theorist Edwin Patterson felt the need to offer an "An Apology for Consideration."[92] A detailed analysis tends to leave commentators using terms like *inconsistent* and *anomalous*.[93] However, there is no indication that the doctrine of consideration is going away, even if its importance has been somewhat reduced by the availability, under some circumstances, of recovery for contract-like transactions in which consideration was absent. Promissory estoppel (often called by its *Restatement* location, "Section 90" reliance[94]) is the primary example, but one should also note the options of unjust enrichment (restitution, quasi-contract) and promissory restitution ("Section 86"[95]). These alternatives to making a claim on the contract are discussed in Section D. Later in the book we will also come across other statutory or court-created exceptions to the requirement of consideration.[96]

In earlier decades, courts sometimes spoke of the doctrine of "mutuality of obligation," a notion that was related to consideration and that indicated that if one party to an agreement was not bound, then the other party could not be either.[97] This doctrine, to whatever extent it ever was a clear doctrine, has largely faded – there are too many circumstances in which the law does make one party bound and the other not (e.g., option contracts, offers for unilateral agreements after the offeree has begun performance, subcontractor bids). However, one can still find cases in which courts seem to refuse enforcement on "mutuality" grounds.[98]

C. STATUTE OF FRAUDS

There are a number of provisions and principles of contract law that have the motivation, or at least the effect, of encouraging parties to put their agreements into writing. Most prominent is the statute of frauds, which is discussed in this section, and the parol evidence rule, which is discussed in Chapter 4, Section D.

The original Statute of Frauds was enacted in England in 1677: it was a statute that dealt with a variety of potential frauds but is best known today for its provisions requiring that certain types of agreements be in writing.[99] Like subsequent statutes

---

[92] Milsom 2003: 45; Wright 1936; E. Patterson 1958.
[93] E.g., C. Fried 1981: 35. A detailed (and still critical) examination of the doctrine and its various possible functions is given in Wessman 1993, 1996, 2008.
[94] *Restatement (Second) of Contracts* § 90.
[95] *Restatement (Second) of Contracts* § 86.
[96] For example, in the treatment of firm offers, discussed in Chapter 3, Section A, and modifications, discussed in Chapter 5, Section B.
[97] E.g., *E. I. Du Pont De Nemours & Co. v. Claiborne-Reno Co.*, 64 F.2d 224 (8th Cir. 1933).
[98] E.g., *Pick Kwik Food Stores, Inc. v. Tenser*, 407 So.2d 216 (Fla. Ct. App. 1981); *Gull Laboratories, Inc. v. Diagnostic Technology, Inc.*, 695 F. Supp. 1151 (D. Utah 1988). For a defense of "mutuality of obligation," see Ricks 1999.
[99] 29 Car. 2, ch. 3. There is evidence that this statute was enacted in part in response to a loosening in the rules under the writ system, which had earlier encouraged the use of formal (written) agreements

of frauds, the legislation required that certain important categories of agreements be in writing or be evidenced by a writing, to be legally enforceable. The written agreement or other writing must be signed by "the party to be charged" – that is, the party objecting to enforcement.

A couple of matters should be made clear at the beginning. First, under modern statutes of frauds, the precise requirement is not that the agreement be in writing but that there be written evidence that an agreement has been entered into[100] (which could include documents written long after the original agreement was entered into); the agreement reduced to writing is, of course, the best such evidence, but letters, memos, or invoices that refer to or imply the existence of an agreement often suffice. Second, in most states, there is not a single statute of frauds but a large number of them, as every statute that requires that a certain type of transaction be evidenced by a writing is called a "statute of frauds," and most state law codifications make no effort to collect such rules in a single statute (or even a single part of the state code).[101]

Among the common categories of agreements on which a writing requirement has been placed are sales of land, agreements that cannot be performed within a year, and agreements in which one party agrees to be responsible for another party's debt or obligation.[102] The Uniform Commercial Code also has its own statute of frauds, imposing a writing requirement for the sale of goods worth more than $500.[103] The UCC creates four exceptions: (1) (if both parties are merchants) where a writing in confirmation of an agreement is sent, and not objected to within ten days, the recipient of the confirmation can no longer raise the statute-of-frauds defense;[104] (2) where the goods are specially manufactured (i.e., the goods would not be available for easy resale to another) and the seller has substantially begun work or made substantial commitments for materials, the buyer may not raise the defense;[105] (3) a party who admits under oath as part of a court procedure the existence of an agreement cannot raise the defense;[106] and (4) where payment has been made and

---

under seal but had begun to make it easier to enforce (alleged) informal oral agreements. Simpson 1975a: 125. The British Parliament repealed most of the Statute of Frauds provisions in 1954. Decker 1973.

[100] *See, e.g., Crabtree v. Elizabeth Arden Sales Corp.*, 110 N.E.2d 551 (N.Y. 1953) ("writing" consists of payroll cards and informal note prepared for employer).

[101] According to one report, a "search of the Ohio statutes identified over 8,212 statutory provisions with writing or signature requirements:" and a "similar search in Georgia's code produced over 5,500 provisions." National Conference of Commissioners on Uniform State Laws 1988: 4.

[102] *See Restatement (Second) of Contracts* § 110. Louisiana is the one state that does not have a general common law statute of frauds, although it does have writing requirements connected to some specific transactions. *E.g., Louisiana Revised Statutes* § 6:1122 (credit agreements must be in writing).

[103] UCC § 2–201.

[104] UCC § 2–201(2).

[105] UCC § 2–201(3)(a).

[106] UCC § 2–201(3)(b).

accepted, or goods delivered and accepted, the statute cannot be raised as a defense, to the extent (the quantity) of the payment or delivery.[107]

Over the years, one limited exception to the statute of frauds was developed by the Courts of Equity: part performance.[108] This is a quite narrow exception: it applies only to agreements relating to interests in land (the sale or leasing of real property), where one party has performed by occupying the property or made improvements (payment is not considered sufficient performance for this purpose), and where that party is seeking equitable damages (e.g., specific performance – it does not apply to cases where the plaintiff only seeks money damages).[109]

A small number of jurisdictions recognize a broader reliance exception to the statute of frauds, if the promisee has relied on an oral promise, and injustice can be avoided only by enforcement of the promise.[110] However, most jurisdictions have rejected this broad reliance exception because it largely undermines the statute of frauds.[111] (A number of states do recognize a more limited reliance exception: where one party relies on the other party's (false) assurance, either that there currently is a sufficient writing documenting the agreement or that a sufficient writing would be forthcoming.[112])

The development of a series of limitations and exceptions to the statute(s) of frauds reflects our mixed intuitions about the writing requirement: that having a writing requirement can prevent some fraudulent claims, as well as serving other goods (those other goods include the greater clarity and mutual understanding of the terms that come from putting agreements into writing), but that a writing requirement can also lead to, or even facilitate, other forms of fraud. There are sophisticated parties who entice other parties into agreements that fall under a statute of frauds but refuse to put terms into writing or to sign any writings that are created. Thus, they can enter agreements that are not enforceable or that they might be able to enforce but that the other parties cannot enforce against them.[113] In general, there are situations in which one or both contracting parties reasonably think that they are legally (contractually) bound, and third-party observers could have the same view, but a legal system with a writing requirement would refuse enforcement.

It is worth noting that the English legal system, in which the statute of frauds originated, has largely gotten rid of that statute. And neither the UN Convention on

---

[107] UCC § 2–201(3)(c).
[108] The exception has been traced back to *Butcher v. Stapley*, 1 Vern. 363, 23 Eng. Rep. 524 (Ch. 1685), decided only a few years after the enactment of the original Statute of Frauds.
[109] *Restatement (Second) of Contracts* § 129; *Winternitz v. Summit Hills Joint Venture*, 532 A.2d 1089 (Md. App. 1987).
[110] *Restatement (Second) of Contracts* § 139.
[111] *See, e.g., Stangl v. Ernst Home Center, Inc.*, 948 P.2d 356 (Utah App. 1997).
[112] *See Restatement (First) of Contracts* § 178, Comment f.
[113] The UCC statute of frauds, through its merchants confirmation exception, UCC § 2–201(2), largely does away with such one-way enforceability for sales of goods between merchants.

Contracts for the International Sale of Goods (CISG) nor the UNIDROIT Principles contain any provision of this sort.[114] In these legal contexts, it is not that a writing is irrelevant but that the existence or absence of a signed writing is simply one factor among many for the fact-finder to consider in determining whether a (binding) contract exists.

D. OTHER GROUNDS FOR RECOVERY

Consideration doctrine restricted legally enforceable promises to those that had been part of a bargained-for exchange. While the common law rejected the notion of "moral consideration" being sufficient to make a promise legally enforceable, there were some categories of cases in which the moral argument for enforcement was sufficiently strong, and the categories sufficiently cabined, that enforcement has been allowed even without new consideration. The following sections discuss two such exceptions: promissory estoppel and promissory restitution.[115]

1. *Promissory Estoppel*

Restatement (Second) of Contracts, Section 90,[116] holds that if there has been a promise, on which the promisor should reasonably have expected to induce action or forbearance, and the promisee in fact does act or forbear, the promise is enforceable to the extent necessary to avoid injustice. Although promissory estoppel (also known as "reliance" or "Section 90 reliance") was once considered primarily a substitute for consideration in limited exceptional cases, it is now generally considered a separate cause of action.[117]

The idea of promissory estoppel is related to the better-established rule of equitable estoppel: if plaintiff had earlier made a factual claim on which a defendant reasonably relied, than the plaintiff is estopped to rely on the contrary to that factual claim. The difference between equitable estoppel and promissory estoppel is that the first

---

[114] CISG art. 11; UNIDROIT Principles art. 1.2.

[115] There are other limited exceptions, such as promises to revive obligations that had previously been erased by the statute of limitations, a bankruptcy action, or the failure of a contractual condition. *See Restatement (Second) of Contracts* §§ 82, 83, 84. This is not the place to get into the question of whether these other forms are properly considered part of "contract." That topic is considered, in passing, in Chapter 9. For present purposes, it is sufficient to note that these topics are commonly discussed in American contract law courses and that is the main reason they are mentioned in this book.

[116] In the *Second Restatement*, the relevant section is in fact Section 90(1); Subsection 90(2) suggests a rule allowing the enforceability of charitable promises without consideration or reliance. The rule suggested by Section 90(2) has been adopted in only one jurisdiction, Iowa. *See Salsbury v. Northwestern Bell Telephone Co.*, 221 N.W.2d 609 (Iowa 1974). Promissory estoppel had been the entirety of Section 90 of the first *Restatement of Contract Law*; and today, almost every reference one finds to "Section 90" is to § 90(1).

[117] For the history of this development, see Metzger & Phillips 1983.

depends on a statement regarding the current state of affairs, whereas the latter goes to a future action.

The idea that there should be recovery on a promise based on reasonable reliance, even in the absence of consideration, has deep historical roots[118] and has been recognized in other jurisdictions.[119] When the first *Restatement of Contracts* introduced Section 90 promissory estoppel, the doctrine was grounded primarily on three lines of cases: promises within families, charitable pledges, and promises for worker pensions.[120] In these three areas, it is common for promises to be made without any expectation of a return promise (or action), and for the promisee to change its position in reliance upon the promise. However, Section 90 is written in general terms, and courts have applied it to enforce promises in areas far outside the three topic areas mentioned.

It is common for students, when they first learn of promissory estoppel, to see it everywhere. With just a little creativity, it is not hard to discover promise, reliance, and injustice in almost every story of promises not kept or negotiations that break down. However, it is equally easy to see why – and how – courts come to the point of rarely recognizing such claims.[121] From the court's perspective, people should know that one should not rely on promises that are not part of enforceable contracts, or rely on oral promises that contradict the written contract, or rely on promises not reduced to a writing where the statute requires a writing, and so on. Lawyers will argue – and courts will generally accept – that to be too quick or too generous in accepting reliance claims will undermine the predictability and certainty of transactions, as well as encouraging false claims.

In analyzing Section 90 claims, the fourth criterion (injustice can only be avoided by enforcing the promise) is basically a conclusion that follows from the first three criteria and that is a function of the strength of those three: the clearer the promise, the more reasonable the reliance, and the more extensive the reliance, the more it will seem that injustice can only be avoided by enforcing of the promise. (The remedies available, or not available, for promissory estoppel claims are discussed in Chapter 6, Section C.)

---

[118] In St. Germain's work of 1580, the "Student" states "if he to whom the promise is made have a charge by reason of the promise, which he hath also performed, then in that case he shall have an action for that thing that was promised, though he that made the promise have no worldly profit by it." St. Germain 1874: dialogue 2, ch. 24, at 177. And, according to one commentator, if the idea is in St. Germain, it likely has far older roots: A. W. B. Simpson describes *Doctor and Student* as having been "produced by paste and scissors plagiarism and rearrangement of material taken from confessors' manuals, the ultimate source being a fourteenth-century Franciscan." Simpson, 1975b: 251 (footnote omitted). J. H. Baker finds a view comparable to promissory estoppel established in English law in the fifteenth century. J. H. Baker 2002: 339.

[119] For English law, see *Central London Property Trust Ltd. v. High Trees House Ltd.*, [1947] KB 130; Treitel 2004: 52–54.

[120] *See* Boyer 1952.

[121] Promissory estoppel claims are successful in less than 10 percent of the cases in which they are raised. Hillman 1998: 589–590.

2. *Promissory Restitution*

Section 86 of the *Restatement* allows for recovery ("to the extent necessary to prevent injustice") where a promise has been made "in recognition of a benefit previously received."[122] The seminal case for promissory restitution is *Webb v. McGowin*,[123] where Webb saved McGowin's life, and McGowin subsequently promised to make regular payments to Webb for the rest of Webb's life. McGowin did so, but after his own death, his estate stopped payment, and Webb sued. The court strained to find justifications that partook of restitution (if one can claim compensation for saving another person's cattle, why not for saving his life?) and in implied promise (that from the promise of payment one could somehow presume a prior request for the action of saving McGowin's life). The *Restatement* standard circumvents such strained reasoning by creating an express, if limited, exception to the consideration requirement.

It is important to add that the *Restatement* also adds limitations even to this already-limited exception: no recovery will be allowed if it is clear that the benefit was intended as a gift,[124] if the promisor was not unjustly enriched, or if the benefit of the subsequent promise is disproportionate to the original benefit.[125] The indications are that Section 86 has not been much used, by either courts or litigants.[126]

3. *Restitution/Unjust Enrichment*

Although promissory reliance and promissory restitution involve the enforcement of promises in the absence of consideration, the large category of "unjust enrichment" (also called "restitution" and "quasi-contract"[127]) can justify recovery for interactions that did not even involve a promise. Unjust enrichment is an equitable doctrine, or set of doctrines, that starts from a vague injunction: that someone who is unjustly enriched at the expense of another person must compensate that person. From that broad starting principle, it is important to note (1) that courts apply the principle narrowly and sparingly, and (2) that over time courts have established relatively

---

[122] *Restatement (Second) of Contracts* § 86(1).

[123] 27 Ala. App. 82, 168 So. 196 (1935).

[124] The structure of the section would make it seem that the person opposing enforcement of the promise would be the one with the burden of showing that the benefit conferred was intended as a gift. This contrasts with the approach of the *Restatement (Second) of Restitution* §§ 116, 117, where emergency work to save a person's health or property is compensable only if there was an intention to charge – that is, the person seeking recovery has the burden to prove that he or she intended to charge money for the service rendered. Assuming that actions done in emergency situations are often done without clear or articulated purposes, which party has the burden of proof in cases arising from such events can be crucial in the outcome.

[125] *Restatement (Second) of Contracts* § 86(2). A few states have statutory provisions whose effect is similar to Section 86. *E.g.*, California Civil Code § 1606.

[126] *See* Butterfoss & Blair 2010.

[127] The terminology in this area is notoriously imprecise and used differently by different writers.

specific rules for the application of the principle in various fact situations.[128] For example, there are special sets of rules for when someone can recover for emergency health care or the emergency saving of property.[129]

As with other equitable doctrines (including some of the equitable defenses discussed later in this chapter), it is probably best to understand the cause of action of unjust enrichment as a recourse available in cases of extreme injustice, but one that courts will be reluctant to use in less extreme cases, for fear of upsetting reliance and predictability. Among the contract-like settings in which some courts have allowed unjust enrichment recovery are (1) subcontractors who have not been paid for their work (by their contracting partners, the general contractor), suing owners who have not paid the general contractor or anyone else for the work in question,[130] and (2) contractors who had not been paid by the tenants who hired them, then suing the owners of the property[131] – but even with these sorts of claims courts are far more likely to deny recovery than to grant it.[132]

As is discussed in Chapter 6, Section C, restitution is also important as a basis of recovery for breaching parties or for parties in contracts that would have lost money.

E. FORMATION-BASED DEFENSES

If one starts with freedom of contract as a strong principle underlying the formation doctrines of contract law, then certain limitations on enforcing agreements seem to follow naturally. Freedom of contract (and its correlate, freedom *from* contract[133]) is an image, or an ideal, of competent actors choosing for themselves what obligations they will take upon themselves: the value of autonomy invoked has little place when there are significant questions about either the actor's basic competence or the actor's basic knowledge (or ability to obtain basic knowledge) about the transaction in question. This section looks at a number of the defenses to validity (or enforceability) of agreements based on the parties circumstances or actions at the time of the agreement's formation.

---

[128] The most recent rethinking of the principles in this area, the *Restatement of the Law (Third) of Restitution and Unjust Enrichment*, was recently completed (2010) and published (2011) by the American Law Institute.

[129] *Restatement (Second) of Restitution* §§ 116, 117; see also *Restatement (Third) of Restitution and Unjust Enrichment* §§ 20, 21.

[130] *See, e.g., Commerce Partnership 8098 Limited Partnership v. Equity Contracting Co.*, 695 So. 2d 383 (Fla. App. 1997).

[131] *See, e.g., Idaho Lumber, Inc. v. Buck*, 710 P.2d 647 (Idaho App. 1985).

[132] The *Restatement* expresses the general principle as follows: "If the claimant renders to a third person a contractual performance for which the claimant does not receive the promised compensation, and the effect of the claimant's uncompensated performance is to confer a benefit on the defendant, the claimant is entitled to restitution from the defendant as necessary to prevent unjust enrichment." *Restatement (Third) of Restitution and Unjust Enrichment* § 25(1).

[133] E.g., Macaulay 2004.

1. *Misrepresentation and Nondisclosure*

Where one party misrepresents facts, and the other party relies on those misrepresentations in entering the agreement, the innocent party has the right to rescind the agreement.[134] Misrepresentations of facts can be intentional or innocent.[135] Intentional misrepresentation is also known as "fraud," and is actionable both in contract law and in tort law. In contract law, one has the remedy of rescission; in tort law, one has the opportunity to obtain damages, and sometimes punitive damages (the latter being generally unavailable in contract law, see Chapter 6, Section B).

The party seeking to prove intentional misrepresentation (as a contractual claim[136]) must prove that there was a representation, that it was false, that the speaker knew the claim to be false, that it was made with the intention to deceive, that it related to a matter material to the transaction, that it was relied on, and that it caused damage.[137] With innocent misrepresentation, the elements of knowing falsehood and intention to deceive fall out, but courts then tend to put greater weight on showing the materiality of the deception and the reasonableness of the reliance on it before granting rescission.

One issue with misrepresentation[138] raises a larger problem. There seems to be no sharp line between the type of deception contract law considers unacceptable – the type of deception that will justify allowing the other party to rescind the agreement – and the types of deception that are implicitly treated as acceptable (allowing the other party no remedy).[139] The fuzziness of the lines is manifest in the idea of "puffing" (the sort of exaggeration found in advertisements) – clear examples of intentional misrepresentations but treated as not actionable because reasonable contracting parties are supposed to expect these forms of distortion and not to rely on their veracity. In the end, the lines drawn between acceptable and unacceptable forms of negotiation and persuasion seem a matter of judgment and a product as much of policy and pragmatism as of strict morality.

---

[134] There are also, if rarely, more serious forms of misrepresentation: misrepresentation as to the nature of a document being signed (e.g., saying that it has no legal effect when it does): such "fraud in factum" or "fraud in execution," as contrasted with "fraud in the inducement," results in a contract that is void, not just voidable. Farnsworth 2004: § 4.10, at 236–237.

[135] A misrepresentation can also be "reckless" in the face of possible falsehood, and, as in the criminal law, recklessness here is often treated as the legal (and moral) equivalent of intentionality. *See Restatement (Second) of Contracts* § 162(1)(b), (c) & Comment b.

[136] The elements of intentional misrepresentation (usually going by the label "fraud") as a tort law claim may be different.

[137] In some jurisdictions, assertions of fraud (intentional misrepresentation) need to be shown by clear and convincing evidence, a higher burden of proof than the usual standard of preponderance of the evidence.

[138] A similar line of analysis can be offered for duress (*see* Unger 1986: 66–75; Kelman 1987: 22–25), and perhaps also undue influence and unconscionability.

[139] E.g., Kelman 1987: 21–22.

Although in general it takes a deceptive statement to give the other party a right to rescind, in limited circumstances, parties will be allowed to rescind an agreement based on deception that occurs without express (mis)representations. These include concealment (which will often be treated as the moral and legal equivalent of a misrepresentation[140]) and nondisclosure.

The basic rule of American (and Anglo-American) transactions had been, and to a significant extent still is, "caveat emptor", "let the buyer beware" (this is also the starting point of the analysis of warranties, the topic of Chapter 4, Section E). The basic standard, as regards disclosure, was stated in an early-nineteenth-century U.S. Supreme Court decision, *Laidlaw v. Organ*.[141] The case involved a purchase of tobacco at a time when the War of 1812 had just ended. The buyer was aware of the Treaty of Ghent, ending the war (and likely increasing the price of tobacco significantly), but the seller was not. The seller asked the buyer if he was aware of any news "calculated to enhance the price or value" of tobacco; the buyer remained silent. Both the trial court and the Supreme Court agreed that a defense of fraud could not be grounded on the buyer's failure to disclose his knowledge of the peace treaty.[142] The Court noted that the seller should have insisted on an answer to his question.

American contract law has slowly, and grudgingly, developed rules that in a few contexts there is an obligation (usually by the seller, occasionally by the buyer) to disclose information to the other party. The *Restatement* lists four categories: (1) where disclosure is required to prevent a prior representation (true when made) from becoming false (e.g., if a representation was made about the zoning classification of a piece of land, but the zoning board subsequently met and changed the classification); (2) where the party knows that disclosure is needed to correct the other party's error as to a material matter and failure to disclose would be contrary to good faith and fair dealing; (3) where the party knows that disclosure is needed to correct the other party's error regarding the content of a writing embodying or evidencing the parties' agreement; and (4) where the parties are in a fiduciary relationship (e.g., lawyer-client).[143] Three of the four are fairly narrow exceptions. The second, "good faith" exception is fairly broad and has been held to apply mostly to "big ticket" items (e.g., the sale of a house) and to circumstances in which the buyer is not well positioned to learn the information for him- or herself.[144] On the whole, though, what obligations of disclosure parties have are set almost entirely by state and federal consumer protection statutes and regulations.

---

[140] Farnsworth 2004: § 4.11, at 239.
[141] 15 U.S. (2 Wheat.) 178 (1817).
[142] However, the Supreme Court remanded the case for further consideration of a claim of express misrepresentation.
[143] *Restatement (Second) of Contracts* § 161.
[144] E.g., *Hill v. Jones*, 725 P.2d 1115 (Ariz. App. 1986), review denied (Oct. 1, 1986).

2. Mistake

Where the parties, at the time of the agreement, shared a mistaken belief regarding some significant aspect of the object of the contract, the courts will sometimes, under their equitable powers, grant a rescission. (This is the doctrine of mutual mistake; unilateral mistake is discussed later.)

The traditional common law rule made the ability to obtain a rescission turn on the distinction between mistakes as to the "essence" of the object rather than just its quality or value. If this analysis was not confusing enough – sounding as it did of Aristotelian metaphysics – the confusion was increased by the paradigm case. In *Sherwood v. Walker*,[145] the Michigan Supreme Court asserted that where the parties buying and selling a cow mistakenly believed that the cow was barren (when she was, in fact, carrying a calf), that was in fact a mistake going to the essence of the object of sale. The sense in which mistaking a cow capable of breeding for a barren cow "goes to the very nature of the thing,"[146] although it may make a kind of intuitive sense, gives little guidance as to how to decide the next case, involving facts other than barren and nonbarren cows.[147]

The *Restatement* prefers a different approach, focusing on (1) whether the mutual mistake goes to a basic assumption of the agreement and materially affects the agreed exchange of performances, and (2) whether it is a mistake for which one party has assumed the risk. This form of analysis would seem to tend against the granting of rescissions, for it is common for contracts to include provisions that could reasonably be read as a buyer's assumption of risk,[148] and, even where there is no express provision, it would be easy to claim that buyers usually assume the risk that objects will not be as valuable or as useful as they assume and hope. Still, like most of the equitable defenses, mutual mistake remains present for those rare cases in which the court feels strongly from the circumstances that enforcement of the agreement would be deeply unfair (perhaps because of a suspicion of sharp practices in the formation process, but practices that fell short of actionable misrepresentation or duress).

In extreme cases, courts will allow rescission even when the mistake was not mutual but was made only by the party seeking to rescind (i.e., unilateral mistake). In general, these are cases where the other party has been at fault in some way, because it contributed to the mistake (e.g., through ambiguous or potentially misleading instructions in the specifications in a contract bidding case), because the mistake was so egregious that the other party must have known of the mistake (and thus to

---

[145] 33 N.W. 919 (Mich. 1987).

[146] *Id.* at 923.

[147] Charles Fried reflects the view of many when he describes the analysis under the classical test as "nonsense." C. Fried 1981: 62.

[148] This is most obvious in cases where the agreement includes an "as is" clause, or a clause stating that the buyer has had the chance to inspect the object of sale.

enforce the agreement would be to allow the other party to take advantage of the error in a context where that would be unfair), or in some other way the enforcement of the agreement as written would be "unconscionable" (often because of the severe harm that enforcement would cause the plaintiff and the relative lack of injury that nonenforcement would cause the defendant).[149]

The traditional rule had been that rescission for unilateral mistake would be only for "clerical" or "mathematical" errors – as contrasted to errors of judgment. However, many jurisdictions have relaxed or ignored those constraints.[150] Similarly, although some courts still use language that indicates that rescission for unilateral mistake will not be allowed if the plaintiff had been negligent, it is not easy to find cases in which a plaintiff commits an error egregious enough to warrant its seeking rescission without that plaintiff's also being negligent in some way. It is probably more accurate to describe the nonnegligence requirement as one of the plaintiff's having acted in good faith and having been less than grossly negligent.[151]

Overall, though, it is important to recall that courts, reluctant in general to authorize equitable claims or defenses, are likely to be especially reluctant to allow a party to get out of a contract based on its own mistake.

3. Duress

A party's ability to avoid obligations under a contract on the basis of duress has a long history, going back to Roman law and continuing through the medieval law of English writs.[152]

Originally, duress as a defense to the enforcement of an otherwise valid contract was available only where a transaction had been coerced through a serious physical assault or a threat of the same.[153] Starting in the eighteenth century, courts began increasingly to allow avoidance of contractual obligations for economic pressure (sometimes labeled "duress of goods," and, later, "economic duress").[154]

To the extent that the idea was that relief should be available where a party's action was not voluntary,[155] the extension of the doctrine from physical violence to severe economic pressure makes perfect sense. The downside of the extension is that the rule went from a relatively bright-line standard of no physical violence or threat of physical violence to a less easily cabined set of criteria.

Under the modern doctrine, the defense of duress is available when one party enters an agreement because of the coercive or improper threats of the other party,

---

[149] *See Restatement (Second) of Contracts* § 153. As with mutual mistake, under the *Restatement* standard, a party cannot recover if it in some way bore the risk of the mistake. *Id.* at §§ 153, 154.

[150] *See, e.g., Wil-Fred's, Inc. v. Metropolitan Sanitary District*, 372 N.E.2d 946 (Ill. App. 1978).

[151] *See Restatement (Second) of Contracts* §157 & Comment a.

[152] *See, e.g.,* Simpson 1975a: 99, 537; Buckland 1963: 416–417.

[153] Dawson 1947: 254–255.

[154] *Id.,* 255–262.

[155] *Id.,* 254.

threats that leave the threatened party no reasonable alternative but to enter the agreement. Where there has been duress, the resulting agreement is voidable at the election of the victimized party.[156] The agreement can also be ratified, either through express statement or, implicitly, through acceptance of benefits (which, for many courts, will include inaction for a significant time after the threat has passed). For most jurisdictions, the categories of "coercive" or "improper" acts include but extend beyond illegal actions.[157]

A common concern is that parties facing hard economic times could always make a tenable case of duress for many of the agreements they enter (especially agreements settling claims or modifying existing agreements). As Judge Posner has pointed out, it is actually not to the benefit of a struggling commercial company to have the power to disavow any and all contractual agreements it enters, for that fact will discourage other parties from entering contractual arrangements with it.[158] So courts are reluctant to find duress merely on a showing of "no reasonable alternatives" for the party claiming duress, combined with some arguable misfeasance in negotiations by the other party. Courts will usually ask for something more: either a (causal) nexus between the misfeasance of the other party and the distressed state of the party claiming distress or evidence that the other party consciously took advantage of the first party's difficult circumstances.

Roberto Unger wrote critically of the American contract law doctrine of duress, that it "serve[s] as a roving commission to correct the most egregious and overt forms of an omnipresent type of disparity."[159] One can accept this description of many of contract law's equitable doctrines while seeing the availability of such doctrines to use in the most egregious cases as a benefit of the system rather than a defect.

4. Undue Influence

Undue influence is a doctrine better known in the law of wills (where weak and vulnerable people seem frequently to be talked into writing wills in favor of trusted friends, lawyers, and clergy, who have taken undue advantage of their weakness or fear), but it is also recognized in contract law. Where one party uses over-persuasion and the other party is susceptible to influence (how much of the second is needed

---

[156] More precisely, economic duress makes agreements voidable at the election of the victim. The narrower traditional understanding of duress, in which force or threat of force had been used, was usually treated as making the agreement not merely voidable but in fact void.

[157] See *Austin Instrument, Inc. v. Loral Corp.*, 272 N.E.2d 533 (N.Y. 1971) (threat to breach contract can be "improper act" for purposes of proving duress); *Totem Marine Tug & Barge, Inc. v. Alyeska Pipeline Service Co.*, 584 P.2d 15 (Alaska 1978) (same). Not all jurisdictions follow this extension. E.g., *Farm Credit Services of Michigan's Heartland, P.C.A. v. Weldon*, 591 N.W.2d 438, 447 (Mich. App. 1998) (Michigan restricts duress to illegal acts).

[158] See *Selmer Co. v. Blakeslee-Midwest Co.*, 704 F.2d 924, 927 (7th Cir. 1983) (Posner, J.).

[159] Unger 1983: 629.

depends on how much of the first is present), the victim of the undue influence has the right to rescind the agreement.

For many courts and commentators, the paradigm case of undue influence, against which other fact patterns are compared, is *Odorizzi v. Bloomfield School District.*[160] In that case, the plaintiff, a schoolteacher, had been arrested for homosexual activity and questioned, and then had been without sleep for almost two full days. At that point, two of the plaintiff's supervisors came to his house and sought his resignation, telling him that they had his best interests at heart; that he did not have time to consult an attorney; and that if he did not resign, they would fire him and publicize his arrest. The plaintiff resigned, but was able to withdraw his resignation, as it had been the product of undue influence.[161] The court offered an influential list of the factors the court should consider in determining whether "over-persuasion" had occurred:

> The pattern usually involves several of the following elements: (1) discussion of the transaction at an unusual or inappropriate time, (2) consummation of the transaction in an unusual place, (3) insistent demand that the business be finished at once, (4) extreme emphasis on untoward consequences of delay, (5) the use of multiple persuaders by the dominant side against a single servient party, (6) absence of third-party advisers to the servient party, (7) statements that there is no time to consult financial advisers or attorneys.[162]

If a number of these elements are simultaneously present, the persuasion may be characterized as excessive, and the "over-persuaded" party will be allowed to rescind the agreement.

There are many fact patterns in which colorable claims of both duress and undue influence could be brought. Much may turn on whether one can identify a "wrongful act" for the purpose of duress and whether the party seeking to avoid enforcement was sufficiently vulnerable or susceptible for the purposes of undue influence.

As with duress, undue influence can be viewed as combining concern about whether the vulnerable party sufficiently consented with a desire to police improper negotiating tactics by the other party.

5. *Minority*

Minority (sometimes known as "infancy") is a limitation on the ability of children under the age of majority to enter fully binding agreements. This defense goes back, in Anglo-American law, to 1292, and the outlines of the doctrine were well settled by

---

[160] 246 Cal. App. 2d 123, 54 Cal. Rptr. 533 (Ct. App. 1966).
[161] In a narrow sense of the term, this is not a contract case, but it is frequently placed in contract law casebooks and taught as part of contract law courses. Whether the letter of resignation is best thought of as a contract or not, the question of whether the signer properly consented is exactly the same as will occur in contract cases.
[162] *Odorizzi*, 246 Cal. App.2d at 133.

the fifteenth century.[163] Minors have a limited legal power to disaffirm agreements they have entered; because of this ability, many vendors will not enter transactions with minors without a competent adult as a cosigner.

Some states have modified their minority doctrine to allow sellers – at least those who acted in good faith (i.e., both without knowledge that the buyer was underage and without overreaching) – to be compensated when the minor disaffirms and returns the goods purchased; the compensation in these cases is measured either by the benefit the minor received from the good or from the depreciation of the good's value.[164] Additionally, state legislators have regularly created limited exceptional categories (often including medical treatment, insurance, or financing) where minors of a certain age could enter fully binding agreements.[165]

States differ on how they treat minors' misrepresentations of their age: some hold that such misrepresentations remove (by estoppel or otherwise by equity) the minor's power to disaffirm. Other states reach a similar result by saying that the minor still has the power to disaffirm, but the other party would have a tort action for fraud to recover any losses. A few courts seem to hold the misrepresentation as being of no consequence and still allow the lying minor full rights of rescission.[166]

There is a related doctrine, from outside contract law, that holds parents liable for the reasonable market value of "necessaries" that their minor children have purchased. (This, in principle, makes sure that vendors of basic goods will be willing to deal with minor purchasers, despite the general right minors have to disaffirm agreements.) How widely "necessaries" are defined varies significantly from state to state.

6. *Mental Incapacity*

A contract made by someone who is not mentally competent is at least voidable[167] at the insistence of that person.[168] As with minority, mental incapacity deals with an outside boundary, beyond which we are no longer willing to assume that parties are the best judges of their own best interests and that they are in a good position to protect themselves. Mental incapacity creates more difficult practical problems

---

[163] *See* Note 1948: 829 & n. 1, citing Y. B. 20 & 21 Edw. I at 318 (1292); *see also* Williston 1920–1924: vol. 1, § 223, at 438–439.

[164] The two measures will often be similar, but not always, as when the object's value diminishes for reasons that give no benefit to the buyer, as in the truck that was damaged by a third party in *Dodson v. Shrader*, 824 S.W.2d 545 (Tenn. 1992), a case in which the court also offers a good overview of the alternative approaches to minority purchases.

[165] Examples from Massachusetts statutes are given in *Sharon v. City of Newton*, 769 N.E.2d 738, 746 n. 9 (Mass. 2002).

[166] Farnsworth 2004: § 4.5, at 227–228.

[167] In some jurisdictions, the agreement is void.

[168] Of course, if the person in question has ongoing incompetence, the avoidance will be made by the person's guardian in the person's name.

than minority, because of the lack of a clear, bright line between competence and incompetence, and because there is no easy way for contracting parties to check competence (as one could check a driver's license for age in relation to the defense of minority, discussed in the prior subsection).

The doctrine is an equitable doctrine, so the court's willingness to offer a remedy will usually turn on the particular facts of the case. When a transaction occurs where the other party did not know of the incompetency, generally rescission will be allowed only if the parties can be returned to the status quo. Where, however, the other party knew or should have known about the incompetency, or in some way took advantage of the incompetency, rescission may be allowed even if the goods cannot be returned.[169]

7. Intoxication

In general, voluntary intoxication at the time the contract was entered, by itself, is not an excuse to the obligation to perform under an otherwise valid contract. However, most jurisdictions (and the *Restatement*) hold that parties can rescind an agreement if, at the time of signing, the other party "has reason to know" that the first party, because intoxicated, cannot understand the transaction, or cannot act in a reasonable manner in relation to it.[170]

F. THEORETICAL IMPLICATIONS

Formation issues, and the alternative grounds for recovery, raise some of the hardest questions for those who wish to theorize about contract law at a general level.

For those who would see contracts as being about protecting the autonomy or respecting the consent of parties, or otherwise enforcing their promises (or, more abstractly, the acts of their will), the actual rules of enforcement seem to raise a series of challenges (or to evoke a series of objections). Objective approaches to formation, combined with alternative (contract-like) grounds of obligation, such as promissory estoppel, create circumstances in which parties are bound even though they had not intended to bind themselves. This is the reasonable compromise between empowering the individual and protecting the reasonable reliance and reasonable expectations of parties with whom the individual deals (and interested third parties as well).

The doctrine of consideration remains as puzzling and problematic for theorists as it is for students. One can come up with interests that the doctrine can be said to

---

[169] *See Restatement (Second) of Contracts* § 15; *Hauer v. Union State Bank of Wautoma*, 532 N.W.2d 456 (Wis. App. 1995) (bank acted in bad faith with incompetent lender; lender allowed to rescind the loan and recover her collateral even though all the loan proceeds had already been spent).
[170] *Restatement (Second) of Contracts* § 16. At least one jurisdiction does not allow a party to rescind an agreement based on intoxication. *Burroughs v. Richman*, 13 N.J.L. 233 (1832).

serve,[171] but it serves such interests poorly and awkwardly at best.[172] It seems a part of contract law best suited for a primarily historical explanation rather than any sort of normative justification.

Electronic contracting has raised doctrinal and practical problems that were not resolved well by existing law. Judges have largely ignored existing doctrine to come up with a result that they, and at least a few commentators,[173] consider most workable. When law changes in significant ways – whether the agent of change is the legislature or the courts – it creates a challenge for any legal theorist who offers a theory of contract law generally rather than merely this jurisdiction's contract law of today (a topic that is revisited in Chapter 9).

SUGGESTED FURTHER READING

Offer and Acceptance

Melvin Aron Eisenberg, "The Revocation of Offers," *Wisconsin Law Review*, vol. 2004, pp. 271–308 (2004).

Karl Llewellyn, "On Our Case-Law of Contract: Offer and Acceptance," Parts 1 & 2, *Yale Law Journal*, vol. 48, pp. 1–36 (1938), 779–818 (1939).

Objective and Subjective

Joseph M. Perillo, "The Origins of the Objective Theory of Contract Formation and Interpretation," *Fordham Law Review*, vol. 69, pp. 427–477 (2000).

Unilateral Contracts

Mark Pettit Jr., "Modern Unilateral Contracts," *Boston University Law Review*, vol. 63, pp. 551–596 (1983).

Consideration

Peter Benson, "The Idea of Consideration," *University of Toronto Law Journal*, vol. 61, pp. 241–278 (2011).

Melvin Aron Eisenberg, "The Principles of Consideration," *Cornell Law Review*, vol. 67, pp. 640–665 (1982).

Lon L. Fuller, "Consideration and Form," *Columbia Law Review*, vol. 41, pp. 799–824 (1941).

Roy Kreitner, "The Gift beyond the Grave: Revisiting the Question of Consideration," *Columbia Law Review*, vol. 101, pp. 1876–1957 (2001).

Val D. Ricks, "The Sophisticated Doctrine of Consideration," *George Mason Law Review*, vol. 9, pp. 99–143 (2000).

---

[171] *See, e.g.,* Fuller 1941.
[172] *E.g.* C. Fried 1981: 38–39.
[173] *E.g.,* E. Posner 2010: 1193–1194.

Gift Promises

Melvin Aron Eisenberg, "Donative Promises," *University of Chicago Law Review*, vol. 47, pp. 1–33 (1979).
_____, "The World of Contract and the World of Gift," *California Law Review*, vol. 85, pp. 821–866 (1997).

Statute of Frauds

John Kidwell, "Ruminations on Teaching the Statute of Frauds," *St. Louis University Law Journal*, vol. 44, pp. 1147–1462 (2000).

Promissory Estoppel

Benjamin F. Boyer, "Promissory Estoppel: Principle from Precedents," Parts 1 & 2, *Michigan Law Review*, vol. 50, pp. 639–674, 873–898 (1952).

Misrepresentation and Nondisclosure

Richard Craswell, "Taking Information Seriously: Misrepresentation and Nondisclosure in Contract Law and Elsewhere," *Virginia Law Review*, vol. 92, pp. 565–632 (2006).
Melvin Aron Eisenberg, "Disclosure in Contract Law," *California Law Review*, vol. 91, pp. 1645–1691 (2003).

Mistake

Melvin Aron Eisenberg, "Mistake in Contract Law," *California Law Review*, vol. 91, pp. 1573–1643 (2003).
Anthony T. Kronman, "Mistake, Disclosure, Information, and the Law of Contracts," *Journal of Legal Studies*, vol. 7, pp. 1–34 (1978).

Duress and Undue Influence

John P. Dawson, "Economic Duress – An Essay in Perspective," *Michigan Law Review*, vol. 45, pp. 253–290 (1947).
Grace M. Giesel, "A Realistic Proposal for the Contract Duress Doctrine," *West Virginia Law Review*, vol. 107, p. 443–498 (2005).

Minority

Cheryl B. Preston & Brandon T. Crowther, "Infancy Doctrine Inquiries," *Santa Clara Law Review*, vol. 52, pp. 47–80 (2012).

4

Interpretation

The previous chapter dealt with issues of formation. In practice, questions of whether there is a valid contract are probably less common than questions of what the parties' (valid) contract *means*. This chapter looks at the rules, standards, and presumptions that govern this often-crucial question.[1]

A. OBJECTIVE AND SUBJECTIVE

An issue that came up with formation (see Chapter 3, Section A) reappears in interpretation: should interpretation focus on the parties' subjective (individual, perhaps idiosyncratic) understanding of terms, or should it instead adopt an objective approach, interpreting terms according to some "plain meaning," dictionary, or "reasonable person" perspective? In the formation context, the question was whether an agreement resulted when two parties appeared to agree on the same terms (e.g., by express assent to a verbal proposal or by signing a written offer) but understood the agreement differently. Assuming that there is a valid agreement, the interpretation question is how the differently understood terms are to be applied. As discussed in the prior chapter, American contract law responds to formation issues in an objective way. With interpretation, the inclination remains largely objective but with some notable modifications.

The *Restatement* states that where the parties understand a term in the same way, that is how it should be applied;[2] however, where they understand a contractual term differently, if one party knew or had reason to know of the other party's

---

[1] A related issue this chapter does not discuss here the issue of who decides: whether an interpretive question is to be left to the judge or given to the jury. Although this can vary from state to state, generally factual questions of what the parties intended are given to the jury; most other interpretive questions are questions of law for the judge.

[2] *Restatement (Second) of Contracts* § 201(1). There is at least one (non-U.S.) jurisdiction in which a court has held that even clear evidence of a shared (unconventional) understanding of a term would

different understanding, the first party will be held to the second party's different understanding.[3] The "had reason to know" part of the rule is likely sufficient to hold parties to a "reasonable person's" (or "plain meaning") understanding of a term, as long as one party so understood the term.[4]

One corollary of an objective approach to interpretation is what is sometimes called "the duty to read."[5] Like the "duty to mitigate," this is not really a duty (see Chapter 6, Section B) but is rather a legal presumption or the negation of a potential line of defense. Contracting parties will not be allowed to defend against enforcement on the basis that they have not read the terms in question from a written contract or that they could not read the terms in question (because they are illiterate, or only literate in a language other than the language in which the contract was written). Courts will say that it was up to the party to read or to have the terms read to them or translated for them.

B. DEFAULT RULES, INCOMPLETE CONTRACTS, AND IMPLIED TERMS

As discussed later in this book (in Chapter 8), one basic ideal (or, if one prefers, one basic myth) of contract law is freedom of contract – the idea that one is, and should be, contractually bound only to the extent that one has expressly so chosen. The reality is, inevitably, more complicated: there are many circumstances in which parties are held to terms to which they did not assent, or at least did not expressly or "fully" assent. Three related topics in contract law that raise this issue of less-than-full assent to terms are the interpretive issues surrounding implied terms, default rules, and "incomplete contracts." The basic question here is how to construe agreements regarding matters on which the agreement appears to be silent or where the parties' preferences are not stated with sufficient clarity.[6]

Implied terms are terms that the court reads into an agreement. It is common to distinguish "implied in fact" terms from terms "implied in law."[7] Implied-in-fact terms are said to be those terms that derive from the parties' actual understanding of their agreement – what both parties would have said about some issue had you

---

be irrelevant to interpreting a term in an agreement, if the objective meaning of that term were different. *Brambles Holdings Ltd. v. Bathurst City Council*, 52 NSWLR 153, [2001] NSWCA 61 (Court of Appeal of the Supreme Court of New South Wales, deciding that "general commercial waste" includes "liquid waste," despite both parties having a contrary understanding).

3 *Restatement (Second) of Contracts* § 201(2).
4 Or at least would be willing so to claim during litigation.
5 *See, e.g.*, Macaulay 1966.
6 Craswell (2012) discusses the way in which the conclusion of whether there is a "gap" in an agreement is tied in with the policy judgment regarding what burdens (e.g., of salience or clear expression) will be imposed on parties attempting to opt out of particular default rules.
7 A comparable distinction can also be found at the formation stage, with courts sometimes finding agreements "implied in fact," on the basis of the parties' actions, whereas some unjust enrichment claims are characterized as obligations "implied in law."

asked them at the time the agreement was signed. Implied-in-law terms, by contrast, are imposed regardless of party intentions and understandings; they are grounded on statutory prescription or on the basis of fairness, efficiency, or some other public policy or objective. The obligation of good faith in the performance or enforcement of a contract (discussed in Chapter 5, Section D) is a term implied in law,[8] as are the mandatory "cooling off" periods one finds imposed on certain kinds of consumer contracts.

Of course, the line between implied in law and implied in fact can often be blurry or quite thin. This is exemplified by the line of cases implying an obligation of "reasonable efforts" or "best efforts" where there is an exclusive deal.[9]

The Uniform Commercial Code offers a number of terms that cover matters such as delivery, payment, and damages; these terms apply unless the parties expressly agree to contrary terms on the same topics.[10] This contrasts with "mandatory" terms, which the parties are not free to modify, even by express agreement.[11] Terms that apply unless the parties agree otherwise are known as "default terms" or "default rules,"[12] and they are present in the law regarding all kinds of contracts, not just the sales of goods covered by the UCC.

Beyond the particular and practical aspects of UCC default terms, there has grown a general debate about default rules in contract law, connected with a discussion about how judges should respond to "incomplete contracts." A variety of different approaches have been offered as to how legislators and judges should set default rules, including (1) selecting those that are most efficient (that maximize efficiency[13]); (2) selecting those that most people would have selected had they chosen (majoritarian default, a criterion that may overlap significantly with the efficiency criterion);[14] (3) selecting those that force parties to divulge crucial information, to undermine asymmetric information situations (penalty defaults);[15] (4) selecting only terms that

---

[8] *See* UCC §§ 1–203, 2–103(j). In revised UCC art. 1, the good-faith provisions appear in §§ 1–302(b) & 1–304.

[9] *See, e.g., Wood v. Lucy, Lady Duff-Gordon,* 222 N.Y. 88, 118 N.E. 214 (1917); UCC § 2–306(2); Farnsworth 1984.

[10] *E.g.,* UCC §§ 2–307 (delivery in single lot or several lots); 2–308 (place of delivery), 2–309 (time of shipment, termination rules), 2–314 (implied warranties), 2–719 (modifying remedies).

[11] This famously includes the nonwaivable duty of good faith; UCC § 1–203.

[12] *"Default"* here seems to be used in analogy to the default settings in computer hardware and software. These ideas have legal applications outside of contract law: the use of default rules is also important in corporate charters, wills (as contrasted with intestate succession), and other areas of law.

[13] As Craswell points out, efficiency might require a more complex calculation than simply counting heads: if part of the population wants one default and a different part wants a different default, an efficiency calculation would need to incorporate an evaluation of how costly it would be for each segment to contract around a disfavored default, such that a default might be inefficient even if favored by a majority of contracting parties. Craswell 2012.

[14] *See* Charny 1991; *cf.* Ayres & Gertner 1999.

[15] Ayres & Gertner 1989; but see E. Posner 2006, who challenges the existence of penalty defaults, with Ayres 2006 responding, and Adler 1999 raising some questions about the operation of penalty default rules in cases like *Hadley v. Baxendale.* (*Hadley* is discussed in Chapter 6, Section B.)

the parties could be said to have consented to (consent theory);[16] and (5) selecting the terms that are more favorable to the party with the greater bargaining power (as this reflects the likely bargain that would have been struck).[17]

Examples of default rules include that sales of goods come with implied warranties,[18] and that consequential damages are generally available,[19] but that such damages will be available only up to the normal or expected level.[20] The parties are allowed to contract around these default rules through express terms in their agreement.[21]

In talking about default rules, one must also develop a view about what a party needs to do to "opt out" of the default rule.[22] Default rules are said to have different amounts of "stickiness," which indicates the difficulty of contracting around them.[23] There may be a requirement that agreements to change the default rule be in writing and that the writing use particular language, and under those circumstances the courts might even raise questions about the voluntariness (and thus the validity) of the new terms.

Some judges and commentators have argued that it is best to think of contract defenses like impossibility, impracticability, and frustration as default rules filling in "gaps" in incomplete contracts.[24] Those doctrines are considered at greater length in Chapter 5, Section C.

C. RULES OF INTERPRETATION

Sometimes commentators distinguish interpretation from construction; according to this distinction, *interpretation* refers to efforts to determine what the parties actually meant, whereas *construction* refers to the rules for the application of the agreements' terms grounded on other policies and not directed primarily at determining the parties' intentions.[25] Although many of the rules of interpretation mentioned in this section are truly "interpretive" rules in this sense, some, as we will see, are better understood as rules of construction. (As the line between interpretation and construction is often far from clear, and the distinction between the two does not

---

[16] Barnett 1992b. In this analysis, "consenting to a term" would include silence, at least in those circumstances in which the default term is well known or easy to discover, and it would not be costly to contract around it. Barnett 1992b: 866.

[17] Ben-Shahar 2009.

[18] UCC §§ 2–314, 2–315.

[19] UCC § 2–715.

[20] *Hadley v. Baxendale*, 9 Ex. 341, 23 L.J. Exch. 179; 2 C.L.R. 517; 18 Jur. 358 (1854).

[21] *See, e.g.*, UCC §§ 2–316 (exclusion or modification of warranties), 2–719 (modification or limitation of remedy); *Hadley v. Baxendale*.

[22] *See* Ayres & Gertner 1989: 120, Klass 2009: 1462; Craswell 2012.

[23] E.g., Goldberg 2006: 3.

[24] A related argument is that courts should respond to incomplete contracts by enforcing relationship-enforcing norms. E.g., Macneil 1978, 2001.

[25] E.g., E. Patterson 1964: 833–836.

reflect any doctrinal rules, the remainder of this text uses the terms interchangeably.)

1. *Canons of Interpretation*

There are rules, principles, or canons that are established and followed to varying extents in the interpretation of contracts. Some of these are borrowed from or overlap those used in statutory interpretation.[26] Steven Burton helpfully summarized a number of the major canons:

> One canon holds that all of the words of an agreement should be construed wherever possible as consistent with one another – to produce a harmonious whole. Another holds that all of the words in an agreement should be given effect if possible.... A third holds that specific terms prevail over general terms if there is a conflict. A fourth, *expressio unis est exclusio alterius* (when one thing is expressed, all excluded things are omitted), is not often used. *Ejusdem generis* provides that, when general, catch-all words ... follow a sequence of specific words ..., the general words have the discrete characteristics of the specific words. *Noscitur a sociis* says that words or terms in a contract should be understood with reference to those that accompany them. And a word's meaning in one part of a contract is presumed to be its meaning wherever it appears.[27]

One canon of interpretation distinctive to contract law is "*contra proferentem*,"[28] under which an ambiguous word or phrase is construed in a way least favorable to the party who drafted it. This principle of interpretation is most often applied with insurance agreements and other agreements in which there is a significant imbalance in sophistication and bargaining power, and the agreement is on a standard form. The principle offers a sort of "punishment" for those who would use ambiguous language in their agreements (perhaps hoping to leave one impression with consumers but to argue for a different reading if and when the clause's meaning is litigated), and (thus) gives those drafting contracts a reason to use unambiguous language in their form contracts.

2. *Plain Meaning*

At least since the end of the nineteenth century, commentators have been skeptical of the idea of legal texts having clear or "plain" meaning. Oliver Wendell Holmes Jr. wrote dismissively on the matter: "It is not true that in practice ... a given word

---

[26] E. Patterson 1964; *cf.* Llewellyn 1950.
[27] Burton 2009: 59–60 (footnotes omitted). For a slightly fuller list, see E. Patterson 1964: 853–855.
[28] This is short for "*omnia praesumuntur contra proferentem.*" It is an approach to interpretation that goes back to Roman Law. Zimmermann 1996: 639–642.

or even a given collection of words has one meaning and no other. A word generally has several meanings, even in a dictionary."[29]

However, although commentators may have strong doubts about "plain meaning," the vast majority of courts do not. There is a convergence here, between the commonsense view that words (and sentences and contractual provisions) have clear meanings and the judicial (and party) interest in resolving what disputes one can at an early stage of litigation.[30] Under American legal practice, a conclusion that a contract has a clear or plain meaning allows the court to resolve the matter at the summary judgment stage; a conclusion that the agreement is ambiguous likely sends the case to (an expensive) trial.[31]

As is discussed in the next section, the notion of plain meaning also plays an important role in whether and when other evidence will be admitted and considered in the interpretation of written agreements.

D. PAROL EVIDENCE RULE

1. *The Rule(s)*

The parol evidence rule[32] is, in a sense, the flip side of the statute of frauds, discussed in Chapter 3, Section C.[33] Recall that the statute of frauds makes certain categories of agreements unenforceable unless there is written evidence of the agreements. The parol evidence rule is a rule that excludes certain evidence when an agreement has been reduced to a (signed) writing, thereby creating a possible incentive to reduce agreements to writing.[34] The parol evidence rule deals with the admission of other ("extrinsic") evidence to help in the interpretation of a written document.[35] Although

---

[29] Holmes 1899: 417.
[30] Under American law, if a dispute turns on the meaning of a contract, and the contract is unambiguous, the trial court will resolve the matter at summary judgment, without a full trial. However, if the contract is ambiguous, and thus there are reasonable factual disputes about its meaning, an (expensive) trial would be required.
[31] Though not in the case of insurance agreements, as discussed in Chapter 7, Section B.
[32] One sometimes sees the term as the *"parole* evidence rule" (and not only by students on exams). Both spellings refer to an old English usage, meaning oral; *"parol"* has the advantage of not encouraging confusion with the term for criminals under state supervision.
[33] Although the parol evidence rule is recognized, in some form, in all U.S. jurisdictions, as mentioned in Chapter 2, Section E, there is nothing comparable to the parol evidence rule in the UN Convention on Contract for the International Sale of Goods (CISG). *See* CISG § 8(3) (prescribing the consideration of all relevant factors in determining the parties' intentions).
[34] As with the statute of frauds, the ultimate policy question is whether the fraud and misunderstanding prevented by the rule is worth more than the mischief the rule enables.
[35] The parol evidence rule is thus, in this straightforward sense, a rule of evidence. However, for many American law purposes it is treated differently than other evidence rules: for example, (1) a federal court sitting in a diversity case, in which it is required to apply federal procedural rules and state substantive law rules, will apply the state parol evidence rule; and (2) many states hold that an

the term *"parol"* refers to oral testimony, the rule itself applies to all "extrinsic" evidence: that is, all evidence other than the document being interpreted. The rule goes back more than four hundred years.[36] The basic idea of the rule is that parties should be able to intend a writing to incorporate their entire agreement, and if the parties have done so, that agreement should then be immune from claims that the agreement was something other than what the document states.[37]

Essentially, the parol evidence rule holds that once a writing is determined to be the final and complete agreement of the parties (at least as to some issues), no evidence external to the document will be allowed in to supplement or contradict the writing.[38] Evidence can, however, be brought in for other purposes, such as to resolve an ambiguity,[39] to establish a later or entirely collateral agreement,[40] or to prove some doctrinal defense to enforcement of this agreement (e.g., duress, undue influence).

If the document is not integrated, or is integrated for only some topics, other evidence can be admitted (in the case of a "partial integration," for issues other than those already covered by the written agreement). The problem is how to answer the threshold question. There are two possibilities, each of which raises obvious problems.

One option is to make the threshold determinations, relating to integration, based only on a close examination of the document itself (the "four corners" approach). The alternative is to consider extrinsic evidence. The argument against considering extrinsic evidence is that to allow it in, even for answering threshold questions,[41]

---

objection based on the parol evidence rule is not automatically waived if the party fails to raise it when the evidence is first introduced, as would be the case with other evidentiary rules. The parol evidence rule is also different from most evidence rules in excluding not certain *kinds* of evidence, but in excluding evidence submitted *for particular purposes* (to alter or supplement the meaning of a writing).

[36] *See Countess of Rutland's Case* (1604) 5 Co. Rep. 25b, 77 ER 89 (K.B.).

[37] A somewhat more cynical view is that the parol evidence rule, at least in contemporary times, is mostly "a device to control juries," in that we do not trust juries' ability to distinguish probative extrinsic evidence from misleading or fraudulent evidence. *Zell v. American Seating Co.*, 138 F.2d 641, 644–646 (2d Cir. 1943) (Jerome Frank), rev'd, 322 U.S. 709 (1944) (per curiam).

[38] At least one state, Montana, has codified its parol evidence rule (and much of the remainder of its rules of contract law). *Montana Code Annotated* § 28-2-905.

[39] Some courts and commentators distinguish "patent" and "latent" ambiguity (and this distinction has been attributed to Sir Francis Bacon). Farnsworth 2004: §7.12, at 464. Under this distinction, a latent ambiguity is one not obvious from the text alone but becomes apparent when extrinsic evidence is allowed in to show the surrounding circumstances. Under this analysis, some extrinsic analysis might be allowed in, even when the text seems to have a plain meaning. *See, e.g., Bohler-Uddeholm America, Inc. v. Ellwood Group*, 247 F.3d 79, 92–94 (3d Cir. 2001).

[40] As is discussed in the next subsection, the parol evidence rule, on its own, will not exclude evidence of subsequent modifications, but a "no oral modification" clause may limit the evidence that can be admitted to prove such modifications.

[41] Where a jury is used as the ultimate fact finder, parol evidence rule questions will be decided with the jury absent. Even where the judge is the fact finder, threshold questions relating to the parol evidence rule will be determined separately. One cannot expect a judicial fact finder to wipe her memory clean

would be to undermine the basic point of the parol evidence rule. The argument for allowing in the evidence for the threshold inquiries is that documents cannot conclusively announce their own integration.

It is especially hard to make judgments on integration when agreements are silent on the topic, although contracts can certainly seem complete, even without the presence of a "merger" or "integration" clause (a clause declaring that the text contains the entire agreement of the parties). However, agreements can, and often do, include such clauses; in contrast, such declarations need not always be believed (as similarly with provisions that declare that both parties fully understand all terms or that the parties are signing the agreement without any pressure).[42]

Both using extrinsic evidence to help decide the threshold question and refusing to use such evidence have their difficulties, but one or the other approach must be chosen. American jurisdictions split on the matter: those who refuse to consider extrinsic evidence are said to be applying a Willistonian approach (named after Samuel Williston, a contract scholar associated with the classical approach to contract law in general and to the parol evidence rule in particular; and with the First *Restatement of Contracts*).[43] The Corbinian approach (named after Arthur Linton Corbin, a contract scholar, whose views on contracts in general and the parol evidence rule in particular were incorporated in the Second *Restatement of Contracts*)[44] allows the court to "glance" at extrinsic evidence in determining whether the agreement is in fact complete and unambiguous. Thus, in broad outline, Willistonian approaches tend to err on the side of excluding evidence, whereas Corbinian approaches tend to allow the evidence to be seen, if only by judges making the necessary threshold judgments as to whether the evidence can be admitted.

Willistonians emphasize the value of putting contractual terms in writing and the importance of protecting those who have relied on the agreements being enforced as written. Corbinians emphasize the importance of determining the parties' intentions in interpreting an agreement, and they believe that extrinsic evidence should be admitted to the extent (though only to the extent) that it helps in ascertaining that intent.[45]

---

of parol evidence raised in the threshold inquiry, if that evidence is subsequently excluded from the trial; however, the court will not be able to rely on excluded evidence in the findings of fact and ultimate conclusions of law. Improper use of excluded evidence could lead to a reversal on appeal.

[42] To use an analogy, I can point a gun to your head and make you sign an agreement that contains a provision stating that there was no gun pointing to your head.

[43] A good example of the Willistonian approach is *Hershon v. Gibraltar Building & Loan Ass'n, Inc.*, 864 F.2d 848 (D.C. Cir. 1989) (applying Maryland law).

[44] A good example of the Corbinian approach is *Taylor v. State Farm Mutual Automobile Insurance Co.*, 854 P.2d 1134 (Ariz. 1993); see also *Restatement (Second) of Contracts* §§ 212–216, with particular emphasis on the Official Comments to those sections.

[45] In the Corbinian approach, the court examines the extrinsic evidence to determine whether the written document is "reasonably susceptible" to the interpretation being offered by the party presenting the evidence.

As noted, the parol evidence rule does not exclude evidence admitted for the purpose of resolving an ambiguity. Some analyses of the parol evidence rule treat ambiguity as a second threshold question: whether the text has a plain meaning[46] or is ambiguous, with extrinsic evidence being admitted if the text is ambiguous (or at least "reasonably susceptible" to more than one reading).[47] However, little seems to turn on whether a court (or commentator) treats the exclusion of outside evidence for unambiguous terms (and their admission for ambiguous terms) as an aspect of the parol evidence rule or as a general rule of interpretation.

The different approaches to considering threshold questions with the parol evidence rule are often paralleled by different approaches to one of the exceptions to the parol evidence rule. In general, the parol evidence rule does not exclude evidence offered to show that there is some doctrinal defense to the enforcement of the agreement. It makes sense, that if the evidence is coming in, not to show the meaning of the contractual document or agreement, but rather to show that there was duress, mental incapacity, mutual mistake, or some other defense to enforcement, that the parol evidence rule should have no application. In contrast, there is one doctrinal defense that causes practical and theoretical issues: misrepresentation. In general, intentional misrepresentation (and even some forms of innocent misrepresentation) can be the grounds for refusing enforcement of an agreement (a topic covered in Chapter 3, Section E). However, when the misrepresentation claim is that the other party represented that the written agreement meant something different from what its words stated (or that the other party would never enforce the agreement to the full force of its literal meaning), then the misrepresentation claim converges on the sort of claim that the parol evidence rule was meant to prevent. Courts that follow a Willistonian approach to the parol evidence rule tend to refuse extrinsic evidence for this sort of misrepresentation claim[48] (allowing it only for a different and narrow category of misrepresentation claims: claims that the other party misrepresented the basic nature of a document – for example, not telling the other party that the document being signed was a legal contract or falsely denying that it was a personal guarantee). By contrast, courts that follow a Corbinian approach tend to allow extrinsic evidence in for all forms of misrepresentation claims, arguing that a party should not be allowed to benefit from its own fraudulent acts simply because it is able to enshrine the fraud in a written document with an integration clause.[49]

The UCC has its own parol evidence provision, which expressly allows "a writing intended by the parties as a final expression of their agreement" to be "explained or supplemented" by usage of trade, course of dealing, and course of performance.[50]

---

[46] On "plain meaning," see Subsection C(2).

[47] *See, e.g., Taylor v. State Farm Mutual Automobile Insurance Co.*, 854 P.2d 1134 (Ariz. 1993).

[48] *E.g., Sherrodd, Inc. v. Morrison-Knudsen Co.*, 815 P.2d 1135 (Mont. 1991).

[49] *Hill v. Jones*, 725 P.2d 1115 (Ariz. 1986).

[50] UCC § 2–202. "Trade usage" is the way terms are understood within a trade community. UCC § 1–205(2). "Course of dealing" reflects the dealings between these contracting parties in prior

This approach to the parol evidence rule reflects the idea that the parties' understanding of the terms of their agreement will reflect the customary understandings of their business community and will be reflected in the way they perform this, and prior, agreements (for if one party had thought that the other party's performance was inconsistent with the agreement's terms, some objection would likely have been raised), and that such evidence should normally be admitted to help interpret the meaning of a sale of goods agreement.[51] However, note that under the language of the UCC parol evidence rule, course of performance, course of dealing, and trade usage were to come in only to "explain" or "supplement" a written agreement, not to contradict it. Nonetheless, many courts have allowed in those categories of evidence even when the understanding of the agreement they support seems to contradict the written terms.[52]

At a practical level, one can see the beneficial purposes that can be served by the parol evidence rule, even in its robust, Willistonian common law (non-UCC) version. First, one can imagine a party going to the trouble to make sure that the transactors' shared understandings, reached perhaps after lengthy and painstaking negotiations, were reduced to writing, and then becoming upset upon hearing the other party deny in court that the written document accurately reflects the parties' agreement. Any threat of that happening often would undermine much of the incentive to reduce agreements to writing.

Second, imagine an owner of an apartment building who writes a detailed lease to constrain tenants from doing things that might harm the long-term value of the property; a common provision in such circumstances states that tenants cannot have pets.[53] The agreement will likely also have an integration or merger clause, stating that no oral promises or representations beyond the written agreement would be valid. Imagine further that the owner has employees whose job it is to find tenants, with the agents' compensation being based in part on their success in finding new

---

contracts. UCC § 1–205(1). "Course of performance" is the dealings between these parties in the performance of the same agreement that is before the court. UCC § 2–208. These considerations are also accepted as relevant to interpretation in non-UCC cases, but they have no special status in relation to the non-UCC parol evidence rule. *See Restatement (Second) of Contracts* § 203.

51 Sharp criticisms have been raised against the UCC's incorporation of customs into the meaning of contractual terms, based on the claim that such customs are rarely present and are frequently contested, and that the standards and meanings parties might apply when a relationship is going well are different from what the parties would want to apply when a relationship is at its end. *See, e.g.,* Bernstein 1996, 1999.

52 The important case here, followed by many (but not all) other courts, is *Nanakuli Paving & Rock Co. v. Shell Oil Co.,* 664 F.2d 772 (9th Cir. 1981) (trade usage and course of performance evidence admitted to prove a requirement of price protection when prices went up, even though contract's term was to pay the posted price).

53 This example makes the general point clearly, but it is not hard to come up with many other examples of principals, agents, and contracting partners, where the conflicting incentives will create the same dynamic, where the principal wants the written agreement to have priority over the oral representations of its own agents.

tenants. When a potential tenant asks about the no-pets provision, she is told by the agent, "Don't worry about that provision; it is never enforced" (or enforced only for really big pets or for really bad tenants). The agent has an incentive to say that (whether it is true or not), as the agent's short-term interests conflict with the owner's long-term interests. When the tenant is evicted for keeping a pet and relies on the agent's oral promises, the owner wants, reasonably, to be able to rely on the written agreement, the integration clause, and the parol evidence rule.[54]

At the same time, one does not have to search hard to find examples of the representations being excluded being made not by some agent of the principal (where the two may have conflicting interests) but by the principal herself. For example, where an owner of a house tells potential buyers, falsely, that the house does not have termites, there does not seem to be a strong argument in either policy or ethics for allowing evidence of that lie to be excluded on the basis of a merger clause[55] in the subsequent sales agreement.[56] Nonetheless, some jurisdictions will allow a merger clause to exclude evidence of an alleged fraud by a principal.[57]

Two responses to such cases, on behalf of a party trying to enforce the merger clause (and to use the parol evidence rule to exclude testimony regarding other purported promises) would be as follows: (1) the merger clause should be considered evidence that no promises were in fact made, evidence at least formally confirmed by the signature of the party now claiming otherwise – that is, with a merger clause in place, courts should assume that those asserting the existence of other promises or representations are lying; and (2) the merger clause is a rule of construction, even more for the parties than for the courts: directing the parties not to construe ambiguous comments as promises or representations. At the least, the merger clause is a warning to the parties signing an agreement with such a provision that it must get any representation into the written agreement, at the risk of its not being enforced.

Already mentioned is the case of the owner whose agents make unauthorized promises. Other story lines involve people making promises contrary to the writing because the organization (for understandable reasons of efficiency) demands the use of a single form to cover a wide range of transactions. And consider a circumstance in which an official makes promises about how an agreement will be enforced – and intends to follow through on those promises – but the official is subsequently replaced, or the company purchased, or in some other way management policy from

---

[54] It should be emphasized that whether a representation is made by a principal or an agent is not expressly part of any doctrinal rule, and the distinction is only occasionally raised in court opinions, but the factual difference, and its moral implications (agents claiming a proposed written contract does not mean what it says versus principals making a similar claim), does seem to explain a portion of the court outcomes.

[55] A "merger clause" or "integration clause" is a provision in a written contract indicating that the written agreement is the entire agreement between the parties (thus excluding any (claims of) separate oral or written promises, representations, warranties, and so on).

[56] *Hill v. Jones*, 725 P.2d 1115 (Ariz. 1986).

[57] *See, e.g., Sherrodd, Inc. v. Morrison-Knudsen Co.*, 815 P.2d 1135 (Mont. 1991).

above is changed. (On their face, the doctrinal rules are not contingent on the factual circumstances, but with these doctrines, as with others, the court's perceptions of the underlying facts affect their application of the rules – especially rules with as much room for judgment as the parol evidence rule.)

2. *Trusting Writings versus Trusting Face-to-Face Promises*

As one looks at the statute of frauds (discussed in Chapter 3, Section C) and the exceptions that were developed by the courts and the UCC drafters; the parol evidence rule, its court-developed and UCC exceptions, and the quite different approaches (Corbinian and Willistonian) to it; and the further complications of "no oral modification" clauses and how they have been treated by courts and the UCC (discussed herein), one can begin to discern a pattern, an ongoing dynamic.[58]

On the one hand, there is the interest in encouraging parties to put agreements into writing, using the incentive of telling them that they will be allowed to rely on the writing being enforceable, even in the face of faulty or fraudulent memories of contrary oral promises. On the other hand, there is the reality that in commercial transactions, promises are often made that go beyond, or even contradict, what is on the written form (especially when the writing is a standard form, not produced especially for this particular transaction), and such oral assurances need to be enforceable if injustice is to be avoided.

Of course, as noted already, one's view of the whole process, one's view of which rule(s) are better, will depend on whom one believes in the particular case or on which sort of scenario (fraudulent claim of oral agreement or modification, or nefarious use of written terms to override authentic oral assurances or agreement) one believes to be more common. Some commentators have noted that the recent tendency toward greater "formalism" in American contract law – giving clearer priority to written agreements over possibly conflicting oral assurances or contrary reasonable expectations – tends to favor big companies over consumers and smaller businesses.[59]

One can see one example of the dynamic between courts and well-counseled clients with "no oral modification" clauses. The parol evidence rule may prevent evidence of oral modifications that occurred prior to or contemporaneous with the signing of an agreement, but it does not exclude evidence of subsequent modifications. Provisions in agreements requiring that any subsequent modifications must be in a signed writing are known as "no oral modification" clauses. Courts, in non-UCC cases, have sometimes held such provisions to be unenforceable, on the freedom-of-contract grounds that parties have the right to modify their agreements subsequently, whether orally or in writing. By contrast, the UCC expressly authorizes the use of

---

[58] A version of this dynamic is nicely outlined in Knapp 1998: 1322–1323.
[59] Mooney 1995: 1170–1171.

"no oral modification" clauses.[60] However, courts may interpret actions in which parties seem to be acting in accordance with an oral modification agreement as a waiver of the "no oral modification" requirement. Parties respond to such rulings by putting "no waiver" clauses in their contracts. Courts will treat the combination of "no oral modification" and "no waiver" provisions as creating a sort of "private statute of frauds," but they might respond by focusing on the exceptions to the UCC's statute of frauds, such as the exception for goods received and accepted or for payments made and accepted.[61]

E. WARRANTIES

Warranties are express or implied assertions that the goods being sold are of a certain description or meet a certain standard. Where a warranty is made and the object turns out not to meet the standard or description, then the buyer can sue for breach.

In the well-known, and strange, 1603 case of *Chandelor v. Lopus*,[62] the seller, a London goldsmith, had "affirmed" to the buyer, a foreign merchant, that a jewel being sold was a "bezar stone" (a stone from an animal's digestive system, thought to have magical properties), and the buyer purchased the object for the then-steep price of one hundred pounds. When the buyer found out (we are not told how) that the object was in fact not a bezar stone, he sued. The buyer prevailed initially (at King's Bench), but on appeal (at Exchequer Chamber), the court held that the plaintiff could not prevail, because he had not claimed either that the seller knew the object not to be a bezar stone or that the seller had "warranted" that it was.

Chandelor somehow became a foundational case for "caveat emptor" – "let the buyer beware" – the view that the common law courts will not intervene to undo a one-sided agreement entered by a gullible, vulnerable, or ignorant buyer. The courts would have buyers seeking certainty regarding the value or quality of the object being purchased demand a guaranty or warranty by the seller – and, under *Chandelor*, if not under more recent cases, that the warrantor had to in fact expressly use that magic word; mere affirmation was insufficient.

No magic words are necessary under current American law (or under the law of most other jurisdictions). For the sale of goods, warranties can arise from an affirmation, a promise, a description, or a sample or model.[63] The concern, then, is

---

[60] UCC § 2–209(2).

[61] The last few back-and-forth arguments can be found in *Brookside Farms v. Mama Rizzo's Inc.*, 873 F. Supp. 1029 (S.D. Texas 1995); the UCC statute of frauds and its exceptions are in UCC §2–201. *Brookside* is one of those cases in which the outcome (allowing enforcement of the oral modification) seems clearly correct, primarily because the other party did not seriously contest that the modifications had been agreed to. The equities of the case might have seemed far different if the other party denied that any such agreement had been made.

[62] (1603) Cro. Jac. 4, 79 Eng. Rep. 3 (K.B.).

[63] UCC § 2–313. Subsection 2 expressly holds that the use of particular words is not necessary to create a warranty, nor need the seller have intended to make a warranty.

that it may take too little to ascribe a warranty to a seller in a context in which the seller was merely "puffing" – the sort of general and superficial talk associated with media advertisements and salespeople, the sort of praise that cautious consumers have learned to (and are expected to) discount or ignore. For that reason, the relevant UCC provision warns that "an affirmation merely of the value of the goods or a statement purporting to be merely the seller's opinion or commendation of the goods does not create a warranty."[64]

Needless to say, here, as with the doctrine of misrepresentation (see Chapter 3, Section E), the dividing line between clear statements of fact and mere opinion is not always easy to discern and frequently becomes the grounds for litigation.

F. INTERPRETATION AND FAIRNESS

As already discussed in a prior section (Section B, discussing default rules), there are situations in which the court's interpretation of a contractual term seems to blur the line between determining what the parties intended at the time they entered the agreement and ignoring party intentions to impose terms that the courts consider fair.

The blurring of the distinction occurs because (1) we have doubts that the parties would in fact have agreed to truly one-sided terms, or terms that leave one party very vulnerable to the other party; (2) we suspect that if the party did agree to such terms, it was because of ignorance, misrepresentation, or improper pressure; and (3) in any event, we (however one understands the "we" in the judicial enforcement of agreements: the court, the law, the state, or the public) do not want to be complicit with what is considered injustice.

In the area of insurance agreements, courts and commentators have developed a doctrine of "reasonable expectations."[65] The doctrine, which many trace back to work by Robert Keeton,[66] has been recognized in one form or another in a majority of American jurisdictions (though far from all of them). However, only in perhaps six to ten of those jurisdictions has the doctrine been accepted in its most extreme form: by which the court will enforce the reasonable expectations of the insured,[67]

---

[64] UCC § 2–313(2).

[65] Under many of its formulations, the doctrine of "reasonable expectations" would apply more generally, at least to other "adhesion contracts." *See, e.g., Restatement (Second) of Contracts* § 237, Comment f. One can also find occasional cases applying the doctrine to non-insurance adhesion contracts, but these are very few (outside the State of Arizona, where the doctrine seems to be used much as the doctrine of unconscionability is in most other states; Braucher 2008: 213–221); the vast majority of the cases where the doctrine of "reasonable expectations" has been applied are disputes involving the interpretation of insurance policies.

[66] *E.g.*, Keeton 1970.

[67] It is rare, but one can find an occasional case in which the "reasonable expectations" doctrine, or something close to it, has been used for the insurer's benefit. *See Central Bearings Co. v. Wolverine Insurance Company*, 179 N.W.2d 443 (Iowa 1970).

even when there is contrary unambiguous language in the policy. In less robust versions of the doctrine, the insured's reasonable expectations are protected only where there is an ambiguity in the policy terms or where the insurance company or its agents have done or said something affirmatively to mislead the insured regarding coverage.[68]

G. CHOICE OF LAW AND CONFLICT OF LAWS

Parties commonly place in their agreements provisions declaring that the agreement is to be governed by the law of a particular state or country.[69] Parties may prefer that an agreement be governed by law with which they are familiar, or that is well developed (as, for example, corporate law is in Delaware), or that is more inclined to enforce certain sorts of provisions.

The justification for enforcing choice of law provisions is straightforward. First, allowing parties to choose applicable law seems another example of deference to the parties' freedom of contract. Second, parties could include a series of individual provisions; a choice-of-law provision is effectively the incorporation of a large number of individual provisions (the applicable norms of the state or country chosen). If courts will enforce individual provisions, why should they not enforce the "package of norms" that comes with a choice-of-law provision?

Not all choice-of-law provisions will be enforceable in all states. First, the UCC and (for agreements other than the sale of goods) a number of state laws restrict (enforceable) choice-of-law provisions to states having some relation to the transaction.[70] Second, when facing an agreement with a choice-of-law provision, basic conflict of laws principles authorize the forum state (the state whose court is hearing the case) to refuse to apply some rule from the choice-of-law state if that law is contrary to the strong public policy of the forum state.[71]

Where the parties have not expressly chosen which law is to govern their arrangement (or where their choice has not been enforced for some reason), questions can arise as to which law to apply, especially where the parties come from different states (or different countries), where the agreement is signed in a different state from that in which the parties reside, where the subject matter of the agreement is in a different state from that in which the parties reside, or where the agreement is simply

---

[68] Schwarcz 2007: 1427–1429.

[69] The provision might also refer to the rules of an international treaty, like the CISG or a set of contract principles unconnected with any governmental body, like the UNIDROIT Principles (both discussed in Chapter 2, Section E). Additionally, some agreements include "choice of forum" clauses, requiring that any dispute be heard in a particular court ("Which court?" being a separate question from "which law?"). The enforceability of such provisions is beyond the scope of the current work.

[70] Under the original UCC art. 1, this restriction appeared in § 1–105; in the Revised UCC art. 1, it is § 1–301.

[71] *Restatement (Second) of Conflict of Laws* § 187(2).

being enforced in a state other than the state in which the agreement was entered. In general, a court will apply the law of the state (or country) that has the strongest connection to the agreement.[72]

H. THEORETICAL IMPLICATIONS

That parties are frequently held to meanings they did not ("subjectively") intend, and may be unable to enforce agreements actually entered into, because of some formal requirement not met (e.g., lack of a writing), seems to offer a challenge for those who think of contract law in terms of freedom of contract, autonomy, and enforcement of promises. Objective rules of interpretation (like objective rules of formation) and formal requirements reflect more the interest in protecting reasonable reliance and reasonable expectations, and generally promoting certainty and predictability, particularly (though not exclusively) in commercial transactions.

In general, the rules of contract interpretation balance a host of conflicting (or at least potentially conflicting) values: not only the values behind subjective and objective approaches but also the set of values and practices that emphasize being able to rely on what was put into writing (and perhaps never relying on what is not in writing) versus the values and practices of relying on the other party's word (and handshake). There are issues of trust, not only between parties but also regarding how much trust we have in juries and judges (e.g., in the way we keep certain alleged agreements or alleged terms away from a jury under the statute of frauds or the parol evidence rule).

SUGGESTED FURTHER READING

Interpretation Generally

Aharon Barak, *Purposive Interpretation in Law.* Princeton, NJ: Princeton University Press, 2005, ch. 13 ("The Interpretation of Contracts").

Steven J. Burton, *Elements of Contract Interpretation.* Oxford: Oxford University Press, 2009.

Kent Greenawalt, *Legal Interpretation: Perspectives from Other Disciplines and Private Texts.* Oxford: Oxford University Press, 2010, ch. 9 ("Contracts").

Avery Wiener Katz, "The Economics of Form and Substance in Contract Interpretation," *Columbia Law Review*, vol. 104, pp. 496–538 (2004).

Edwin W. Patterson, "The Interpretation and Construction of Contracts," *Columbia Law Review*, vol. 64, pp. 833–865 (1964).

Richard A. Posner, "The Law and Economics of Contract Interpretation," *Texas Law Review*, vol. 83, pp. 1581–1614 (2005).

Steven Shavell, "On the Writing and Interpretation of Contracts," *Journal of Law, Economics and Organization*, vol. 22, pp. 289–314 (2006).

---

[72] *Restatement (Second) of Conflict of Laws* § 188; *see generally* Weintraub 2010: § 7.3D, at 529–537.

Parol Evidence Rule

Margaret N. Kniffin, "Conflating and Confusing Contract Interpretation and the Parol Evidence Rule: Is the Emperor Wearing Someone Else's Clothes?" *Rutgers Law Review*, vol. 62, pp. 75–129 (2009).

Eric A. Posner, "The Parol Evidence Rule, the Plain Meaning Rule, and the Principles of Contractual Interpretation," *University of Pennsylvania Law Review*, vol. 146, pp. 533–577 (1998).

James B. Thayer, "The 'Parol Evidence' Rule," *Harvard Law Review*, vol. 6, pp. 325–348 (1893).

Choice of Law and Conflict of Laws

Erin Ann O'Hara, "Opting Out of Regulation: A Public Choice Analysis of Contractual Choice of Law," *Vanderbilt Law Review*, vol. 53, pp. 1551–1604 (2000).

5

Performance

Much of the work of contract lawyers consists in advising clients on how to respond to developments after an agreement has been signed: in particular, whether a certain outside event, defective performance, failure of performance, or threat not to perform would justify nonperformance, or different performance, on behalf of one's client. The present chapter looks at the various and interrelated questions that arise in the performance of an agreement.

A. CONDITIONS

1. *On-Off Switches*

A condition is an on-off switch. It is either an event that creates an obligation to perform under the contract where one had not been before or an event that removes or modifies an obligation to perform that had previously been in effect.[1] The *Restatement* offers the following, somewhat awkward, definition: "A condition is an event, not certain to occur, which must occur, unless its non-occurrence is excused, before performance under a contract becomes due."[2] As is discussed here, it is important to distinguish conditions from promises (although on rare occasion a provision can be both a condition and a promise).[3]

Distinctive to conditions is an if-then structure: stating that if certain things do (or do not) occur, then obligations to perform under the contract will arise

---

[1] Older discussions of conditions had referred to "condition precedent" and "condition subsequent" depending on whether the condition came before, and turned on, an obligation, or came after, and turned off or modified the obligation. However, the *Second Restatement* and recent commentators have largely abandoned that terminology.

[2] *Restatement (Second) of Contracts* § 224.

[3] The *Restatement* creates a presumption that, when in doubt, a contractual term is to be treated as a promise rather than a condition. *Restatement (Second) of Contracts* § 227.

(or evaporate). One common condition occurs with the sale of a house, where a buyer's obligation to purchase may be conditioned on the buyer's ability to obtain financing.

Conditions can be express, implied, or constructive: an express condition is one written (in clear terms) into the agreement; an implied condition is one that is derived from the other terms of the agreement or the general structure of the transaction (the condition is implied on the basis of the parties' intentions); and a constructive condition is one implied by the courts on the basis of fairness or policy considerations. Although constructive conditions are in principle independent of the parties' intentions, parties can usually override them by express agreement to contrary terms.

A standard example of a constructive condition involves the timing and dependence of performance: that where one performance of a contract takes much more time than another (e.g., building a house versus paying money), the shorter performance is not due until the longer performance is finished.[4] As noted, such constructive conditions can be, and usually are, overridden by express terms (e.g., setting the schedule for when the owner must make payments to the builder, frequently set amounts for the completion of distinct parts of the project).

As is discussed here (in Section B4), the failure of a constructive condition is sometimes excused for "substantial performance" (performance that is only slightly defective relative to what the contract demands), but courts have been reluctant to extend that excusing doctrine to express conditions.[5]

2. *Excuse of Failure of Condition*

Although a breach of a promise generally results in damages, a failure of a condition can have more radical consequences, often entirely ending one party's obligation to perform. To mitigate the harsh consequences of (failures of) conditions, the Courts in Equity developed a series of doctrines by which a failure of a condition could be "excused." These doctrines include waiver, estoppel, and forfeiture.[6] The sharp division between Law and Equity no longer exists in American law, but the fact that these are equitable doctrines retains significance: like other equitable doctrines

---

[4] *See, e.g.*, Farnsworth 2004: § 8.11, at 544–547; *Restatement (Second) of Contracts* § 234. Where the two performances take about the same amount of time (e.g., paying money and handing over a deed), neither is due until the other has been proffered. *Id.*

[5] *See, e.g., Oppenheimer & Co., Inc. v. Oppenheim, Appel, Dixon & Co.*, 660 N.E.2d 415 (N.Y. 1995). One commentator has argued that courts, as an (unwritten) rule, forgive all, or nearly all, nonmaterial failures of condition. Childres 1970. Although there may be truth to this as a general observation of court behavior, there are prominent exceptions like the refusal to recognize "substantial performance" as an exception in *Oppenheimer.*

[6] Some courts also recognize "prevention" as the basis for excusing a failure of a condition. Prevention occurs when one party actively prevents the occurrence of the conditioning event and then pleads the failure of the event to occur as the basis for nonperformance. *See* Murray 2011: § 111, at 695–696.

and defenses, they involve all-things-considered judgments by the court in an effort to do justice between the parties. A court is unlikely to excuse a party from the failure of a condition unless the equities of the situation are strongly in that party's favor.

Waiver is the intentional giving up of a right, although "intentional" here can mean not only express statements that one is relinquishing a right but also any action inconsistent with one's rights at a time when one knows the facts necessary to ground one's claim of right. Thus, an insurance company that investigates a claim filed two days past the deadline given in the insurance policy for filing such claims will be held to have waived its right to deny the claim solely on the basis of the missed deadline.[7] Waiver is also commonly more express or intentional: if the purchase of the home depends on my obtaining bank financing, and I am unable to do so, I can choose to waive that condition (if, for example, I am obtaining financing through a relative); the seller cannot rely on the failure of condition to avoid performance if I choose to waive that condition.[8] (Only the party the condition is meant to benefit has the right to waive it.)

Waiver is, in this sense, a "one-person game." When one party does or says something that is inconsistent with its legal rights, nothing further need be proved regarding the other party (e.g., by way of reasonable reliance). However, waiver is generally only allowed for only minor ("nonmaterial") conditions, generally, procedural or technical conditions (e.g., deadlines and writing requirements). By contrast, excuse of a failure of condition on the basis of estoppel is a "two-person game" – one must show that the other party reasonably relied on some statement or action such that it would be unjust to enforce the condition. However, estoppel can apply even to conditions that are "substantive" (i.e., not merely procedural or technical).[9]

Forfeiture is when the enforcement of a (failed) condition would leave one party with little or nothing despite its having invested significant resources, and that loss seems out of proportion to the faultiness of that party's actions under the contract.[10] In one well-known case, *J. N. A. Realty v. Cross-Bay Chelsea*, a tenant was in principle allowed to renew a lease, despite having missed a deadline, because an eviction would have created a loss of the goodwill (and other investments) in the

---

7 For that reason, companies will often place "no waiver" terms in their agreements (in which the parties agree that their actions are not to be construed as waivers, unless there is an express statement to that effect); also, insurance companies sometimes condition investigations into late claims on the insured's first signing a form stating that it agrees that the investigation is not to be understood as a waiver of rights.

8 On waiver generally, see, e.g., Farnsworth 2004: § 8.5, at 523–527; *see also Restatement (Second) of Contracts* § 84.

9 On estoppel generally and its connection to waiver, see Murray 2011: § 112, at 700–704.

10 *See Restatement (Second) of Contracts* § 229. The *Restatement* defines "forfeiture" as "the denial of compensation that results when the obligee loses his right to the agreed exchange after he has relied substantially, as by preparation or performance on the expectation of that exchange." *Id.*, Comment *b*.

restaurant's current location; the only question left to be determined was whether the renewal would have caused hardship for the landlord or innocent third parties.[11] (Although almost all courts will excuse the failure of a condition to avoid "extreme" or "disproportionate" forfeiture, some will not allow this where the failure occurred as a result of the plaintiff's own negligence, as was the case in *J. N. A. Realty*. These courts will restrict equitable relief to failures due to mistake and accident.[12])

B. RESPONSES TO CURRENT AND FUTURE PROBLEMS IN PERFORMANCE

For the practicing lawyer advising a client, one of the most important – and trickiest – set of questions is how to respond to nonperformance or imperfect performance, or the threat of the same. American contract law offers doctrinal rules that are nuanced enough to respond to the complexities of commercial practices. However, it is just that level of nuance that makes it unpredictable as to whether a later court will interpret one's responses as doctrinally justified or unjustified. On the whole, these areas of contract law offer amorphous standards and a great deal at stake: not a good combination. (This is not to imply that clearer or more easily and predictably applied standards would be easy to construct.)

The doctrines vary depending on when the (actual, threatened, or alleged) nonperformance or faulty performance occurs.

1. *Prior to Scheduled Performance: Anticipatory Repudiation and Adequate Assurances*

What happens if one party threatens not to perform (or threatens to perform in ways significantly different from what was promised or to perform only conditional on some action or event, where there are no grounds in the agreement for that condition)? For example, what if someone is under contract to paint a house on July 1, and the painter calls the owner on May 1 and states that she will not be able to do the job? A similar question arises when some action by the promisor makes performance impossible (e.g., the seller in a contract sells the object to a third party).

The prominent commentator Williston had argued that this could not be treated as any sort of breach, for how could one breach before one had any obligation to

---

[11] *J. N. A. Realty Corp. v. Cross Bay Chelsea, Inc.*, 366 N.E.2d 1313 (N.Y. 1977). It appears that neither the landlord nor any innocent third parties had significant equitable claims; on remand, the landlord and the tenant settled the case by agreeing to a long-term lease with an increased rental. Knapp, Crystal & Prince 2007: 804.

[12] *See, e.g., Finkle v. Gulf & Western Manufacturing Co.*, 744 F.2d 1015 (3d Cir. 1984) (applying Pennsylvania law, holding that failure of condition due to mere inadvertence could not be the basis for an excuse of a failure of condition)

perform?[13] However, the modern view is that if one party makes an unequivocal statement that it will not perform (or will not perform except on terms significantly different from what the agreement states[14]), then the nonbreaching party has two options: (1) to do nothing, waiting (for a reasonable time[15]), hoping that the promisor will change its mind, retract its repudiation, and perform according to the contract terms, or (2) to treat the contract as over, either by publicly stating that it (the non-breaching party) is doing so, or by suing for "total breach" of the contract.[16] (There is one quirky, hard-to-justify exception: one has no immediate cause of action where the anticipatory repudiation relates to a future obligation to pay money. This seems to be an area in which the rule can be "explained" only historically and causally – we have this exception because we have always had this exception. However, it is hard to find a reason the exception was developed in the first place or a good reason for keeping it.[17])

Whether a statement is an "unequivocal" refusal to perform according to contract terms may be a judgment call (e.g., what if a promisor states that "it doesn't look likely that it will be able to perform" or if it files for bankruptcy?). Where an innocent party treats a statement as an unequivocal refusal to perform – as an anticipatory repudiation – when it is in fact not, the tables may be turned. An innocent party who overreacts in this way (e.g., by selling to a third party) will be adjudged to have been the repudiating party.

In part because of the uncertainties in determining whether one's contracting party has repudiated an agreement (and the significant penalties for guessing wrong), the Uniform Commercial Code offers the parties recourse when doubts arise that may fall short of an anticipatory repudiation. "When reasonable grounds for insecurity

---

[13] *See* Williston 1901: 428. One state that has followed Williston rather than the modern view (in not allowing the innocent party to sue immediately after an anticipatory repudiation) is Massachusetts. *See Daniels v. Newton*, 114 Mass. 530 (1874); *Cavanagh v. Cavanagh*, 598 N.E.2d 677, 679 (Mass. App. 1992), review denied, 602 N.E.2d 1094 (Mass. 1992); *Pedersen v. Klare*, 910 N.E.2d 382 (Mass. App. 2009). Although even Massachusetts must follow the general rule in sales of good cases, as it has adopted UCC Article 2, which incorporates the general rule for anticipatory repudiation. *See Cavanagh*, 598 N.E.2d at 679; UCC § 2–610.

[14] For example, someone might state that she was happy to paint the house as agreed in the contract but only for twice the price stated in the contract, or only if paid in advance (where the contract had stated that payment would be after the job was completed).

[15] What counts as a reasonable time, as ever, depends on the circumstances. One important circumstance is whether waiting also involves the nonrepudiating party acting in a way that would increase damages should the repudiating party not retract. In the paradigm case for mitigation of damages, *Rockingham County v. Luten Bridge*, 35 F.2d 301 (4th Cir. 1929), the county that had authorized the construction of a bridge told the builder to stop after work had already begun. The builders were not allowed to recover the expenses for work done beyond that point. The implicit holding was that it was not reasonable to wait and hope for a retraction if the waiting included continued work and the piling up of damages. This case is discussed in connection with mitigation of damages, in Chapter 6, Section B.

[16] *See* Farnsworth 2004: §§ 8.20–8.22, at 581–593. The important early case on this issue was *Hochster v. De La Tour*, 2 Ellis & Bl. 678, 118 Eng. Rep. 922 (Q.B. 1853). On "total breach," see Section B(2).

[17] *See* Perillo 2003: § 12.9, at 505–509.

arise" regarding the other party's performance under the contract, one may "in writing demand adequate assurance of due performance" and suspend performance until that assurance is received.[18] If adequate assurances are not received, then the party requesting the assurances can treat the contract as having been repudiated. (As concern about the other party's performance can occur in the middle of contractual performance and before performance has begun, the process of seeking adequate assurances is available during both time periods. The problem of defective performance during the course of the contract is considered at greater length in the next subsection.)

The advantage of the process of seeking adequate assurances is that it gives the innocent party firmer ground for treating a contract as over, if there are reasonable grounds for insecurity and a request for assurance is not responded to adequately. The difficulty is that although this tool potentially solves one problem of judgment (whether there had been an anticipatory repudiation), it does so in a way that raises other difficult judgment calls (did one have "reasonable grounds" for insecurity, and were the other party's assurances "adequate"?). And again, a mistake of judgment can result in one's being treated as the breaching party, liable for significant damages, rather than the nonbreaching party, able to recover for one's losses.[19]

2. Failures in the Middle of Performance

What happens when the failure in performance comes in the middle of the promised actions (e.g., in failing to pay the full third installment when five installments are due; or failing to deliver the appropriate quality of corn this month, when there are still six month's worth of delivery left; or doing a poor job on the foundation for an agreement to build a whole house)?

American contract law has created somewhat intricate rules for how the nonbreaching party is allowed to react to defects in performance that occur in the middle of performance. In rough summary, for trivial defects (sometimes called "nonmaterial" or "partial" breach), the nonbreaching party can sue for damages for that breach itself but nothing else. For very significant defects (sometimes called "material breach"), the nonbreaching party can suspend its own performance, demand corrective action, and sue for damages for the breach itself. If the significantly defective performance is not corrected in a reasonable way in a reasonable time (i.e., "total breach"), the innocent party can treat the contract as over and can sue for damages

---

[18] UCC § 2–609(1). The right to suspend performance is not allowed if suspension would not be "commercially reasonable." *Id.*

[19] *See, e.g., Pittsburgh-De Moines Steel Co. v. Brookhaven Manor Water Co.*, 532 F.2d 572 (7th Cir. 1976) (assurances requested too great relative to insecurity). *See generally* White & Summers 2010: § 7–2, at 273–283.

not only for the breach itself but also for all damages that result as a consequence of that breach (e.g., lost profits on other agreements).[20]

In the sale of goods, there is a special rule for single-delivery agreements: the "perfect tender rule." Under the perfect tender rule, the buyer has the right to reject a delivery "if the goods or the tender of delivery fail in any respect to conform to the contract."[21] The perfect tender rule had once held more broadly in American contract law, even with agreements other than the sale of goods, but it has been undercut significantly by the development of the doctrine of "substantial performance" – discussed in Subsection 4. And even with the sale of goods, in actual practice and as interpreted and restricted by the courts, the perfect tender rule may not be as significant as it at first appears.[22]

3. Modification

What happens if one party, either before it begins performance or in the middle of performance, informs the other party that it will not perform (further) unless it is given more favorable terms than were agreed to in the contract?

Under the classical common law approach, even if the parties agree to modify the terms of an existing agreement, such modifications would not be enforceable. They would be said to fail of consideration (see Chapter 3, Section B), because one side was offering extra money (or extra services) in return for what the other party already had an existing legal duty to do or to pay.[23] The common law rule has been eased somewhat, as reflected by a *Restatement* section, basically giving courts authority to determine whether the modification agreement in question was fair – was it sought in good faith, on the basis of good reasons, and not obtained by coercion.[24]

Modifications of existing agreements are a normal part of business, and such modifications are often sought in good faith, in response to unforeseen difficulties or supplier price hikes, or the like, and such modifications are frequently agreed to by the other party. Because it is a normal part of business practice, the UCC changed the common law rule to make such modifications relating to sale of goods contracts enforceable as a matter of course, without a need to show new consideration.[25]

---

[20] *Restatement (Second) of Contracts* §§ 236, 241–243.
[21] UCC § 2–601. If the agreement calls for a series of deliveries, then there are limits on the ability to reject an installment for a small imperfection, particularly if the defect is easily "cured." UCC § 2–612.
[22] *See* White & Summers 2010: § 9–3, at 415–419.
[23] *E.g., Alaska Packers' Assn. v. Domenico*, 117 F. 99 (9th Cir. 1902). *Alaska Packers'* is the classic case in American contract law on modification. For more on the background to this case, see Threedy 2000.
[24] *Restatement (Second) of Contracts* § 89.
[25] UCC § 2–209(1). Section 2–209(2) notes that parties can validly agree to "no oral modifications" provisions. This is a change from the common law, where such provisions were sometimes held to be unenforceable, on the grounds that parties should retain the plenary power to modify their own agreements. *E.g.,* Murray 2011: § 65, at 291–292.

However, modifications sought in less than good faith are, unfortunately, also a common part of business. A recent book on the construction industry reported:

> [C]onstruction firms often make unrealistically low bids to get jobs . . . but they can count on finding plenty of reasons later to jack the price up enough to allow for a profit. When the building is under way, it becomes prohibitively expensive to fire the contractor and start anew. The owner has become a hostage.[26]

Under UCC law, modifications are policed, not through the consideration doctrine but through the doctrines of duress and good faith.[27] Although both of these doctrines are discussed in greater detail elsewhere (in Chapter 3, Section E, and Section D in this chapter), their application to UCC modification cases warrants a brief elaboration.

In general, to prove duress, one must show a combination of a wrongful act by one party and the lack of a reasonable alternative by the other. For modification, it is important to note that a threat to breach – that is, a threat not to perform where one does not (subjectively) believe that one has a legal justification for nonperformance – can count as a wrongful act.[28] Therefore, modifications coerced through threats of nonperformance may turn out to be unenforceable (if the other element(s) of duress are proved and questions of good faith also point to nonenforcement).

Good faith in a modification context requires that a party not seek a modification without a good reason (where unexpected costs increases from suppliers is a good reason and simply wanting a higher profit is not). Additionally, some courts have held that good faith requires a party who eventually opposes enforcement of a modification to have raised objections at the time the modification was negotiated (that it would be "bad faith" to lead the other party to believe that one had no objections to the modification, only to oppose its enforcement later).[29]

A topic related to modification is the operation of "accord and satisfaction" in relation to moneys due. Where there is a dispute in good faith about the amount owed, one party might send a check with the amount it believes to be due, with the language "payment in full" or "in full satisfaction" or something similar. If the person owed the money cashes that check, that is considered acceptance of the payor's offer.[30]

---

[26] *See, e.g.,* Hagerty 2007.
[27] *See* Farnsworth 2004: § 4.22, at 272–274.
[28] *See, e.g., Kelsey-Hayes Co. v. Galtaco Redlaw Castings Corp.,* 749 F. Supp. 794 (E.D. Mich. 1990).
[29] The standard discussion of good faith in UCC modification cases comes from *Roth Steel Products v. Sharon Steel Corp.,* 705 F.2d 134 (6th Cir. 1983).
[30] *See* Murray 2011: § 65, at 282–284; UCC § 3–305. Under most jurisdiction's understanding of the law, if the creditor notes "with reservation of rights" before cashing the check, this will still be treated as an acceptance of the payor's offer. Murray 2011: § 65, at 283–284; UCC § 1–107.

4. *Failure in Completed Performance: Substantial Performance,*
Divisibility, Restitution

What happens when one party's performance is complete but imperfect relative to the terms specified in the agreement? How or when do such defects in performance affect that party's rights to demand the other party's performance (usually payment) under the same contract? There had been cases in old English contract law that indicated that the obligations under a contract were "independent," such that one need not prove one's own performance under the contract to enforce the other party's duties under the agreement.[31] Whatever the state of the law had been in the independence of promises,[32] by the time of Lord Mansfield's decision in *Kingston v. Preston* in the late eighteenth century, the courts' view was that a proper understanding of most contracts was that one party's performance was a (constructive) condition for the other party's obligation to perform.[33]

It has already been discussed (Section 5A) how the courts impose constructive conditions, such that the obligation to pay would come after a performance, such as constructing a house, that takes a significant amount of time. One understanding was that the obligation to pay on a construction contract would not arise until the builder had finished its work – that is, had met every specification in the agreement. However, the view that payment on a construction project was conditioned on the perfect completion of the construction work was modified by the landmark case of *Jacob & Youngs v. Kent*.[34] *Jacob & Youngs* involved the construction of a house in which the builder was alleged to have deviated in a small way in its construction of the house. Under the contract, the builder was to have used a certain brand of pipe but in fact had used a different brand for much of the building. It was assumed, for the purpose of the litigation, that the type of pipe used by the builder was of equivalent quality to the type specified. The New York Court of Appeals (in an opinion written by Judge Benjamin Cardozo) had to face two questions: should the builder be able to "claim on the contract," and how should the damages be formulated? The builder was not seeking the full contract price but was seeking compensation based on the contract – the contract price, reduced by the damages caused by the builder's defective performance (a level of damages the builder claimed to be minimal).

The damages question is considered in greater detail later (in Chapter 6, Section D). As for the more basic question, the defendant had argued that a breaching builder cannot demand payment at all, or at least not based on the contract price

---

[31] E.g., *Nichols v. Raynbred*, Hob. 88, 80 Eng. Rep. 238 (K.B. 1615) (seller seeking purchase price of cow did not need to plead the delivery of the cow).

[32] McGovern 1978 argued that in many areas English law had not accepted the independence of promises.

[33] *Kingston v. Preston*, discussed in *Jones v. Barkley*, 2 Doug. 689, 99 Eng. Rep. 437 (K.B. 1773).

[34] *Jacob & Youngs v. Kent*, 230 N.Y. 239, 129 N.E. 889 (1921). For more on the background of the *Jacob & Youngs* case, see Danzig & Watson 2004: 95–118.

(at most, the argument went, it might have an "unjust enrichment" claim, which would likely amount to far less than the contract price).[35] As already mentioned (in Subsection B(2)), in sales of goods cases, the seller is required to offer "perfect tender" – precisely what was specified in the contract – and if the seller does not, then the buyer has the right to reject the goods, even if the defect or deviation was minor. The person who requested the building of the house in *Jacob & Youngs* argued that this was also the rule for the construction agreement in that case.

The court, however, emphasized that although the parties could have expressly agreed to a perfect tender rule, without such language, the court would not lightly ascribe that intention to the parties in a construction case. Unlike the sale of a particular movable good, with construction contracts it is the case both that perfect performance is unlikely (with the hundreds, if not thousands, of specifications in the agreement) and that the builder will be unable merely to take the subject of the contract back – it is not a good that can be returned in the mail but an immensely heavy object constructed on the other party's land. It would not seem likely that a builder would have agreed to (or would have understood itself to have agreed to) having a substantial forfeiture of pay as the penalty for even trivial defects in performance.[36]

Jacob & Youngs held that where the breach is insignificant relative to full performance (and taking into account whether the breach was intentional or negligent), the breaching party should be able to sue on the contract (with any claim, of course, subject to offset for the damages caused by the breach). This is the doctrine of "substantial performance."[37]

If a breaching party's deviation from the contractually prescribed performance is not small enough to allow use of the doctrine of substantial performance, the only remedy may be suing "off the contract" for restitution, that is, seeking the fair market value for the benefits conferred on the nonbreaching party (that amount to be offset by the damages caused by the breach). The availability of restitution for a breaching party is considered at greater length in Chapter 6, Section D.

An intermediate option, between the near-full recovery of the doctrine of substantial performance and what is usually a significantly reduced recovery of claiming under restitution,[38] is the option of divisibility. Here, if the contract can be recharacterized as a series of smaller performance obligations, the breaching party can recover the full amount for the parts that were completed, even where the extent of the breach on the overall contract was substantial.[39]

---

[35] The restitutionary claim for breaching parties will be discussed in Chapter 6, Section D.

[36] *See Jacob & Youngs*, 129 N.E. at 890–891; Fried 1981: 120–123.

[37] *See* Farnsworth 2004: § 8.12, at 547–553.

[38] As is discussed in Chapter 6, Section D, a few jurisdictions do not even allow breaching parties to seek restitution, so a breaching party in those jurisdictions ends up with nothing.

[39] *See, e.g., Carrig v. Gilbert-Varker Corp.*, 50 N.E.2d 59 (Mass. 1943) (on agreement to build thirty-five homes, builder finished only twenty, but contract treated as divisible, and builder allowed to recover for the twenty homes finished); *see generally* Farnsworth 2004: § 8.13, at 553–556.

C. IMPOSSIBILITY, IMPRACTICABILITY, AND FRUSTRATION OF PURPOSE

The idea of excusing the obligation to perform on the basis of changed circumstances has a long history. A doctrine of impossibility goes back to Roman law,[40] and medieval canon law recognized an implied condition that a contract was no longer binding if conditions changed (*clausula rebus sic stantibus*). The extent to which this doctrine was recognized in the canon law and in the European civil codes varied greatly across jurisdictions and over time,[41] but there are indications that it played an important, if indirect, role in the development of the English law of impossibility.[42]

Although the general principle announced by the English common law courts was that contractual obligation was absolute,[43] there were existing exceptions for certain forms of subsequent events that made performance impossible.[44] If, subsequent to the execution of a contract, government action made the performance of the agreement illegal (or, under some case law, imposed requirements that made performance impossible), then the duty was discharged.[45] If a party indispensable to performance were to die, then the obligation to perform was discharged. Thus, there is an excuse for nonperformance when a famous painter contracted to paint a portrait dies but not when someone hired to paint a house dies.[46] Similarly, if an object necessary to performance is destroyed, performance is excused. This is the well-known case of *Taylor v. Caldwell*, where the music hall rented for performance was destroyed by fire shortly before the performance, and the person renting the hall was held not to be liable for breach of contract.[47]

Sometimes the subsequent event does not make performance impossible but makes it nearly impossible – vastly more difficult and likely vastly more expensive. This is the doctrine of impracticability;[48] arguably the first impracticability case, *Mineral Park Land Co. v. Howard*,[49] involved an obligation to extract gravel that was excused when it became ten to twelve times more expensive. However, courts are generally reluctant to allow this defense, so some quite extraordinary changes in costs have been held insufficient to ground an impracticability defense.[50]

---

[40] Gordley 2004: 513–514.
[41] Zimmermann 2001: 80–83.
[42] Gordley, 2004: 521–522, 525.
[43] *See Paradine v. Jane*, 82 Eng. Rep. 897, 897 (K.B. 1647).
[44] Farnsworth 2004: 619–622.
[45] *See Abbot of Westminster v. Clerke*, 1 Dy. 26b, 73 Eng. Rep. 59 (K.B. 1536); *see also Louisville & N.R.R. v. Motley*, 219 U.S. 467 (1911); UCC § 2–615(a).
[46] *See, e.g., Mullen v. Wafer*, 480 S.W.2d 332 (Ark. 1972); *see generally Restatement (Second) of Contracts* § 262; Farnsworth (2004: 620–621). The principle was first raised in *Hyde v. Dean of Windsor*, 78 Eng. Rep. 798 (Q.B. 1597).
[47] *Taylor v. Caldwell*, 122 Eng. Rep. 309 (K.B. 1863).
[48] UCC § 2–615.
[49] 156 P. 458 (Cal. 1916).
[50] *See, e.g., Karl Wendt Farm Equipment Co. v. International Harvester Co.*, 931 F.2d 1112 (6th Cir. 1991) (loss of $2 million a day insufficient to ground impracticability defense).

When the subsequent event does not make performance impossible or even very difficult but simply pointless, the courts have occasionally excused nonperformance under the doctrine of frustration. In the leading case, *Krell v. Henry*,[51] a room was rented to observe a coronation procession for King Edward VII, but the coronation was subsequently cancelled as a result of the king's illness. If anything, courts have been even more reluctant to grant relief based on frustration than on impracticability.[52]

It is conventional to speak of these doctrines as involving implied terms: that they excuse performance in those instances where the parties themselves would not have expected performance to be due under the agreement. Where the parties promise performance, they will be held to that promise, regardless of effort or fault, but it is always open to the parties to agree that under certain circumstances, no performance will be due. One can find the roots of this approach in the original and paradigmatic "absolute obligation" case, *Paradine v. Jane*,[53] from 1647. In that case, a tenant had been thrown off his land by a foreign militia, but the court held the tenant still liable for rent, for even if possession of the land had become impossible, the contractual obligation to pay the rent had not. In *Paradine*, the court stated:

> [W]hen the party by his own contract creates a duty or charge upon himself, he is bound to make it good if he may, notwithstanding any accident by inevitable necessity, because he might have provided against it by his contract.[54]

By this reasoning, it is not so much (Anglo-American) contract law that imposes strict liability but the parties themselves. It would be open to the parties, by express language, to forgive an obligation to perform or to pay, based on "acts of God," warfare, labor trouble, or unexpected financial difficulty (and one can find such provisions in many contracts – such terms are generally called "force majeure" clauses).[55] It is just a small step from there to say that the parties may have had an unstated but shared understanding that was never translated into express contractual terms, and the doctrinal rules (the defenses of impossibility, impracticability, and frustration) are simply reflections of those unstated shared understandings.

---

[51] [1903] 2 K.B. 740 (C.A.).
[52] *See* Farnsworth 2004: § 9.7, at 634–640. There is also a question of what to do if and when an agreement has been voided on the basis of frustration or a related doctrine. Most courts allow parties to recover payments already made as part of an unjust enrichment claim. For criticism of that approach, see Goldberg 2010.
[53] 82 Eng. Rep. 897 (K.B. 1647).
[54] *Paradine v. Jane*, 82 Eng. Rep. at 897. For more on the background and implications of *Paradine v. Jane*, see Pryor & Hoshauer 2005: 349–359.
[55] *See, e.g., Restatement (Second) of Contracts*, Ch. 11, Introductory Note ("The obligor who does not wish to undertake so extensive an obligation [strict liability] may contract for a lesser one by using one of a variety of common clauses"). In some contracts, parties include a clause with the contrary purpose and effect, known as a "Hell or high water" provision, under which the parties make clear that performance is due even in the face of strikes, military action, government regulation, acts of God, and so on.

The argument against seeing these doctrines as implied terms based on the parties' unstated but shared understandings is that parties' understandings vary greatly, from person to person, and from transaction to transaction, and it would be unlikely, at best, for the current doctrine to capture everyone's understandings in every case. One could, of course, argue that the doctrine fits most people's understandings, and it is always open for the remainder to write into their agreements express provisions indicating their contrary understanding. This returns us to the earlier discussion (see Chapter 4, Section B) of the different and competing justifications for default rules: majoritarian, efficiency, and penalty- and information-forcing.

D. GOOD FAITH

The Uniform Commercial Code introduced an unwaivable duty of "good faith in . . . performance and enforcement,"[56] which the *Second Restatement* then provided as well for agreements not covered by the UCC.[57] The doctrine of good faith precedes the enactment of the UCC (and can be found in the legal systems of other countries[58]), but the UCC provisions spurred universal recognition and application in American law.[59]

The nature of this "good faith" obligation (not to be confused with an obligation of good faith in negotiation[60]) is notoriously difficult to explain or apply. Judge Richard Posner helpfully summarized the idea behind the obligation: it is a duty between contracting parties more exacting than the tort obligation not to defraud but less exacting than a fiduciary obligation; it is an intermediate obligation that reflects the fact that contracting parties in a cooperative venture are at various points particularly vulnerable to one another.[61] Of course, that range of possible application

---

[56] UCC § 1–203.

[57] *Restatement (Second) of Contracts* § 205.

[58] For example, see the German BGB § 242, which arguably influenced Karl Llewellyn's own ideas about "good faith" for the UCC. Some commentators find "good faith" in two early English cases written by Lord Mansfield. *Kingston v. Preston*, 2 Doug. 689, 99 Eng. Rep. 437 (K.B. 1773), and *Carter v. Boehm*, 97 Eng. Rep. 1162, 1164 (K.B. 1766), but the concept was not generally accepted by the English courts at that time.

[59] *See* Beatson & Friedmann 1995, for a discussion of the similarities and differences in contractual good faith across North American and European jurisdictions.

[60] There is no general obligation in contract law to negotiate in good faith, although certain forms of extreme bad-faith negotiation – duress, undue influence, and misrepresentation (discussed in Chapter 3, Section E) – make any consequent agreement subject to rescission. Also, in highly exceptional cases, parties can reach an interim, partial agreement, which the courts will interpret as imposing an obligation to negotiate in good faith. *See, e.g., Itek Corp. v. Chicago Aerial Industries*, 248 A.2d 625 (Del. 1968); *Channel Home Centers v. Grossman*, 795 F.2d 291 (3d Cir. 1986). This is discussed briefly in Chapter 3, Section A. In European and international contract law, "good faith" generally extends to precontractual behavior as well. *See, e.g.*, Hesselink 2004: 279; UNIDROIT *Principles of International Commercial Contracts* art 2.1.15 ("Negotiations in Bad Faith").

[61] *Market Street Associates Ltd. Partnership v. Frey*, 941 F.2d 588, 593–95 (7th Cir. 1991) (Posner, J.); *see also* Rakoff 2007.

leaves much still to be decided, and court decisions and commentators have not been able to agree on standards.[62] The New York Court of Appeals in 1933 famously summarized the rule as imposing "an implied covenant that neither party shall do anything which will have the effect of destroying or injuring the right of the other party to receive the fruits of the contract."[63]

Some commentators have argued that good faith is often easier to understand in terms of what it excludes, in terms of the kinds of activities that will be condemned as "bad faith," and thereby considered not authorized by the agreement, even when those actions seem to fall within the contract's express wording.[64] For example, in *Tymshare, Inc. v. Covell*,[65] the express language of a contract gave the employer discretion to alter the terms on which bonuses were earned, including the power to do so retroactively, but the court held that good faith prevented the exercise of this power where it was motivated solely by a desire to reduce the commissions due a particular employee.[66]

At the same time, it is also frequently stated that "good faith" cannot override clear language. This has led to controversy over whether "good faith" limits the ability of banks to call in loans where there is an express provision giving the bank the power to demand repayment at any time.[67] The current tendency of courts in general seems to be toward upholding express language, rejecting arguments that discretion is limited by "good faith." And certainly where there is a carefully crafted provision reserving the right to act in a way that might otherwise seem one-sided, "good faith" will have no role.[68] This makes sense, once one remembers that good faith is about protecting reasonable expectations, and making a prerogative sufficiently clear to the other party will remove any reasonable contrary expectation.

Beyond this general (and unwaivable) obligation of good faith in performance, "good faith" plays a role in other rules in contract law; for example, under the UCC, good faith restricts the occasions on which one can seek a modification of an existing contract (see Subsection (B)(3)),[69] restricts the variation of demand in a requirements contract or supply in an output contract,[70] and restricts a party's contractually granted discretion to fix a price.[71] Outside the UCC, "good faith" has

---

[62] E.g., Rakoff 2007.
[63] *Kirke La Shelle Co. v. Paul Armstrong Co.*, 188 N.E. 163, 167 (N.Y. 1933).
[64] E.g., Summers 1968.
[65] 727 F.2d 1145 (D.C. Cir. 1984) (Scalia, J.).
[66] *Id.* at 1154.
[67] *Compare K.M.C. Co., Inc. v. Irving Trust Co.*, 757 F.2d 752 (6th Cri. 1985) ("good faith" limits lender's right) *with Kham & Nate's Shoes No. 2, Inc. v. First Bank*, 908 F.2d 1351 (7th Cir. 1990) ("good faith" does not limit lender's right).
[68] *See, e.g., Third Story Music, Inc. v. Waits*, 41 Cal. App. 4th 798, 48 Cal. Rptr. 2d 747 (1995) (express language reserving the right not to market Tom Waits's music held not to be constrained or overridden by "good faith").
[69] UCC § 2–209, Comment 2.
[70] UCC § 2–306(1); *see also Empire Gas Corp. v. American Bakeries, Inc.*, 840 F.2d 1333 (7th Cir. 1988).
[71] UCC § 2–305(2).

a role in determining the validity of some agreements with mentally incompetent parties (see Chapter 3, Section (E)(6)) and the application of subjective satisfaction clauses. As to the last, where a contract makes one party's satisfaction with the product a condition of payment, the presumption is that an objective standard is to be applied, such that the party to be paid need only show that a reasonable person in the obligor's position would have been satisfied.[72] However, there are types of transactions, usually turning on aesthetics (e.g., the painting of a portrait), where subjective satisfaction is intended, and in such cases all that is required is that the judgment of satisfaction be exercised in good faith – that is, that it be sincere and reported honestly.[73]

Good faith may be thought to exemplify a more general phenomenon: interpretation of contractual provisions that blurs the line between "implied in fact terms" (terms implied by courts in contracts on the basis of the parties' apparent common intentions) and "implied in law terms" (terms implied on the basis of fairness, efficiency, or some other public policy, regardless of party intent).[74]

E. THEORETICAL IMPLICATIONS

The rules relating to performance show the regular oscillation in American contract law between holding parties strictly to the terms to which they agreed and constraining interpretation and enforcement in the name of reasonableness and fairness. Many of the rules come out of the old Equity Courts, where judges unapologetically claimed to be acting in the name of justice, but modern commentators have shown that these same doctrines can often be recharacterized or rationally reconstructed as being about enforcing the parties' likely intentions (and the limits of their actual agreement).

The doctrines relating to performance are rules that are meant to help parties work through disputes, or at least guide their actions if they decide to end rather than merely clarify or adjust an ongoing relationship. Scholars of both law and economics and law and society have raised questions regarding the extent to which the rules in action serve their intended purposes.[75]

SUGGESTED FURTHER READING

Conditions

Robert Childres, "Conditions in the Law of Contracts," *New York University Law Review*, vol. 45, pp. 33–58 (1970).

---

[72] *Restatement (Second) of Contracts* § 228.
[73] *See id.*, Comment a. For a good discussion of satisfaction clauses, see *Morin Building Products Co. v. Baystone Construction, Inc.*, 717 F.2d 413 (7th Cir. 1983) (Posner, J.).
[74] On implied terms, see, e.g., Farnsworth 2004: §§ 7.16–7.17, at 483–500.
[75] E.g., Macaulay 1989, 2003; Macneil 1978; Braucher 2012; Bernstein 1996, 1999; Schwartz 1992.

Edwin W. Patterson, "Constructive Conditions in Contracts," *Columbia Law Review*, vol. 42, pp. 903–954 (1942).

Anticipatory Repudiation and Adequate Assurances

R. J. Robertson Jr., "The Right to Demand Adequate Assurance of Due Performance: Uniform Commercial Code Section 2–609 and Restatement (Second) of Contracts Section 251," *Drake Law Review*, vol. 38, pp. 305–353 (1988–1989).

Keith A. Rowley, "A Brief History of Anticipatory Repudiation in American Contract Law," *University of Cincinnati Law Review*, vol. 69, pp. 565–639 (2001).

Good Faith

Jack Beatson & Daniel Friedmann (eds.), *Good Faith and Fault in Contract Law*. Oxford: Oxford University Press, 1995.

Edward J. Imwinkelried, "The Implied Obligation of Good Faith in Contract Law: Is It Time to Write Its Obituary?" *Texas Tech Law Review*, vol. 42, pp. 1–21 (2009).

Robert S. Summers, "The General Duty of Good Faith – Its Recognition and Conceptualization," *Cornell Law Review*, vol. 67, pp. 810–840 (1982).

———, "'Good Faith' in General Contract Law and the Sales Provisions of the Uniform Commercial Code," *Virginia Law Review*, vol. 54, pp. 195–267 (1968).

Impossibility, Impracticability, and Frustration of Purpose

Melvin Aron Eisenberg, "Impossibility, Impracticability, and Frustration of Purpose," *Journal of Legal Analysis*, vol. 1, pp. 207–261 (2009).

James Gordley, "Impossibility and Changed and Unforeseen Circumstances," *American Journal of Jurisprudence*, vol. 52, pp. 513–530 (2004).

Richard A. Posner & Andrew M. Rosenfeld, "Impossibility and Related Doctrines in Contract Law: An Economic Analysis," *Journal of Legal Studies*, vol. 6, pp. 83–118 (1977).

Richard E. Speidel, *Contracts in Crises: Excuse Doctrine and Retrospective Government Acts*. Durham, NC: Carolina Academic Press, 2007.

6

Enforcement and Remedies

Prior to the nineteenth century, remedies at common law were the largely unregulated province of the jury.[1] By contrast, current contract law offers substantial rules and principles to guide the award of damages for breach of contract. The basic principle is that damages should compensate the innocent party for moneys lost due to the breach. This compensatory principle is both the objective and the limit of contract damages: the courts should try to ensure that parties are compensated, but they also are to guard that damages do not go beyond compensation.[2]

As is discussed here, compensation is also to be understood narrowly, with a handful of exceptions: innocent parties cannot recover punitive damages, damages for pain and suffering (emotional distress damages), or attorney's fees. Because of these restrictions on damages and others to be mentioned, innocent parties are almost assured of *not* being fully compensated for their losses.[3]

A. SUBSTANTIVE (FAIRNESS) CONSTRAINTS AND PUBLIC POLICY

1. *Fairness Constraints*

If, as has been argued, contract law is essentially about respecting party choice,[4] then it is especially anomalous when the courts refuse to enforce what the parties have

---

[1] Simpson 1979: 549–551.

[2] On this, and on most of the topics discussed in this chapter, there are both significant convergences and significant divergences across national jurisdictions. *See generally* Treitel 1988; Saidov & Cunnington 2008.

[3] If only because plaintiffs (in the United States) must sustain their own costs of litigation (outside the exceptional case in which payment of fees was expressly authorized by a provision of the contract that was breached or where a statute authorizes an award of fees). This is, of course, true of other private law litigation in the United States, but at least in an area such as tort law, a jury might well make up for the costs of litigation by increasing the award in some amorphous area like pain and suffering. Knapp, Crystal & Prince 2007: 920.

[4] E.g., B. Fried 2007, 2012.

agreed to. However, while we might value autonomy generally, and party choice in agreements in particular, there are sometimes conflicting values, and freedom of contract may sometimes need to give way. This section reflects situations in which the courts (and, on occasion, legislatures) make judgments that particular contractual terms or certain sorts of transactions are not to be enforced, even though the parties might have wanted (or at least assented to) enforcement.

Most legal systems, whether common law, Roman law, or civil law, seem to have had some mechanism for refusing enforcement of egregiously unfair agreements.[5] Under Roman law (grounded on a text in Justinian's Code, and later elaborated by medieval commentators), if property was sold for less than half of its just price, the seller had a right to sue (under a doctrine that became known as "*laesio enormis*"[6]) to avoid the sale – although the buyer could maintain the sale by paying the difference between the sale price and the just price.[7]

A related legal (and moral) principle added by the medieval church was that property should not be sold at an unjust price.[8] However, one should not overstate the stringency of that doctrine: "just price" here meant "the price fairly agreed upon in the market, without fraud or deceit, though with one qualification, namely, that it was also required, in the case of food or other necessities, to be sufficiently low to permit the poor to afford them."[9] Additionally, there are skeptical commentators who have argued that many of the common law and Roman law doctrines allowing parties to avoid enforcement of unfair contracts seem to have worked, not for the benefit of the poor and downtrodden but for the well-off.[10]

A common academic response to claims of one-sided agreements is the argument that such agreements inevitably will be rare, at least in competitive markets.[11] If some term (e.g., a warranty for a good sold, the right to consequential damages, or a right

---

[5] E.g., Angelo & Ellinger 1992.

[6] More precisely, "*laesio ultra dimidium vel enormis.*" E.g., DiMatteo 1997: 120.

[7] Zimmermann 1996: 259–270; Kaser 1980: 212–213; Gordley 1990: 401–402. Thomas Aquinas (1947: II-II, q. 77), noting that the law could not forbid all that is contrary to virtue, affirms the Roman law rule of voiding unfair agreements only when the injustice is extreme (here, paying half the just price).

[8] E.g., de Roover 1958.

[9] Berman 2003: 161 (footnote omitted).

[10] A. W. B. Simpson wrote (in response to Morton Horwitz's praise of the common law implied warranty doctrine): "In England, the implied warranty arose in the context of the sale of horses. The poor did not buy horses; they walked. The doctrine of *laesio enormis* in the civil law protected landowners; in England the case law in chancery on sales at low value and on 'catching bargains' with expectant heirs appears to have largely performed the same function.... [I]n the main, I doubt if [the poor's] lot was much improved by the existence of an implied warranty of quality on the sale of victuals, or made worse by some detail of the rules for the assessment of damages. It was their misfortune to be outside the world in which such luxuries as legal actions at common law or bills in equity much mattered." Simpson 1979: 601; *see also* Gordley 1991: 148 ("Before 1750, nearly all the cases in which courts of equity found a contract to be unconscionable concerned either necessitous heirs who had sold their inheritance at a low price or the repercussions of the South Sea Bubble" (footnote omitted).).

[11] E.g., Bebchuk & Posner 2006.

to bring class actions or to avoid arbitration) is worth more to a consumer than it is to the vendor, then it is profitable to insert the term in the agreement at a price attractive to both parties. And if current sellers or vendors in the market (irrationally, inefficiently) refuse to offer the term, some competitor will.

Commentators also note that even if individual consumers may be ignorant regarding terms or have cognitive biases that prevent them from protecting their own interests, such biases may not be present among consumers treated in the aggregate.[12] And, some commentators add, it may at times be sufficient to constrain sellers that a sophisticated minority of consumers read, understand, and compare contract terms.[13]

These are substantial objections, and not to be dismissed lightly, although one might wonder whether they apply to all cases and circumstances. Or, to put the point differently, one wonders whether it is exactly in cases under this rubric that behavioral economics (the objections of "bounded rationality" and "cognitive defects") have their greatest power against a rational choice model.[14]

For example, imagine a consumer contract with a mandatory arbitration provision (and, for the sake of argument, imagine it to be a particularly one-sided provision: requiring consumer challenges under the contract to be brought under great expense in a faraway country, where the consumer's rights are limited and the vendor is not similarly restricted[15]). How much would it be worth to a consumer *not* to have that provision in the agreement?

Theorists of bounded rationality and cognitive defects would point out (among other things): (a) that overly optimistic consumers (and employees, who frequently face comparable terms in their employment agreements) are unlikely to focus on dispute-related terms, because they assume that there will never be a dispute (or, at least, they underestimate the likelihood of such a dispute); (b) the "endowment effect" means that parties value an entitlement far less when they do not have it than when they do (thus, how much you would have to pay a consumer to give up her right to bring disputes to court, or an employee to give up her right to be fired only for cause, will almost always be far greater than what that person would pay to obtain such rights, if those rights were not already in the contract); (c) cognitive effort tends to be limited, which, when combined with the natural tendency to focus on salient terms (i.e., terms made prominent by advertising or media coverage), means that consumers will rarely focus on, and even more rarely challenge, terms limiting their rights.[16]

---

[12] Schwartz & Wilde 1983.

[13] *E.g.*, Gillette 2004. For a direct response, see Bar-Gill 2012.

[14] *See, e.g.*, Sunstein 1997; Korobkin 2000, 2003; Bar-Gill 2008, 2012.

[15] For an example of an egregiously one-sided arbitration provision, although this one is in an employment agreement, see *Hooters of America, Inc. v. Phillips*, 173 F.3d 933 (4th Cir. 1999). I think the argument would still work for a fairer and more reasonable provision, although a one-sided provision makes the point clearer.

[16] On bounded rationality generally, and its effect on consumer choices, see, e.g., Kahneman 2011. For some of the points in the text here, I am indebted to Daniel Schwarcz.

Although sometimes the agreement challenged in court has unfair terms as a result of oppression and sharp practices, terms that appear to be one sided are often (at least arguably) a predictable consequence of circumstances. Cross-collateral terms may be a commercially reasonable way to sell high-priced items to consumers with bad credit; a job with lower wages and no job security may be the only terms on which an employer would (or perhaps should) take a chance of employees with a poor job history or a criminal record. The alternative to a sale or an employment contract on bad terms may be no sale or no job at all. And that is not likely to be the preference of the consumers and employees offered these opportunities, however one sided. Of course, there may be transactions so exploitative or degrading that we want to discourage them, or at least avoid any government imprimatur of them, however much the parties themselves may seek them, but that is not a conclusion one should reach too quickly.[17]

Although casebooks and teachers might prefer the cases in which the downtrodden prevail over those who would oppress them, the real-world story is that claims to avoid the enforcement of one-sided provisions rarely prevail. In the (still-rare) instances in which one-sided agreements are refused enforcement, it is much more likely to be under state and federal consumer protection rules than under the amorphous common law (or UCC) unconscionability doctrine or other contract law doctrines.[18] The unconscionability doctrine is considered in greater detail in the next subsection.

2. *Unconscionability*

Modern unconscionability doctrine appeared as a provision of the Uniform Commercial Code[19]:

> If the court as a matter of law finds the contract or any term of the contract to have been unconscionable at the time it was made, the court may refuse to enforce the contract, or it may enforce the remainder of the contract without the unconscionable term, or it may so limit the application of any unconscionable term as to avoid any unconscionable result.[20]

---

[17] *Cf.* Wertheimer 1996.

[18] There are, one should note, pockets of cases in which, for a variety of moral and policy reasons, unconscionability does seem to be more frequently accepted as a serious defense to enforcement, as in premarital agreements and mandatory arbitration agreements. The topic of premarital agreements is considered at greater length in Chapter 7, Section F.

[19] There are earlier references in American law both to the term and to the idea of refusing full enforcement due to unfairness. *See, e.g., Scott v. United States,* 79 U.S. (12 Wall.) 443, 445 (1870) ("If a contract be unreasonable and unconscionable . . . a court of law will give the party who sues for its breach damages, not according to its letter, but only such as he is equitably entitled to").

[20] UCC § 2–302(1). For the legislative history of this provision, showing how the scope was expanded and the terms made less specific, see Leff 1967. The UNIDROIT Principles have a comparable provision. UNIDROIT Principles art. 3.10.

The doctrine is not, however, limited to sales of goods; it has been recognized as a potential defense to enforcement for all types of agreements.[21]

The doctrine of unconscionability serves two distinct, if overlapping, objectives. First, it allows the courts to invalidate transactions perceived as too unfair to be given judicial (or governmental) imprimatur. Second, it gives the courts a basis for invalidating transactions for which there is evidence – but insufficient direct proof – of other doctrinal defenses to enforcement, such as duress, undue influence, or mutual mistake.[22]

The standard understanding of unconscionability is that it requires showings of both procedural unfairness and unfairness in substantive terms ("procedural unconscionability" and "substantive unconscionability"), on a kind of sliding scale, where a showing of greater unfairness on one means that less unfairness need be shown on the other. Procedural unfairness could entail anything from sharp business practices to terms in obscure language hidden in small print to inequality of bargaining power. A few courts have suggested that rescission might be allowed on the basis of "pure price unconscionability," even without any finding of procedural unfairness.[23]

The case most often cited in connection with the unconscionability doctrine is *Williams v. Walker-Thomas Furniture*,[24] in which the court noted that the unconscionability doctrine could in principle have been applied to a cross-collateral agreement.[25] Consumer contracts, especially those on standard forms, have remained the primary locus for unconscionability claims, but there are also occasional cases involving business plaintiffs. On the whole, though, only a quite small percentage of unconscionability claims prevail.[26] The standard is amorphous, and the cases hard to predict. One commentator referred to the cases in which

---

[21] *See Restatement (Second) of Contracts* § 208.

[22] Epstein 1975.

[23] *See, e.g., Gillman v. Chase Manhattan Bank*, 534 N.E.2d 824, 829 (N.Y. 1988); *Maxwell v. Fidelity Financial Services*, 907 P.2d 51, 59 (Ariz. 1995).

[24] 350 F.2d 445 (D.C. Cir. 1965). For more on the case, see Spence 1993–1994.

[25] Under the agreement, purchasers of items at a store paid in installments and were not held to have paid off any of their purchases until all were paid off; thus, any failure to pay would warrant repossession of all the items purchased. The lower courts had considered themselves without power to evaluate the transaction under the doctrine of unconscionability because the relevant UCC provisions had not been in force in the District of Columbia at the time of the transaction. In *Williams*, the Court of Appeals for the D.C. Circuit, sitting as an appellate court for the District of Columbia, held that the trial court could have applied the doctrine of unconscionability as a matter of common law. Although *Williams* strongly hinted that the cross-collateral term, at least as applied to the parties before the court, was unconscionable, the issue was left to the lower court to decide on remand, after an evidentiary hearing. (No hearing was held; the parties settled, with Walker-Thomas dropping all claims against Williams and paying her the reasonable value of the items that had been taken from her. Macaulay 1989: 579.) For an argument that such terms are in fact reasonable, see Epstein 1975. For some details of the doubtful techniques used by Walker-Thomas salespeople, see Greenberg 1980.

[26] Once a term is invalidated on the basis of unconscionability or some related doctrine, the question remains what should be put in its place. Various alternatives are considered and evaluated in Ben-Shahar 2011.

agreements were refused enforcement on the basis of unconscionability as "two parts sentiment and one part common sense."[27]

3. *Public Policy*

Courts will declare some contracts "void as contrary to public policy" for a variety of types of transactions in which the state does not want to give its imprimatur to an agreement. The range of agreements include agreements to restrain trade, agreements to pay debts based on illegal gambling, agreements to pay for a criminal act, prostitution agreements, and surrogacy agreements.[28] This topic also covers mundane transactions, such as agreements in which one party has failed to obtain a license required for transactions of this sort (e.g., to run a hotel, to lend money, to perform construction work).

When faced with an agreement held to be contrary to public policy, two questions arise: (1) Should the agreement nonetheless be enforced?; and (2) Even if the agreement is unenforceable, should one or both parties be allowed a remedy in restitution for whatever performance of the agreement has already occurred (e.g., moneys paid or services rendered)?

It goes without saying that where the legislature has offered clear direction regarding enforcement or the availability of restitution, the courts must follow that direction. Far more often, however, the legislature is silent (e.g., establishing a licensing requirement but including no language regarding contractual agreements with parties who have failed to obtain the relevant license). Many courts will then apply a multiple-factor analysis, taking into account the importance of the public policy, the relative culpability of the parties, whether nonenforcement will help effect the public policy, and whether nonenforcement will leave one party unjustly enriched. Even where the court treats the agreement against public policy as automatically void, some relief might be available through divisibility of the contract or (as earlier mentioned) restitution.[29]

B. LIMITATIONS ON REMEDIES

The basic objective of breach of contract remedies are to place the nonbreaching party in the same position it would have been in had the contract been fully performed or had the contract never been entered. Alternative measures of damages are elaborated in the next section. There are also significant constraints on what

---

[27] Fried 1981: 105.

[28] On the public policy exception generally, see *Restatement (Second) of Contracts* §§ 178–179. The public policy doctrine also constrains what can be covered in a noncompete provision ("restrictive covenant") in an employment or partnership agreement. This topic will be discussed in Chapter 7, Section A, in relation to employment agreements.

[29] *See, e.g., Restatement (Second) of Contracts* §§ 181, 184; Murray 2011: § 90, at 595–598.

damages courts will award, which are summarized in this section. The four main constraints are: (1) causation, (2) certainty, (3) foreseeability, and (4) mitigation.

1. *Causation*

A defendant in a breach of contract suit will be held liable only for the losses caused by his or her breach. Causation here is understood much as it is elsewhere in the law (e.g., in criminal law and tort law): minimally, that it must have been the case that, but for the breach, the damage would not have occurred ("but-for causation").[30] To put the same point a different way, if the defendant can show that the plaintiff would have suffered the same loss even if the breach had not occurred, then the defendant will not be liable to pay compensation.[31]

2. *Certainty*

A plaintiff in a breach of contract suit will be liable only for those losses that can be proved "with reasonable certainty."[32] This term is meant to reflect a middle position: on the one hand, not allowing plaintiffs (or juries) to impose liability for losses that are highly speculative; and on the other hand, not requiring proof to a level of certainty unlikely in any discussion of counterfactual futures (as the uncertainty as to what would have happened under full performance is created by the defendant's breach, the defendant should not be able to avoid all liability just because of that uncertainty).

There are some more specific rules that have grown out of this general doctrine. For example, a number of jurisdictions have a per se rule that new businesses will not be allowed to recover for lost profits, because the profits of businesses with no track record are thought to be too speculative to allow proof (there is some indication of a trend of jurisdictions getting rid of this per se rule, although, of course, this still leaves a very hard burden of proving with reasonable certainty what profits a business would have made that never even began).

3. *Foreseeability*

The third constraint, foreseeability, is sometimes called "*Hadley* foreseeability," after the foundational case on the topic.[33] Plaintiffs will be able to recover only normal (usual, expected) damages, unless they had informed the defendants at the time

---

[30] In tort law, there are sometimes other limitations on causation – for example, the idea that the defendant's action was a sufficiently "proximate" cause of the plaintiff's injuries. Limitations comparable to proximate cause may occur in contract cases – though not expressly under that rubric – through analyses either of "causation" or of "certainty."

[31] For a more detailed discussion of causation in contract law and how it relates to causation elsewhere in the law, see Hart & Honoré 1985: 308–324; Moore 2009: 513–571.

[32] *Restatement (Second) of Contracts* § 352.

[33] *Hadley v. Baxendale*, 9 Ex. 341, 23 L.J. Exch. 179, 2 C.L.R. 517, 18 Jur. 358 (1854).

of contracting of unusual damages that might result (e.g., that they had especially profitable agreements with other parties that were dependent on competent performance of the subject agreement). The *Hadley* standard of foreseeability at the time the agreement is entered can be contrasted with the tort standard of limiting damages based on foreseeability at the time of the wrong.[34] In contract law the focus is not on the time of the wrong – the breach – because focusing on the time of agreement allows parties to make decisions based on the level of risk they are taking on (in the face of extraordinarily high liability, parties might ask for a higher price, insert terms limiting liability, or simply refuse to enter the agreement).

It is indeed the *Hadley* doctrine as a whole, and not merely the timing of the foreseeability test, that shows a marked difference between contract law and tort law: where tort law punishes wrongdoing by creating civil liability for full compensation for losses, contract law creates obligations for partial compensation to make costs predictable.[35]

One prominent commentator has argued that the shape of the *Hadley* doctrine reflects the particular commercial and legal circumstances of the decision (e.g., the early stages of industrialization, the underdeveloped commercial law and agency law, and the personal liability of principals for the misdeeds of their companies),[36] whereas others, doubting this view, emphasize the extent to which the *Hadley* rule incorporates principles borrowed from the civil law.[37]

There was once a competing (though similar) principle, under which consequential damages would be available only if it appeared that the parties had made a "tacit agreement" to cover that risk. However, although this test had the support of the eminent American legal figure Justice Oliver Wendell Holmes Jr.,[38] it has not been generally accepted. That said, the concept of thinking of damages and other baseline rules of agreements in terms of what the parties had agreed or would have agreed has regained prominence through the support of law and economics theorists.[39]

4. Mitigation

Mitigation refers to the nonbreaching party's actions or omissions directed toward reducing the amount of damage the breach causes.[40] Most obviously, this involves

---

[34] Eisenberg 1992 argues that contract law should adopt something like the tort standard of proximate cause, although he would have the parties protected by disclosure rules.

[35] *Cf.* Shiffrin 2007: 724.

[36] *See* Danzig 1975; Danzig & Watson 2004: 48–94.

[37] For the grounding of the *Hadley* rule in civil law in general, and Robert Pothier's treatise work in particular, see Perillo 2005: 269–276; Simpson 1975b: 273–277. For a response, see Danzig & Watson 2004: 62–73.

[38] *Globe Refining Co. v. Landa Cotton Oil Co.*, 190 U.S. 540, 543 (1903).

[39] *Cf.* Epstein 1989.

[40] Expenses incurred in efforts to mitigate, even if those efforts yield no results, are recoverable from the breaching party. *See Restatement (Second) of Contracts* §347, Comment c.

not acting in a way that will "pile on" the damages. This can be seen in the standard case cited on the topic of mitigation, *Rockingham County v. Luten Bridge Co.*,[41] in which a construction company continued work on a bridge, despite being told in clear language to stop by the commissioning county government. The construction company was able to recover damages for the breach, including lost profits, but was not allowed to recover for expenses incurred after the contract was repudiated.

Along with a requirement that one desist from piling up damages, mitigation also involves obligations on the nonbreaching party to do actions that will reduce damages. For example, an improperly dismissed employee must seek alternative employment; an improperly dismissed construction company must seek alternative building jobs, or at least sell off the materials it had bought for the job; and the seller of goods must find a new buyer.

The usual phrase is "the duty to mitigate," but there is no such duty, in any conventional sense of duty. Duty implies sanction for noncompliance, but no contracting party who fails to reduce its damages will ever be threatened with jail or even be subject to a civil fine. Mitigation simply refers to the outer limit of recoverable damages: if a court determines that certain damages were reasonably avoidable, the nonbreaching party will not be able to recover those damages.[42] As Melvin Eisenberg points out, contract law, through its duty of mitigation (and a few other doctrines) comes closer to imposing a duty to rescue (a duty to use affirmative effort to prevent significant harm to another) than criminal law or tort law ever did in the common law tradition.[43]

A number of interesting practical and theoretical issues arise under mitigation: for example, when a seller of goods or provider of services enters a second contract after the first one has been breached, under what circumstances will or should the second contract be treated as a mitigating contract? And after an employee is improperly terminated, under what circumstances will an opportunity for employment (either with the original employer or a third party) be held as potential mitigation (i.e., reducing the amount of damages that can be claimed)?

The question of "mitigating contracts" comes up most often with sales of goods and construction work, but it can be raised in other areas as well (even with some personal service contracts). When one agreement is breached, and the nonbreaching party enters another agreement after the breach, should the income or profits of the second contract be considered mitigation of the losses caused by breach of the

---

[41] 35 F.2d 301 (4th Cir. 1929). For the background and context regarding the case, see Richman 2007. Recall that this case was also discussed in connection with anticipatory repudiation, in Chapter 5, Section B.

[42] *See* Farnsworth 2004: § 12.12, at 779–780.

[43] Eisenberg 2002.

first contract?[44] The answer depends on whether the second contract was possible only because of the breach of the first contract. If I own one car, and I have a contract to sell it to you, you breach, and then I sell it to a third party, then the sale to the third party is a mitigating contract. Without the breach, it would not have been possible; I have only one car to sell, and if you had gone through with the agreement to purchase the car, the car would not have been mine to sell to the third party.

The analysis is more intricate, but still basically the same, for car dealers who have many cars to sell, but who many have more potential buyers than cars to sell. If they can get only thirty versions of a popular model each month, and there are more than thirty interested buyers, than the car dealer will be able to get the profits on only thirty sales, whether some buyers renege on their contracts or not. If, however, the supply of these cars is flexible, and the dealer can get as many cars as it has deals, then the breach of one car loses the dealer the profits on that one sale, even if the particular car that was being sold to the reneging buyer is later sold to another buyer.

With employment contracts, an improperly discharged employee, for mitigation purposes, need only take a comparable job, "comparable" understood both in terms of type of work and in terms of status and prestige. Sometimes the only comparable job available is with the same employer that breached the agreement. Predictably, this frequently can be awkward (to put it mildly), but the employee may need to take that job (or have the damages that can be recovered reduced by the amount the job would have paid), unless the employee can show "special circumstances" (e.g., that the employee had been a victim of sexual harassment at that workplace).[45]

Although the doctrine of mitigation does not require a wrongfully terminated employee to take a position that is not "comparable," if the employee does take a noncomparable position (perhaps out of a reasonable desire to be able to pay accumulating bills), the money earned will be deducted from the damages available. Most jurisdictions do not require employees to prove that they made reasonable efforts to mitigate; rather, the burden of proving a failure to make reasonable efforts

---

[44] On "mitigating contracts," and "lost volume" sellers, see, e.g., Farnsworth 2004: § 12.10, at 771–778; *Restatement (Second) of Contracts* § 347, Comment f; *see also Jetz Service Co. v. Salina Properties*, 865 P.2d 1051 (Kan. App. 1993) (supplier of coin-operated laundry equipment can recover profits on contract, even though some of the machines from the breached agreement were used in subsequent agreements; supplier had large supply of machines available).

[45] The most famous case on this topic is probably *Parker v. Twentieth Century-Fox Film Corp.*, 474 P.2d 689 (Cal. 1970), in which the court concluded, over a strong dissent, that Shirley MacLaine was not required, for mitigation purposes, to star in a western (for the same employer) after her agreement to star in a movie musical had been breached. For a quite different reading of *Parker*, seeing the agreement at issue in the case as a "pay or play" contract, see Goldberg 2006: 279–312. A more conventional example is *Fair v. Red Lion Inn*, 943 P.2d 431 (Colo. 1997) (en banc) (employer wrongfully terminated employee, then offered her the same position; court held that duty to mitigate required her to take the position).

to mitigate is placed on the breaching employer. A few jurisdictions go even further and require the employer to prove both that the employee failed to use reasonable efforts and that such efforts would have led to comparable employment.[46]

These practical and doctrinal issues aside, mitigation raises questions because of its tensions with ideas about both the morality and efficiency of performance. From the perspective of deontic theory, the problem is that mitigation seems to reduce or undermine appropriate compensation (as corrective justice or, if you will, punishment) for the breaching party. From the perspective of efficiency, mitigation – viewed as an effort to encourage parties to reduce losses where it is efficient to do so – may lead to suboptimal incentives for potential breaching parties. Let me take the two points in turn.[47]

As to the first point, mitigation effectively imposes a duty on the nonbreaching party to reduce the damages due from the breaching party.[48] This seems contrary to the moral status of the plaintiff as an innocent party, and the breaching party as the party responsible for making the innocent party whole.[49] It is true that the duty to mitigate can be seen, in some cases, as consistent with a general duty not to increase other people's burdens unnecessarily,[50] but the general duty to mitigate seems to extend significantly beyond any such narrow moral duty.

As to the second point, the problem of incentives is difficult. Damages in private law matters are paid by the defendant to the plaintiff. It will commonly be the case that the damages set, even if that amount creates the optimal incentives for one party (regarding not only the incentives to perform and not to breach but also incentives regarding, for example, preperformance reliance and investment, and renegotiation), it is very possible (and perhaps probable) that the same amount will create suboptimal incentives for the other party. For example, although we may want to give contracting parties incentives to minimize their losses – and thus the duty to mitigate – doing so may have the effect of creating too weak of an incentive to avoid breach for the other contracting party.

On the topic of incentives, the availability of mitigation – and other doctrines that limit damages, such as foreseeability, the infrequent availability of specific performance, and the unavailability of punitive damages and emotional distress damages – means that there will be lower liability costs to the seller, which will in

---

[46] *See, e.g., Stewart v. Board of Education of Ritenour Consolidated School District*, 630 S.W.2d 130 (Mo. Ct. App. 1982) (improperly discharged teacher made no efforts to find other work, but school board failed to show that she could have found a job if she had tried).

[47] Of course, one could define the objectives of breach of contract damages (the focus of the next section) in a way that already incorporates current rules of mitigation. However, this would be to resolve a difficult moral, conceptual, or policy dispute by fiat – which is always possible but rarely helpful.

[48] I say "effectively imposes a duty" because, as earlier mentioned, mitigation is not, strictly speaking, a duty. There is no sanction for failure to mitigate. It is only the case that an opportunity to mitigate will limit the damages the innocent party can recover from the breaching party.

[49] Shiffrin 2007: 724–726.

[50] C. Fried 2007: 7–8, 2011.

turn mean lower overall costs to buyers.[51] Having or not having these higher levels of liability, and the corresponding higher costs, will also have distributional effects that need to be taken into account.[52] The evaluation of the mitigation doctrine, in terms of efficiency, "wealth maximization" or utilitarianism (or even in terms of justice or fairness), is thus far from straightforward.

5. *Unrecoverable Damages*

In general, attorney's fees, emotional distress damages, and punitive damages are not available in breach of contract cases.

For attorney's fees, this reflects a basic rule of civil litigation in the United States: each party pays its own attorney's fees, win or lose. This "American rule" contrasts with the rule in many other jurisdictions (e.g., England), in which the attorney's fees of winning parties are paid by the losing parties. There are exceptions. First, parties are allowed to include provisions in their agreements providing that attorney's fees will be paid by the losing party when a contract is enforced. Second, some statutes (e.g., many state and federal consumer protection statutes) may provide for an award of attorney's fees. Third, a court rule may authorize an award of attorney's fees (e.g., the Federal Rule of Civil Procedure imposing attorney's fees as a possible sanction for frivolous actions in litigation[53]).

Although emotional distress damages are available as a matter of course in tort cases, they are almost never available for breach of contract cases. Courts sometimes refer to the exceptional cases in which such damages are available, a category involving transactions in which emotional distress is the likely result of a breach, but that exception is applied narrowly in American law (unlike, for example, English law, where a comparable exception is applied more broadly to allow emotional distress damages for agreements for holiday travel[54]). There are idiosyncratic exceptions: where the breach of contract involves bodily harm (as with a contract for medical care, which is then negligently given), agreements involving the treatment of corpses or the delivery of messages about death, and agreements with common carriers.[55] A standard case involving negligence and property, however predictable the resulting emotional distress, will not ground damages for that distress.[56]

Punitive damages are not available for breach of contract cases, with the exception, in many jurisdictions, of cases involving insurance companies and bad-faith failure to honor claims or to settle cases within policy limits. (That aspect of insurance contract law is discussed in Chapter 7.) California briefly experimented with

---

[51] Craswell 2012.
[52] *See id.*
[53] *Federal Rules of Civil Procedure*, Rule 11.
[54] Peel 2007: 1039–1040.
[55] *Restatement (Second) of Contracts* § 353, Comment a.
[56] *Erlich v. Menezes*, 981 P.2d 978 (Cal. 1999).

allowing punitive damages for bad-faith breach of contract but eventually rejected that doctrine as being too hard to apply and creating too much commercial uncertainty.[57]

It should be noted that emotional distress damages and punitive damages can arise out of a breach of contract if the other party's action can be characterized as an independent tort (e.g., fraud), as those sorts of damages would be available in connection with a tort claim.

C. MEASURING DAMAGES: EXPECTATION, RELIANCE, RESTITUTION

In general, the remedy available for breach of contract is money damages. Equitable remedies (discussed in Section E) are available only in extraordinary circumstances.[58]

There are three measures of money damages available, from which the plaintiff must usually make an election: expectation damages, reliance damages, and restitution. Roughly, expectation damages are meant to put the plaintiff (the nonbreaching party) in the same position it would have been had there been full performance; reliance damages are meant to put the plaintiff in the same position it would have been in had the contract not been agreed; and restitution is meant to put the breaching party in the same position it would have been had the contract not been agreed.

1. *Expectation Damages*

As noted, expectation damages are meant to put the nonbreaching party in the same position it would have been in had the agreement been performed. To transform this general principle into specific damage awards, a variety of formulas have been offered.

One standard measure of expectation damages is the difference between "contract" and "market": that is, at the time of the breach, the difference between the price set by the contract and the price that would have been available in the marketplace from alternative suppliers or purchasers. If one had a futures contract to purchase one thousand bushels of corn at $3.50 per bushel on June 1, but the seller reneges, and, on June 1, the market price is at $4.00 per bushel, then one has the

57 The California experiment begins with *Seaman's Direct Buying Service, Inc. v. Standard Oil Co.*, 686 P.2d 1158 (Cal. 1984), and ends with *Freeman & Mills, Inc. v. Belcher Oil Co.*, 900 P.2d 669 (Cal. 1995).
58 Civil law countries tend to be much more favorable to specific performance. Laithier 2005: 108–116; Zimmermann 2005: 43–49; Miller 2007. ("German courts simply order the defendant to perform. French courts force him to perform by *astreinte*, that is, by threatening to award large damages if he does not." Gordley 2001c: 14 (footnote omitted).) For a claim that this preference or presumption in favor of specific performance in civil law countries is diminishing, see Lando & Rose 2004. Specific performance (along with, on occasion, public penance) had also been available, as a matter of course, in the church courts in breach-of-faith cases. Helmholz 1975: 424.

right to the contract-minus-market difference of $0.50 per bushel, for one thousand bushels, for a total of $500.00.

One practical problem is that losses due to market fluctuations are not merely hypothetical. The buyer who needs one thousand bushels of corn in early June needs to find an alternative supplier (as a seller of corn whose buyer has reneged needs to find an alternative buyer), and this process is frequently not instantaneous. What happens if the market changes in the interim? For example, consider a buyer with a contract to buy corn at $3.50 per bushel on June 1. The seller reneges on that day the market is at $4.00 per bushel, but by the time the buyer has found an alternative supplier a few days later, the market price is up to $4.10 per bushel. The UCC allows buyers who act reasonably in finding an alternative supplier (what it calls "cover") the right to recover the difference between the "cover" price and the contract price, even if that is greater than the difference between the contract price and the market price at the time of breach.[59] Similarly, the seller whose buyer reneges may recover the full difference between the contract price and the price paid by an alternative buyer.[60]

Finally, a word should be added about "disgorgement." Disgorgement is the idea that the breaching party should have to surrender any gains it obtained because of its breach (as the seller who reneges, and gains a higher profit from a new buyer). Disgorgement is not generally an officially accepted ground or measure of damages in American contract law,[61] but there are a handful of cases that are hard to characterize in any other way. In circumstances in which a breaching party acts badly, eventually obtains significant benefits, and might otherwise owe only a small amount of damages, the inclination to find some way (by stretching existing remedial doctrines) to recoup that party's gain for the innocent party is understandable.[62]

2. *Reliance Damages*

Reliance damages (not to be confused with the cause of action for reliance – that is, promissory estoppel, discussed in Chapter 3, Section D) are the nonbreaching party's out-of-pocket expenses. If expectation damages are about putting the nonbreaching party in the same position it would have been in had the contract been performed, then reliance damages are about putting the nonbreaching party in the same position it had been in before the contract had been entered.

---

[59] UCC § 2–712.

[60] UCC § 2–706.

[61] The opposition to disgorgement as a remedy is connected with the view that contract damages should never be more than compensatory, and (thus) also connected with the idea of "efficient breach," discussed in Section I.

[62] For an argument that disgorgement is more common in American law than is usually believed, see Eisenberg 2006; for the presence of disgorgement-type remedies in U.K. law, see Cunnington 2008.

Reliance damages are subject to all the same constraints as expectation damages, discussed in Section B: causation, certainty, foreseeability, and mitigation. Additionally, if the breaching party can prove (with reasonable certainty) that full performance would have resulted in the nonbreaching party losing money (i.e., a "losing contract"), then damages will be reduced by the amount of that loss.[63] This reflects the idea that one should not do better from litigation than one would from performance.[64]

3. Restitution

Like "reliance," "restitution" can be the name for both a cause of action (which also goes by the name of "unjust enrichment," and was discussed in Chapter 3, Section D) and a measure of recovery, and this has occasionally caused some confusion.

As a measure of recovery, restitution allows the plaintiff to recover the amount by which the defendant was enriched by the nonbreaching party (by payment or services performed) during the course of performance.[65] When a party is suing for breach of contract, one can say that restitution damages have the purpose and effect of putting the breaching party in the same position it would have been in had the breach not occurred.[66] Normally, a party would have little reason to opt for a restitution measure of damages where expectation damages or reliance damages would be available, as these will almost always be larger. However, restitution can be an attractive alternative in some exceptional circumstances.

First, in cases where the nonbreaching party had been part of a losing contract (and the breaching party can prove that loss with reasonable certainty), under expectation damages or reliance damages, the amount the plaintiff would have lost under full performance will be deducted from the amount it would be allowed to recover.[67] When the plaintiff was in a losing contract, there is an odd (but widely accepted) doctrine that the nonbreaching party has the right to sue "off the contract" for

---

[63] *Restatement (Second) of Contracts* § 349.

[64] Although, as will be seen here, there is an exception to this principle for "market value restitution." In the English case of *Omak Maritime Ltd. v. Mamola Challenger Shipping Co.*, [2010] EWHC 2026 (Comm), the principle of not being allowed to do better by litigation than one would have done by performance was applied rigorously to refuse the owners of a boat compensation for wasted expenditures, because the charterer's repudiation had allowed the owners to earn significantly more (on a rising market) by rechartering the boat, more than making up for the wasted expenditures. Thus, even without awarding damages, the owners were already in a better position than they would have been in had the contract been performed, so no further damages were awarded.

[65] Restitution is thus different from disgorgement (discussed in Section C, Subsection 1), which deals with the benefits the breaching party obtained from third parties.

[66] This is in a sense a mirror image of reliance damages, which puts the nonbreaching party in the same position it would have been in had the breach not occurred.

[67] *See Restatement (Second) of Contracts* § 349 (deduction from reliance damages for losses proved with reasonable certainty). As for expectation damages, by definition, one would have no lost profits on a losing contract, and getting one to the same position one would have been in had there been full performance would include taking into account the loss on that performance.

restitution, recovering the full market value of services it rendered, with no deduction for the losses it would have made on full performance, and without the actual contract price being a limit on recovery.[68] This is known as "market value restitution."[69]

Additionally, as discussed in Section D, Subsection 2, both the UCC, for contracts involving the sale of goods,[70] and the vast majority of jurisdictions in non-sale of goods cases,[71] allow the breaching party to recover ("off the contract") on a restitutionary basis, subject to an offset for the damages caused by the breach.

D. SPECIAL CASES

1. *Cost of Completion versus Diminution of Value*

In construction and related cases, where the builder or renovator fails to perform according to the contract specifications, there are two distinct ways to measure the expectation damages that are then due. Each, in its own way, meets the formula of bringing the nonbreaching party to the same position it would have been in had there been full performance.[72] One measure is the cost of finishing the work undone or correcting the work that was defective: a direct and obvious sense of bringing the nonbreaching party to the equivalence of full performance. The other measure involves the breaching party's paying the difference between what the land or building would have been worth under full performance and what it is worth with the defective performance. The difference between the two measures of damages can be substantial, in part because the costs of undoing defective performance can be high and in part because the nonbreaching party might subjectively value expensive modifications that do not raise the (objective) market value of the property significantly – indeed, some requested work might decrease the value of the property.

---

[68] *See, e.g., Restatement (Second) of Contracts* § 373; *United States ex rel. Coastal Steel Erectors, Inc. v. Algernon Blair, Inc.*, 479 F.2d 638 (4th Cir. 1973); Farnsworth 2004: § 12.20, at 825–827; Murray 2011: § 127, at 806–807. The recently published *Restatement (Third) of Restitution and Unjust Enrichment* has suggested that in these sort of cases, the plaintiff should recover only "the market value of the plaintiff's uncompensated contractual performance, not exceeding the price of such performance as determined by reference to the parties' agreement." *Id.*, § 38(2)(b).

[69] This exception has its own exception, as idiosyncratic (relative to other doctrines) as "market value restitution" itself: if the nonbreaching party has performed all its duties under the contract, and all that was left to perform by the breaching party was a payment of money, the nonbreaching party cannot recover in restitution but can recover only the moneys due. *Restatement (Second) of Contracts* § 373(2).

[70] UCC § 2–718.

[71] *Restatement (Second) of Contracts* § 374; see Murray 2011: § 127, at 807–810.

[72] In a different sense, though, the two measures reflect diametrically opposed aspects of contract law damages: the promisee's primary interest in performance versus the promisee's secondary interest in being compensated for any damage caused by a breach of the agreement.

Two paradigm cases on the side of diminution of value are *Jacob & Youngs v. Kent*[73] and *Peevyhouse v. Garland Coal & Mining Co.*[74] In *Jacob & Youngs v. Kent* (a case already discussed relative to other topics, in Chapter 5, Section B), the builder of a house used a type of pipe different from that specified in the contract (it appeared that the quality of pipe was the same; only the manufacturer was different). The court (through Judge Benjamin Cardozo) stated that without express direction to the contrary, and without evidence that the deviation from the contract terms was either significant or willful, the correct measure of damages should be the diminution of value (how much less the house was worth because of the different piping, likely little or nothing) rather than the cost of completion (the substantial cost of tearing out the old plumbing and putting in the type of pipes specified in the contract). Judge Cardozo also emphasized that the cost of completion would be "grievously out of proportion" to the defect.[75]

In *Peevyhouse*, a coal company paid a farmer to strip-mine coal on the farmer's land. The agreement also included an express promise by the coal company to restore the property at the end of the contract period. The coal company did not restore the land, and the farmer sued.

Testimony at the trial indicated that restoring the land would cost $29,000 but would yield an increase in the land's value of only $300. The court, noting that the restoration work was "merely incidental" to the main purpose of the agreement, and that the cost of repair was "disproportionate" to the value to the promise, concluded that the diminution of value was the appropriate measure of damages.[76]

Although *Peevyhouse* came out in favor of the diminution-of-value measure of damages, in many ways by its facts (though not its outcome) it is a paradigm case for cost of completion. There is evidence that the farmers in that case expressly included a provision requiring the coal company to restore the farmland and accepted a lower payment for the coal rights in exchange for that express promise.[77] Additionally, unlike cases involving commercial landowners, commercial property, or property that was sold before litigation, the Peevyhouse family had a personal and ongoing interest in the conditions of the land, which remains scarred from the remedial work not performed (as of 2007, the plaintiffs' family still lived on that land[78]).

In these cases, the courts will sometimes refer to requiring completion (or the payment of its cost) as "economic waste" or as a "windfall" to the plaintiff, indicating a reason for choosing the lesser diminution-of-value measure of damages, although

---

[73] 230 N.Y. 239, 129 N.E. 889 (1921).

[74] 382 P.2d 109 (Okla. 1962). The Oklahoma Supreme Court expressly reaffirmed *Peevyhouse* in 1994 (though by a 5–4 vote), noting that parties who wanted a cost of completion measure of damage could place such a term in their agreements. *Schenberger v. Apache Corp*, 890 P.2d 847 (Okla. 1994).

[75] *Jacob & Youngs*, 230 N.Y. at 244, 129 N.E.2d at 891.

[76] *Peevyhouse*, 382 P.2d at 114.

[77] This and much else come out in the excellent narrative of the case in Maute 2007.

[78] Maute 2007: 301.

courts also seem to focus on whether the breach was intentional or inadvertent and on whether the uncompleted work would directly benefit the innocent party (as was clearly the case in *Peevyhouse* but not in *Jacob & Youngs*).[79]

Although law and economics scholars have, on the whole, favored the diminution of value measure for these sorts of cases,[80] some theorists from that tradition appreciate that concern about economic waste is misguided. Schwartz and Scott make the basic point that construction contracts of this sort involve a prepayment for the service in question,[81] and cost of completion damages should be awarded as a matter of course, for the same reason that market value damages are awarded in standard sale of goods cases.[82]

It should be noted that this is one area in which fault plays a role in the doctrinal rules, one of a scattering of exceptions to the general principle that contract law is amoral,[83] and a matter of strict liability (a topic taken up in Section I).[84]

2. *Restitution for the Breaching Party*

One of the lessons of the classic case of *Jacob & Youngs v. Kent* (discussed in Chapter 5, Section B, and in the previous subsection) is that, generally, full and perfect completion of an agreement is a condition for payment. *Jacob & Youngs* modified or clarified the rule by declaring that (unless there is express language in the agreement) "substantial performance" of the agreement would be sufficient to create a duty of payment (less whatever damages were due for whatever breaches had occurred). Even with this loosening of the rule, it remained the case that those who had breached their agreement in a significant way had no right to sue for payment "on the contract." This left open the question of whether breaching parties could sue "off the contract" on a restitution claim, for the fair value of any benefit conferred through their partial performance of the contract. Some early cases in a few jurisdictions established a blanket rule that breaching parties could not seek recovery, even under the limited form of restitution. In the well-known 1824 case

---

[79] Farnsworth 2004: 788–792. Similar analysis is used in other common law countries. *See, e.g., Tabcorp Holdings Ltd. v. Bowen Investments Pty. Ltd.* (2009) 83 A.L.J.R. 390 (Australian court imposing cost of completion damages on tenant who egregiously and secretly violated lease provision forbidding alteration to premises, even though cost of completion damages was forty times greater than diminution of value).

[80] *E.g.,* R. Posner 2011: 152; Harrison 2007: 273–278.

[81] Some observers suspect frequent outright fraud, with "companies specializing in extracting natural resources from private land, promising remedial work to landowners without ever intending to perform, knowing their damages liability will be limited to diminution of value." Maute 2007: 294 n. 29.

[82] Schwartz & Scott 2008.

[83] Many of the exceptions lie (unsurprisingly) in the equitable side of contract law: one cannot take advantage of another party's reasonable expectations and reasonable reliance (equitable estoppel, promissory estoppel, the doctrine of reasonable expectations in insurance law), one cannot knowingly take advantage of another party's mistake (unilateral mistake doctrine), and so on.

[84] *See* G. Cohen 2009.

of *Stark v. Parker*,[85] the Massachusetts Supreme Judicial Court did not allow an employee hired for a year to recover any part of the wages he was due when he left the employment prior to the end of the year (and with no fault claimed against the employer).[86] The court seemed perplexed that anyone would even question the matter:

> It cannot but seem strange to those who are in any degree familiar with the fundamental principles of law, that doubts should ever have been entertained upon a question of this nature. Courts of justice are eminently characterized by their obligation and office to enforce the performance of contracts, and to withhold aid and countenance from those who seek, through their instrumentality, impunity or excuse for the violation of them. And it is no less repugnant to the well established rules of civil jurisprudence, than to the dictates of moral sense, that a party who deliberately and understandingly enters into an engagement and voluntarily breaks it, should be permitted to make that very engagement the foundation of a claim to compensation for services under it.[87]

As Robert Gordon has pointed out, this rule, in the employment context, can be seen as intended to discourage otherwise migratory farm and factory laborers from leaving (potentially unpleasant and underpaid) employment prior to the end of their contracts.[88]

An 1834 case from New Hampshire, *Britton v. Turner*,[89] led a (slow) trend of cases coming out the other way. The *Britton* court pointed out that denying any recovery for a breaching party effectively punishes a party more harshly for part performance (where the party confers value but receives nothing for it) than for not performing at all. Additionally, the rule of no recovery gives the employer an incentive to try to drive employees away just before the end of their employment contract.[90]

By the time of the *Restatements*, allowing for recovery by breaching parties (subject to deduction for the damage caused and subject to any liquidated damages provision) was the accepted position in most jurisdictions.[91] It is also the rule for the sale of goods under the Uniform Commercial Code.[92]

Although most jurisdictions follow this rule, allowing for recovery in restitution by the breaching party as a matter of course, this approach is not universal. One holdout, Massachusetts, allows for recovery (in cases not involving the sale of goods)

---

[85] 19 Mass. (2 Pickering) 267 (1924).
[86] The employment contract was for $120, and there was evidence that the employee had been paid a total of only $36 prior to leaving his employment. *Stark v. Parker*, 19 Mass. at 285.
[87] *Stark v. Parker*, 19 Mass. at 289.
[88] Gordon 2004: 424–427.
[89] 6 N.H. 481 (1834).
[90] *See id.*
[91] See *Restatement (Second) of Contracts* § 374.
[92] UCC § 2–718.

only if the breaching party shows both that it substantially completed the required contractual performance and that it acted in good faith.[93]

E. EQUITABLE REMEDIES

As discussed in Section C, the starting point of American contract law (and the contract law of most common law countries) is that monetary damages are sufficient. The view of contracting parties is often different: they would prefer the agreed performance to monetary compensation (especially when monetary compensation requires expensive litigation and when the compensation may be, for other reasons, significantly less than the losses incurred[94]). At the same time, some breaching parties might complain that under some factual circumstances, the cost of their performing has become far greater than the harm done by nonperformance, a harm that, in any event, is adequately met by monetary compensation (at amounts lower than the cost of performance).[95]

Judicial orders to perform in old English law were available from the chancellor, who had the discretion to make such orders in appropriate cases. Over time, however, the common law courts and the courts of equity resolved their jurisdictional overlap through a series of principles that included, prominently, that equitable remedies would be available only where money damages were "inadequate."[96]

Under the somewhat idiosyncratic view of the English courts, money damages were never considered adequate for the purchase of land – as each parcel of land was considered unique, and the money to buy a different parcel of land was thus considered an inadequate substitute – and the American courts have adopted that view.[97] Other circumstances in which money damages would be inadequate would include situations in which the various doctrines limiting awards of damages might leave the nonbreaching party without adequate recourse (e.g., because the losses were insufficiently certain).[98] In the sale of goods, a showing that a product purchased

---

[93] E.g., *J. A. Sullivan v. Commonwealth*, 494 N.E.2d 374 (Mass. 1986). For sale of goods cases, Massachusetts has adopted UCC art. 2, including the provision allowing recovery by the breaching party. *Mass. Gen. Laws* ch. 106, § 2–718(2).

[94] Although where performance is available only by court order (i.e., "specific performance"), that performance will also require the significant time and expenditures of litigation.

[95] E.g., R. Posner 1981: 204–205.

[96] When a breaching party's defective performance consists only of a failure to pay money, a judge's order to pay becomes a kind of specific performance, in the sense that it is ordering performance of the contract. However, as money damages, it is not considered an equitable order, and the special requirements for equitable remedies do not have to be met.

[97] Modern justifications for this approach have been offered. Steven Shavell (2006b) argued that for the purchase of goods, parties would likely agree to money damages rather than specific performance, because of the possibility that the production of the good in question would have become difficult or expensive; with the sale of land, however, the subject of the contract already exists, so parties would be more likely to agree to a specific performance remedy.

[98] *See, e.g., City Stores v. Ammerman*, 266 F. Supp. 766 (D. D.C. 1967), aff'd, 394 F.2d 950 (D.C. Cir. 1968).

was unique is also therefore considered necessary – and usually sufficient – to ground an order of specific performance.[99]

Although some commentators (and contracting parties) might look enviously upon legal systems in which specific performance is in principle more commonly or more easily granted, it appears to be the case that even in such systems plaintiffs only rarely seek that remedy. This may merely reflect the practical reality of seeking specific performance even in jurisdictions where it is purportedly easy (or at least easier) to obtain: litigation toward that remedy will be expensive and long, and by the time the remedy is obtained (if it is obtained), perhaps being delayed further by appeals, so much time may have passed that the actual performance of the promise at that point will be either impossible or pointless.[100]

By long-standing rule, injunctive relief is not available to enforce a personal services contract, although a court may be willing to grant a negative injunction requiring a breaching party not to work for competitors.[101] As the courts have recognized from the first case on the issue,[102] there is often only a very thin line between the (acceptable) negative injunction against working for another employer and the (unacceptable) positive injunction requiring a return to the contracting employer. And courts are wary not to grant a negative injunction, "if its probable result will be to compel a performance involving personal relations the enforced continuance of which is undesirable or will be to leave the employee without other reasonable means of making a living."[103]

As a matter of the common law of contracts, courts will generally not order an employer to reinstate an employee who was terminated in breach of contract, although such orders are commonplace (either through courts or arbitrators) under the auspices of many collective bargaining agreements and state and federal civil service regulations.

F. AGREED REMEDIES

Few other topics show sharper distinctions between different theoretical approaches to contract, or disparate treatment across jurisdictions or over time, than the issue of "agreed remedies."

Simply, as parties agreed to other terms relating to their transaction (e.g., price, quality, delivery, payment schedule), they could also agree to what the remedy would

---

[99] UCC § 2–716.

[100] E.g., Lando & Rose 2004: 486.

[101] The original case here is *Lumley v. Wagner*, 1 De GM & G 604, 42 Eng. Rep. 687 (1852), in which an opera singer had agreed to work for one opera house and also had expressly agreed not to appear with any other opera company. When she broke the agreement, the Lord Chancellor granted a negative injunction, requiring that she not sing for any competing opera company.

[102] See *Lumley v. Wagner*, 42 Eng. Rep. at 693.

[103] *Restatement (Second) of Contracts* § 367(2).

be if and when one of the parties fails to perform as promised.[104] In American contract law, agreed remedies are often referred to as "liquidated damages," especially when they approximate the expected or actual losses of the nonbreaching party. However, agreed remedy provisions are referred to as "penalty clauses" when they seem to be far greater than projected or actual losses.[105]

Historically, punitive bonds were common in medieval English transactions: usually to the effect that where one party promised to pay one hundred pounds by a certain day (either as payment for some good, or as repayment of a loan), that party would have simultaneously promised to pay the promisee twice that amount if the original promised amount was not timely paid.[106] However, throughout the seventeenth century,[107] first the equitable courts, and then the law courts as well, became increasingly willing to give relief to defendants subject to a penal bond, holding that they would not have to pay the bond price if they were willing to pay the (smaller amount) of moneys due, plus actual damages (usually, interest and costs). Eventually, this position was solidified by legislation.[108]

Modern American doctrine indicates that agreed remedies will not be enforceable if their purpose is to terrorize the other party into performance. To many people new to contract law, this seems paradoxical. Isn't performance what the parties want, and what those who made contracts enforceable want? Why would it be a bad thing rather than a good thing to have terms that make it more likely that parties will perform as they promised? And from the perspective of the party on whom the "penalty" would be enforced, there might be good reasons to accept – or even to propose – such a provision. To a company trying to establish itself, it can be a way of signaling a commitment to performance or to high-quality performance (comparable to a money-back guarantee).[109]

A separate paradox is that if the parties agree to a bonus for early performance (increasingly common in government construction contracts), such provisions are entirely uncontroversial and raise no doctrinal issues. However, when provisions

[104] Agreements regarding damages to be paid entered into after the breach occurs are an entirely different matter: such "settlement" or "release" agreements are encouraged by the American legal system and will be enforced (within the constraints of other general defenses to contractual enforcement, like fraud or duress) even if the amount to be paid is significantly higher or lower than the actual damages suffered. *See, e.g.,* Farnsworth 2004: § 4.23, at 274–276.

[105] Agreed damages provisions that significantly undercompensate are not subject to the same legal suspicion or the same regulatory rules as agreed damages provisions that appear to overcompensate. In fact, limitations of liability are both common and legally supported – see *Restatement (Second) of Contracts* § 356 & Comment a; UCC §§ 2–718 & Comment 1, 2–719.

[106] Simpson 1975a: 88–128. The precise language of the bond usually involved the party promising to pay the larger amount, with that obligation being defeated if the party paid the smaller amount by the date specified. *E.g., id.,* 90–92.

[107] The evidence is mixed and uncertain regarding the availability of relief against penalties prior to the mid-sixteenth century. J. H. Baker 2003: 823.

[108] Simpson 1975a, 118–122.

[109] E.g., R. Posner 2011: 160.

impose penalties for late performance (although these are even more common in construction contracts), they are said to raise special doctrinal concerns (but such provisions are commonly enforced), even though, from an economic or mathematical perspective, a low fixed price and a later deadline with incentives for early performance is identical to a higher fixed price and an earlier deadline with disincentives for later performance.

Similarly, if a court can be convinced that an obligation to pay a large sum (larger than the value of promised performance) is not a liquidated-damages provision but rather a chosen alternative within a "pay or play" (also called "take or pay") contract, where the contract expressly gives one party the option to perform in a certain way or pay a certain sum (such contracts are common in the natural gas industry,[110] but can be found elsewhere as well), then the provision will be enforced, even though its effect would be identical to a liquidated-damages clause.

Modern economic theorists have come down, fairly consistently, for the enforcement of agreed remedies, even where these vary sharply from reasonable estimates of actual damages.[111] This alternative view is grounded in part in questioning the principle that contract remedies should be primarily about compensation – never more, and only exceptionally, and by express agreement, much less – and partly questioning the idea that parties would never have good reasons to agree to supracompensatory damages (and thus also questioning that such an agreement is usually a sign of overreaching).

A few words on the details of the doctrine: although the rules vary from one jurisdiction to another, most place the burden of proof on the party opposing enforcement of an agreed remedies provision, and the standard is whether damages would be hard to measure or to prove and whether the agreed damages are a reasonable estimate of the anticipated or actual harm caused by the breach.[112] Most courts read this last test as requiring the invalidation of provisions that might have been reasonable estimates at the time the agreement was signed, but which have turned out to overstate significantly the actual damages, although a few courts have read the test a different way: to require enforcement if the provision was a reasonable estimate at the time of execution, even though the ultimate damages turn out to be much lower.[113] Some courts have held that damages that would be unrecoverable in a breach of contract

[110] *E.g.*, Medina 1988. Such agreements also seem to be relatively common in Hollywood. *See, e.g., Locke v. Warner Bros.*, 57 Cal. App. 4th 354 (Cal. App. 1997).
[111] *See, e.g.*, Scott & Triantis 2004, Edlin & Schwartz 2003, Goetz & Scott 1977. Richard Posner lists "the law's refusal to enforce penalty clauses" as one of the "most important contradictions to the efficiency theory of the common law." R. Posner 2011: 319; *see also id.*, 159–163 (on penalty clauses). Judge Posner also proffered his view in a well-known case, *Lake River Corporation v. Carborundum Company*, 769 F.2d 1284, 1288–1292 (7th Cir. 1985) (Posner, J.).
[112] *Restatement (Second) of Contracts* § 356.
[113] *California & Hawaiian Sugar Co. v. Sun Ship, Inc.* 794 F.2d 1433 (9th Cir. 1986).

case, like emotional distress damages, may nonetheless help ground the amount of agreed damages.[114]

A brief word should be added here about agreed remedies that refer to equitable remedies rather than money damages. It is increasingly common for parties to place provisions into agreements – for example, in the restrictive covenants of employment agreements – in which the parties purport to agree to orders for injunctive relief or other equitable remedies should the agreement be breached.[115] There is no indication that courts give such terms any credence: equitable remedies are within the discretion of the courts, and the courts jealously guard their right to make their own judgments about the appropriateness of "extraordinary remedies."[116] (Similar results occur in related fields, as with party agreements to appoint a receiver when a mortgage is foreclosed.[117])

G. THIRD-PARTY RIGHTS AND DUTIES

The basic ideal of contract law, freedom of contract, indicates that contract law is an area in which parties can set their own rules, creating rights and obligations that apply only to the contracting parties, and only because of the contract that they have entered. This section looks at the situations in which rights and duties of third parties (individuals and entities who were not parties to the agreement in question) can also be affected, either by gaining a right to sue on the agreement or because of a transfer of the rights or duties grounded in the contract.

1. *Third-Party Beneficiary*

Until well into the nineteenth century, third parties to a contract could never sue on a contract.[118] Two lines of exceptions developed, each based on a New York case.

---

[114] *See Wassenaar v. Panos*, 331 N.W.2d 357 (Wis. 1983) (provision requiring payment of full salary for terminated hotel manager, upheld, with no deduction for money received from subsequent employment; full salary held to compensate manager for harm to reputation and emotional distress).

[115] *E.g., Valley Medical Specialists v. Farber*, 982 P.2d 1277, 1279 (Ariz. 1999) (provision agreeing to injunction should restrictive covenant be violated).

[116] *See* Laycock 1993: 53 (noting, but criticizing the conventional view of equitable remedies as "extraordinary"); *Restatement (Second) of Contracts* § 359, Comment a ("Because the availability of equitable relief was historically viewed as a matter of jurisdiction, the parties cannot vary by agreement the requirement of inadequacy of damages"); Yorio 1989: 439–452; *see also Restatement (Second) of Contracts* § 364(2) (in appropriate circumstances, specific performance or a negative injunction can be ordered even where the parties have expressly agreed not to authorize that remedy). Although it is hard to find an American case discussing the matter, the Court of Appeal for England and Wales has expressly held that the parties cannot bind the court's discretion through an agreement to grant specific performance. *Quadrant Visual Communications Ltd. v. Hutchison Telephone (UK) Ltd.*, [1993] BCLC 442 (C.A.) at 451.

[117] *E.g., Dart v. Western Savings & Loan Assoc.*, 438 P.2d 407, 410 (Ariz. 1968) ("'no such contract provision should force a court of equity to exercise its discretion in favor of a party who stands in no need of aid.'").

[118] There was a seventeenth-century English case, *Dutton v. Poole*, 83 Eng. Rep. 523 (K.B. 1677), involving a son's promise to pay a daughter's dowry in exchange for the father's promise not to

The first case was *Lawrence v. Fox*.[119] In that case, Holly owed $300 to Lawrence. Holly later loaned $300 to Fox, instructing Fox to repay the money to Lawrence. The court determined (on the basis of analogy to beneficiaries' rights to sue the trustee of a trust) that Lawrence had the right to sue Fox for the money due him under the contract with Holly. The second case was *Seaver v. Ransom*,[120] in which a husband promised his wife he would leave money in his will for the wife's niece (in exchange for the wife signing a will giving the husband use of the wife's house during his life), but then did not do so. The court allowed the niece to sue the husband's estate for the promised money, enforcing the husband's contract with the wife. The first case exemplifies what has been called "creditor beneficiary" cases, the second case "donee beneficiary" cases.[121]

Under American law, intended beneficiaries have the right to enforce the agreement (subject to defenses the promisor would have had against the promisee). The two main questions for practical application are the following: How does one tell whether a third party counts as an "intended beneficiary"? When does the right vest? The first question is hard, because nearly all agreements confer some benefit on third parties, but a wide scope of third-party rights would seem to undermine the freedom of contract of the original parties. The second question is important, because once the third-party right vests, the contracting parties lose their ability to alter their agreement (without the consent of the third party).

Regarding intended beneficiaries, some courts look to whether both contracting parties intended to give the third party rights; others look only to the promisee's intentions, and the remainder take a middle position; asking whether the promisor knew or had reason to know of the promisee's intention.[122] The jurisdictions also vary regarding when the right vests in the third party: ranging from immediate vesting upon the making of the contract, to vesting when the beneficiary learns of the contract and assents to the benefit in some way, to a view that vesting occurs only when the beneficiary relies upon the contract.[123] In any event, it remains open to the contracting parties, by express language to alter the rules of vesting (e.g., under the terms of many insurance policies the insured reserves the right to change beneficiaries, and thus retains that right, regardless of whether the beneficiary assents to the benefit or relies on it).

sell some wood, which seemed to authorize enforcement by (at least some) intended beneficiaries. However, that case was repudiated in *Tweddle v. Atkinson*, 121 Eng. Rep. 762 (Q.B. 1861), and it was not until the Contracts (Rights of Third Parties) Act 1999, ch. 31, that third-party enforcement was firmly reestablished in England. On the history of third-party claims generally, see Holdsworth 1920.
[119] 20 N.Y. 268 (1859).
[120] 120 N.E. 639 (N.Y. 1918).
[121] Although the *Second Restatement* intentionally avoids these labels, it reintroduces categories that are strongly analogous: performance that will satisfy an obligation of the promisee to the beneficiary and performance that is intended to benefit the beneficiary. *Restatement (Second) of Contracts* § 302(1).
[122] E.g., Knapp, Crystal & Prince 2007: 750; *cf. Restatement (Second) of Contracts* § 302..
[123] *See* Farnsworth 2004: § 10.8, at 673–675.

A different set of third-party benefit rules is said to apply to cases in which the government is one of the contracting parties. Here, third parties are often refused the right to enforce an agreement, even where it might otherwise seem that they were the intended beneficiaries of the agreement. There are (at least) two concerns: (1) as to companies providing utility services or like services to the general public under a contract with the government, to allow citizens to sue on that contract would potentially subject the company to massive liability, thus potentially scaring off companies from this important service;[124] and (2) the government choice as to when to enforce an agreement may be part of a policy choice that should be left to officials, not to be affected or overridden by third-party enforcement suits.[125]

2. *Assignment and Delegation*

Another way in which contracts can create rights and duties in third parties is through a transfer or sale of those rights or duties. Following conventional (though far from universal) usage, this text refers to transfers of contractual rights as "assignments" and to transfers of contractual duties as "delegations."

Briefly, assignments of rights are generally allowed (and are crucial to modern commercial life[126]), and, when properly done, they extinguish entirely the rights of the original holder. By contrast, there are significant constraints on the ability to delegate duties (to be discussed), and even when a delegation is successful, the original duty holder's duty is not extinguished; all that occurs is that a successful performance by the replacement duty holder (the delegatee) will discharge the obligation of that original duty holder. However, if the delegatee does not perform (or performs in a defective way), the other party can sue the original duty holder for breach.

Certain types of commercial transactions (involving negotiable instruments and secured transactions) have developed whole codes to cover the intricate rules of their assignment and delegation. These appear in American law under Articles 3 and 9 of the Uniform Commercial Code, respectively, and are not discussed further here.

---

[124] The standard old-case citation here is *H. R. Moch Co. v. Rensselaer Water Co.*, 159 N.E. 896 (N.Y. 1928).

[125] One should keep in mind the extent to which a state or federal executive may have different policy views from those of its predecessor, and thus may choose not to enforce contractual restrictions imposed by the predecessor, or to enforce them only where a violation is particularly egregious. This is the point arguably missed in some of the cases that allow third-party enforcement of government contracts. *E.g.*, *Zigas v. Superior Court*, 174 Cal. Rptr. 806 (Cal. App. 1982) (allowing tenants to enforce Department of Housing and Urban Development agreement with landlord regarding maximum rents).

[126] In business, it is common for payment to come after performance and for performance to require costly outlays (buying supplies, paying employees, and so on); in the meantime, businesses can sell their accounts receivable to a third party or use them as collateral for bank loans, thus reducing significantly their cash-flow problem.

It took the common law a long time (and a fair amount of prompting from the equity courts) to recognize the assignment of a contractual right. The English common law courts finally gave full rights[127] to the assignee near the end of the eighteenth century; American state courts often did not follow until well into the nineteenth century.[128]

In contemporary law, contract law imposes few restrictions on assignment, although state and federal statutory law may impose some selective restrictions based on public policy (e.g., limitations on the ability to assign the right to wages or the proceeds of government contracts).[129] And although the law states that an assignment will not be valid if it increases the burden on the other party, courts have (perhaps surprisingly) generally approved assignments even with the right under a requirements contract and the right to enforce a noncompetition clause in an employment agreement.[130]

There are more significant constraints on the delegations of duties. In particular, if the choice of this particular person to perform a service was central to the contract, delegation will not be allowed (without the consent of the other party).[131] It is understandable that if I hire a famous artist to paint my picture (and at a commensurably high price), I might feel aggrieved if that painter then delegated the job to her new apprentice.

H. BILATERAL STRUCTURE, CORRECTIVE JUSTICE, AND OPTIMAL INCENTIVES

Private law – especially tort law and contract law – is structured bilaterally. The government acts only at the request and on behalf of a complaining plaintiff, and the liability of the wrongdoing defendant is paid to the plaintiff, not to the state. Contrast, for example, criminal law or administrative law, where it is usually the government bringing the action against the alleged wrongdoers, and any monetary sanctions are paid to the state. There are two points to note about the bilateral structure of contract law (and tort law). First, it is one of the strongest pieces of evidence that contract law is related to corrective justice.[132] Although corrective

---

[127] Previously, an assignee would be treated as suing in the name of the assignor and, on that basis, might lose its right if the assignor died or filed for bankruptcy. Farnsworth 2004: § 11.2, at 684.

[128] *Id.* at 682–685.

[129] *See id.*, § 11.4, at 691.

[130] *Id.*, at 692–693. By express agreement the parties can themselves restrict assignment or delegation, although current rules seem to authorize courts at times to ignore or override restrictions of assignment. *See* UCC § 2–210(2) ("a right arising out of the assignor's due performance of his entire obligation can be assigned despite agreement otherwise"); *Restatement (Second) of Contracts* § 322 (creating rules for restricting the interpretation and application of "no assignment" clauses).

[131] *E.g.*, Farnsworth 2004: § 11.10, at 719–722.

[132] The importance of bilateral structure for supporting a corrective justice approach or for criticizing an economic (efficiency) approach is more common in tort law than contract law. For examples from the

justice may be most clearly present in tort law, it seems clearly to play some role in contract law as well, as is shown in the general structure of the victim of the breach seeking compensation from the breaching party, on the basis of the damages caused by the breach.[133]

Second, the tying of the amount the defendant pays with the amount the plaintiff receives means that it is possible – and perhaps common – that one or both will be subject to inefficient incentives. Economists speaking in terms of efficiency want the level of activity to be at a level where overall wealth (understood broadly) is maximized,[134] and this will occur when the costs of an activity are internalized and the benefits of alternative uses of resources are considered. We want contracting partners to have the right incentives to perform or to breach, but we also want them to have the right incentives to invest or to rely on the other party prior to performance, and even the right incentives to mitigate damages. However, even those sympathetic to the law and economics approach note how difficult it is to create (and apply) contract law performance and remedial doctrines in a way that will create just the right incentives for either party, and that it is almost impossible that the resulting level of potential damage liability will create just the right incentives for both parties simultaneously.[135] Thus, even though there are likely good arguments of both fairness and efficiency for doctrines like mitigation that constrain damages, when the result in many cases is a reduction to nothing or nearly nothing, it is hard to believe that this creates this absence of disincentive to breach is optimal.[136]

Some theorists have recently argued that corrective justice may also not be the best explanation or justification for contract law's bilateral structure. The argument, roughly, is that if (corrective) justice were the objective of private law, there would be little reason to confine enforcement to the wronged party. Why should the state or interested third parties not be recruited to make sure that wrongdoers were punished, breached promises were compensated for, and so on. These theorists suggest that contract law might better be understood in terms of a kind of "civil recourse" or "redressive justice," with the government providing parties a forum in which their rights can be enforced and their wrongs redressed.[137]

tort law literature, Coleman (2001: 13–24) emphasizes bilateralism and a corrective justice approach, and Kraus (2007) argues that an economic (efficiency) approach can still be viable in the face of objections based on bilateralism. Smith (2004: 63–64, 180–183) discusses the bilateralism of contract law but in the context of making a different point.

[133] The corrective justice grounding of contract law seems to have been noted as long ago as the Roman Jurist Gaius. Gordley 2002: 11–12. For a contemporary discussion, see Bridgeman 2007; Oman 2012.

[134] *See, e.g.*, R. Posner 2011: 3–20.

[135] *See* Craswell 2001: 26–32.

[136] Similarly, when the costs, delays, and uncertainties of litigation leave most consumers and many other contracting parties with no effective way to enforce their contracts, see Braucher 2012. It does not seem likely that the lack of disincentives in such cases for breach by the other party would be optimal. This line of argument is considered again in Chapter 8, Section B.

[137] *See, e.g.*, Oman 2011, 2012; Gold 2011, 2012. For an argument that the "civil recourse" approach is not an alternative to corrective justice, but a component of it, or a complement to it, see Ripstein 2011.

I. EFFICIENT BREACH AND THE (A)MORALITY OF CONTRACT LAW

"Efficient breach" is the idea, associated with the economic analysis of contract law, that the remedial doctrines of contract law implicitly encourage parties to breach their agreements, when doing so will yield the breaching party profits even after the nonbreaching party in the original agreement is paid expectation damages. There is already an extensive literature on the nature and merits of "efficient breach,"[138] and there will be a later discussion (Chapter 8, Section E) of the concept in connection with the Holmesian idea that contract law imposes at most only an obligation to either perform one's promises or to pay damages.[139] Here these ideas are important mostly for the way they reflect or reinforce a certain view of contract remedies.

One could say, at the least, that the law sends a mixed message. The idea of *pacta sunt servanda* ("agreements are to be kept") is a commonplace of civil law and canon law, and goes back to Justinian's Code.[140] And certainly one can find direct and indirect evidence of the simple moral intuition – that, other things being equal, it is moral to keep one's promises and undertakings, and immoral not to do so – in the actions of judges hearing contract cases and juries deciding them, and not merely in the marginal doctrines in which good faith plays an express role.[141]

Even in the Official Comments to the Uniform Commercial Code (relating to a section dealing with the right to seek adequate assurances of the other party's performance), one finds this:

> This section rests on the recognition of the fact that the essential purpose of a contract between commercial men is actual performance and they do not bargain merely for a promise, or for a promise plus the right to win a lawsuit.[142]

In contrast, the idea that a contracting party has an option to either perform or pay damages also has deep roots (if not quite as antiquated as Justinian's Code), going back at least to a 1617 English case decided by the King's Bench. In *Bromage v.*

---

[138] *E.g.*, Birmingham 1970; Goetz & Scott 1977; Craswell 1988; Friedmann 1989; Gordley 2001a; Shavell 2006a. In the terminology of some economic analysts, it might also be an efficient breach if the motivation for the breach was the costs avoided (that performance would cost the promisor more than paying expectation damages would). *E.g.*, Markovits & Schwartz 2011: 1944.

[139] *See* Holmes 1897: 462; 1963: 236. Holmes emphasized that it is not that one promises to pay damages (if one does not perform), but that one's actions have made one liable to pay damages, just as one's actions can leave one liable to pay tort damages for certain negligent or intentional harms. Holmes 1941.

[140] W. W. Buckland offered the commonsense response to Holmes's analysis: "You don't buy a right to damages, you buy a horse." Buckland 1945: 98. This answer has a certain power to it but seems to weaken in the face of different fact situations: for example, what happens if you think you have bought the horse, but no horse is ever delivered; or if a horse is delivered, but it is defective or varies greatly from the terms agreed on; or the seller had wanted to deliver the horse but unforeseen complications make delivery impossible or nearly so?

[141] There is also growing empirical, experimental evidence for this attitude. *E.g.*, Wilkinson-Ryan & Baron 2009; Wilkinson-Ryan & Hoffman 2010.

[142] UCC § 2–609, Comment 1.

Genning,[143] Sir Edward Coke denied a suit for specific enforcement of a contract on the basis that "this would subvert the intention of the covenantor when he intended it to be at his option whether to lose the damages or perform the lease."[144]

Additionally, the "message" of various remedial doctrines is equally clear. When extracompensatory damages are not available, specific performance is rarely ordered, intentional (or even malicious) breaches of agreements generally merit no greater remedies than other types of breaches,[145] and claims for tortious interference with contractual relations[146] are rarely brought and even more rarely granted,[147] then parties are effectively invited to breach agreements when doing so will be in their economic interest.

At least one theorist inclined to a morality-based analysis of contract law has claimed that there need not be a moral objection to "efficient breach," if the breaching party were to promptly pay compensation, instead of forcing on the nonbreaching party the trouble, the expense (including, prominently, significant and noncompensable attorney's fees), and the uncertainty of litigation.[148] The problem with "efficient breach," from this perspective, is (only) that in practice the nonbreaching party is often subjected to significant uncompensated costs along with the breach of the agreement (and compensation by the breaching party may be slow in coming, if it comes at all[149]).

The topic of the morality of and within contract law is revisited in Chapter 8.

[143] 81 Eng. Rep. 540 (K.B. 1617).

[144] Translation from Law French taken from Simpson 1975a: 597.

[145] There are a handful of contexts in contract law in which the level of fault or innocence of the parties does affect their rights, many of which have already been mentioned in this book. This is most obviously true where the remedies or defenses are grounded in equity – for example, the grounds of promissory estoppel, promissory restitution, and unjust enrichment (Chapter 3, Section D); the reliance exceptions to the statute of frauds (Chapter 3, Section C); the right to rescind based on mistake, duress, and undue influence (Chapter 3, Section E); and the excusal of failures of conditions based on waiver, forfeiture, estoppel, and prevention (Chapter 5, Section A). Additionally, where there is a defect in construction, the choice between diminution of value and cost of completion may turn on the good faith of the breaching party's actions (Chapter 6, Section D). Another example is the rule in some jurisdictions that breaching parties will be denied the right to recover in restitution if their breach was intentional (Chapter 6, Section D). See *Restatement (Second) of Contracts* § 374, Comment b. For an overview of the role of fault in contract law, see the articles in Ben-Shahar & Porat 2010.

[146] The cause of action for intentional interference with contractual relations is conventionally traced back to *Lumley v. Gye*, 118 Eng. Rep. 749 (1853), although scholars have found antecedents of the cause of action going back to classical Roman law. *See* Sayre 1923.

[147] Such claims are occasionally brought and prevail. *See, e.g., White Plains Coat & Apron Co., Inc. v. Cintas Corp.*, 867 N.E.2d 381, 835 N.Y.S.2d 530 (N.Y. Ct. App. 2007). The mystery is why this does not happen more frequently.

[148] C. Fried 2007. Another commentator has argued that "efficient breaches" may often not be immoral, when the breach arose from a contingency on which the parties had not reached any express agreement. Shavell 2009. A third commentator has argued that if it is understood (by party agreement or by the default understanding of the jurisdiction's rules) that a party can renege on its promise as long as it pays damages, then the decision so to renege is hardly a breach (efficient or otherwise). Gordley 2001c.

[149] Macaulay writes: "[I]n my experience, when relational concerns do not matter, many large corporations and their law firms do not efficiently breach. They do not seek to buy their way out of contracts

J. THEORETICAL IMPLICATIONS

The American legal realists argued that legal rights should be equated with, or at least understood in terms of, the remedies available for the enforcement of those rights. This view is revisited in Chapter 9, but for now it is sufficient to note that lawyers would be well advised to tell their clients the difference between agreements in which breach would probably lead to orders for specific performance as against those for which money damages will be the probable remedy, and the difference between circumstances in which something approximating full monetary compensation might be available as opposed to situations in which various limiting doctrines might lead to far lower levels of compensation.[150] Most people would view as quite different contract rights with significant remedial protection and contract rights with uncertain or limited protection.

It is certainly important to one's view of the nature of (American) contract law that there are substantial limitations on the availability of damages (not going beyond compensation for financial losses, and often falling far short of that), as well as secondary limitations on the ability of parties to contract around the default remedial rules. Equally significant is the small role of fault in determining whether a party is liable at all and the extent of any liability.

SUGGESTED FURTHER READING

Damages Generally

Robert Cooter & Melvin Aron Eisenberg, "Damages for Breach of Contract," *California Law Review*, vol. 73, pp. 1432–1481 (1985).
Lon L. Fuller & William R. Perdue Jr., "The Reliance Interest in Contract Damages" (Parts 1 & 2), *Yale Law Journal*, vol. 46, pp 52–96, 373–420 (1936).

Unconscionability

Arthur Allen Leff, "Unconscionability and the Code – The Emperor's New Clauses," *University of Pennsylvania Law Review*, vol. 115, pp. 485–559 (1967).
Seana Valentine Shiffrin, "Paternalism, Unconscionability Doctrine, and Accommodation," *Philosophy and Public Affairs*, vol. 29, pp. 205–250 (2000).

Foreseeability

Barry E. Adler, "The Questionable Ascent of *Hadley v. Baxendale*," *Stanford Law Review*, vol. 51, pp. 1547–1589 (1999).

for anything like the other party's expectation damages. They just breach, at best offer an insulting token settlement, and practice scorched earth litigation tactics, taking out of that unpublished but very real text, *Discovery Abuse for Fun and Profit*" (Macaulay 2000: 782).
[150] Of course, the lawyer should also advise the client that the cost, delays, and uncertainty of litigation might make it inadvisable to seek enforcement of many (perhaps most) contracts. *See, e.g.*, Braucher 2012.

Melvin Aron Eisenberg, "The Principle of *Hadley v. Baxendale*," *California Law Review*, vol. 80, pp. 563–613 (1992).

Richard A. Epstein, "Beyond Foreseeability: Consequential Damages in the Law of Contract," *Journal of Legal Studies*, vol. 18, pp. 105–138 (1989).

Third-Party Rights and Duties

Melvin Aron Eisenberg, "Third-Party Beneficiaries," *Columbia Law Review*, vol. 92, pp. 1358–1430 (1992).

W. S. Holdsworth, "The History of the Treatment of *Choses* in Action by the Common Law," *Harvard Law Review*, vol. 33, pp. 997–1030 (1920).

Stephen A. Smith, "Contracts for the Benefit of Third Parties: In Defense of the Third-Party Rule," *Oxford Journal of Legal Studies*, vol. 17, pp. 643–663 (1997).

Anthony John Waters, "The Property in the Promise: A Study of the Third-Party Beneficiary Rule," *Harvard Law Review*, vol. 98, pp. 1109–1210 (1985).

Specific Performance and Efficient Breach

Melvin Aron Eisenberg, "Actual and Virtual Specific Performance, the Theory of Efficient Breach, and the Indifference Principle in Contract Law," *California Law Review*, vol. 93, pp. 975–1050 (2005).

Agreed Remedies

Charles J. Goetz & Robert E. Scott, "Liquidated Damages, Penalties, and the Just Compensation Principle: Some Notes on an Enforcement Model of Efficient Breach," *Columbia Law Review*, vol. 77, pp. 554–594 (1977).

7

Special Categories of Contract Law

As is discussed at greater length in Chapter 9, there is a sense in which we do not have a single simple and unitary (American) contract law but rather a large number of contract laws, reflecting both different jurisdictions and different topics. Lawrence Friedman once famously argued that contract law was merely the law for the remnants, the principles for transactions too unimportant not to have their own distinct set of statutory or administrative regulations.[1] This is likely an overstatement,[2] but it remains the case that there are many types of transactions, broadly contractual, which have distinctive sets of governing rules. Whole books and courses are devoted to some of these categories; what can be offered here in this chapter is necessarily just a taste of the both the variety and complexity of those subjects.

A. EMPLOYMENT AGREEMENTS

A distinct topic of employment law has developed to cover the many statutory and judicially created special rules that attach to the employer-employee contract. There are state law rules that govern the employment relationship (some of which derive from judicial decisions many decades old), state and federal antidiscrimination rules, and federal labor law rules grounded in statutes and administrative agency action. Additionally, where the employment is a civil service job or one covered by a union, there are state or federal statutory or administrative rules controlling issues of hiring, promotion, firing, and the handling of disputes.

One issue that frequently arises with relation to employment contracts involves noncompetition clauses (i.e., "restrictive covenants"), which we briefly considered

---

[1] Friedman 1965: viii, 23–29. He wrote that modern contract law courses were was like "a zoology course which confined its study to dodos and unicorns." *Id.*, 25.

[2] *See* Macaulay 2011.

earlier (in Chapter 6, Section A).[3] As noted then, the basic question in such agreements is whether the restriction on competition is reasonable in its scope and duration, taking into account the employer's interests (not enforcing some restrictive covenant would discourage employers from giving new employees training, trade secrets, and access to customers), the employees' interests (employees should not be entirely foreclosed from making a living in their area of training), and the interest of third parties (especially with physicians and lawyers, there is a strong public policy that patients and clients should not be prevented from seeing the professional of their choice).[4] Where a noncompetition clause is found to be unreasonable, some courts have the authority to enforce the provision as modified, reduced to reasonable terms. This is known as the "blue pencil" approach.[5] This approach seems justified if one believes that the employer was acting in good faith, and the explanation for its not using a more reasonable (individualized) noncompetition provision might be as innocent as a large company that uses the same employment form for a large number of employees. The "blue pencil" approach seems less justified if one suspects that a noncompetition clause was intentionally written in an overbroad way, perhaps on the employer's hope that most employees would not challenge the provision, and even those who did could achieve nothing beyond the "blue-penciled" reasonable terms.

There was a line of cases in the 1970s and 1980s in which courts creatively used good faith, public policy,[6] and unilateral contract ideas to limit employers' ability to terminate at-will employees.[7] The unilateral contract argument was an intricate claim that employee handbooks that promised procedural or substantive restrictions on termination were offers that were accepted by employees' continuing in their jobs rather than quitting. Many jurisdictions never accepted the good faith–public policy exception to the right to terminate at-will employees, and those jurisdictions that did accept it tended to apply it narrowly, such as by not allowing termination in response

---

[3] These provisions also arise in partnership agreements and agreements to sell a business or practice. The legal analysis is similar in all cases.

[4] *See, e.g., Restatement (Second) of Contracts* § 188; *Valley Medical Specialists v. Farber*, 982 P.2d 1277 (Ariz. 1999) (noncompetition agreement among physicians too broad); *Safety-Kleen Systems v. Hennkens*, 301 F.3d 931 (8th Cir. 2002) (enforcing noncompetition agreement covering salesperson). *See generally* Kesan & Hayes 2012. That an agreement not to work in a given industry and area might be unenforceable was indicated in the case law as long ago as 1414. *Case of John Dyer*, 2 Hen. V (of. 5, pl. 26) (1414). California has a statute that makes restrictions on subsequent employment presumptively unenforceable. *California Business and Professions Code* § 16600.

[5] A few courts will "blue pencil" only where the modification can be achieved by removing (rather than rewriting) contractual provisions. *See, e.g., Valley Medical*, 982 P.2d at 1285–1286.

[6] *E.g., Monge v. Beebe Rubber Co.*, 316 A.2d 549 (N.H. 1974).

[7] "At will" employees are employees with no right to continued employment, who can be fired for (as the expression goes) "good reason, bad reason, or no reason at all," subject only to antidiscrimination statutes.

to employee adherence to criminal law mandates,[8] or not allowing termination to be used as a means to avoid paying a commission that was already earned.[9]

The employee protections offered by the employee handbook as unilateral contract were relatively short lived, as well-counseled employers learned to place clear language in their handbooks indicating that any promises made there were not meant to be legally binding on the company.[10]

B. INSURANCE LAW

Insurance law is a heavily regulated area of law in which the terms of insurance contracts are sometimes set by state law, and the terms are generally reviewed by state agencies (to see whether the terms are contrary to public policy, unreasonably confusing, and so on).[11] There are also a few contract law rules and principles specific to or distinctive of insurance law: (1) the application of a "reasonable expectations" doctrine (in some jurisdictions[12]), which is primarily or exclusively for insurance agreements, under which a term in an insurance agreement, even if nonambiguous, will not be applied if it is contrary to the reasonable expectations of the insured[13]; (2) *contra proferentem* ("construction against the drafter," discussed in Chapter 4, Section C), though a general doctrine of contractual interpretation, is commonly and aggressively used with insurance agreements (and somewhat more hesitantly in other contexts); (3) all (or nearly all) states impose liability (sometimes including multiple liability damages or punitive damages) on insurance companies that negligently or in bad faith fail to settle third-party claims within policy limits[14]; and (4) roughly half of states also impose liability (including, in some cases, multiple liability or punitive damages) for a bad-faith refusal to pay on a first-party claim.

Despite regulatory oversight and the threat of liability, there is growing evidence that insurance companies increasingly fail to pay valid claims and that this is done as

[8] *See, e.g., Thompson v. St. Regis Paper Co.*, 685 P.2d 1081 (Wash. 1984) (cannot terminate for employee compliance with Foreign Corrupt Practices Act).

[9] *See, e.g., Fortune v. National Cash Register Co.*, 364 N.E.2d 1251 (Mass. 1977).

[10] *See, e.g., Lincoln v. Wackenhut Corp.*, 867 P.2d 701 (Wyo. 1994).

[11] However, it is frequently asserted that these agencies have been "captured" by insurance company interests.

[12] Although one article lists thirty-four jurisdictions that have accepted the doctrine of reasonable expectations in some form, Anderson & Fournier 1998: 353–356 n. 57, other commentators have found the doctrine, narrowly understood (as a doctrine distinct from general contract interpretation principles, such as "construction against the drafter"), to be applied in only a handful of states. E.g., Schwarcz 2007: 1427–1430.

[13] *See, e.g., C & J Fertilizer, Inc. v. Allied Mutual Insurance Co.*, 227 N.W.2d 169 (Iowa 1975); *Restatement (Second) of Contracts* § 211, Comment f. The *Restatement* would apply this approach to all standardized agreements, but the handful of courts that apply the "reasonable expectations" doctrine in its strongest form apply it only to insurance agreements.

[14] Hyman, Black & Silver 2010: p. 52 n. 7.

a profit-making strategy.[15] Contract law, as currently structured, seems poorly placed to prevent behavior of this sort (although regulatory oversight has not always proved significantly more efficacious).

C. LANDLORD-TENANT

Apartment leases are the first detailed legal documents many law students see after their legal education begins (and their first opportunity to discover that even legal training may fail to make such documents fully comprehensible). Many states have created mandatory terms for landlord-tenant rental agreements (in a handful of places, including city-based rent control). Landlord-tenant agreements (for personal leases; commercial leases usually are treated differently) are usually subject to distinct rules developed by common law decisions, state statutes, and administrative regulation. Many states impose an implied warranty of habitability on landlords,[16] although there is evidence that a combination of limitations on that doctrine and changes in the housing market have caused this implied warranty to be of little value to tenants today.[17]

As a lease is "an interest in land" (considered so even if the apartment is many feet removed from actual "land"), certain rules and principles related to land transactions usually apply to landlord-tenant agreements: for example, in most jurisdictions, agreements of a certain length (usually a minimum of six or twelve months) or longer must be in writing (the statute of frauds, discussed in Chapter 3, Section C), but certain types of "part performance" will take an otherwise unenforceable oral lease "out of" the statute of frauds (i.e., make it enforceable despite the absence of written evidence of the agreement).[18]

On the remedial side, the traditional rule had been that landlords had no duty to mitigate when a tenant breached a lease. American states are increasingly turning against that rule and holding that landlords must mitigate (by looking for replacement tenants) just like other parties after a breach.[19]

D. REAL ESTATE AGREEMENTS

The sale and purchase of real property is heavily (if not always rationally) regulated. In teaching and scholarship, the topic is usually treated as a special topic within property law or as a topic unto itself.

---

[15] Feinman 2010.

[16] The seminal case is *Javins v. First National Realty Corp.*, 428 F.2d 1071 (D.C. Cir. 1969).

[17] Super 2011.

[18] On the part performance exception to the statute of frauds for interests in land, see *Restatement (Second) of Contracts* § 129; on its application to a lease, see, e.g., *Winternitz v. Summit Hills Joint Venture*, 532 A.2d 1089 (Md. App. 1987), cert. denied, 538 A.2d 778 (Md. 1988).

[19] Knapp, Crystal & Prince 2007: 903–904.

Under state statutes (supplemented by case law) sellers often have detailed duties of disclosure that are in sharp contrast to the general lack of a duty to disclose for the vast majority of transactions.[20] There are also special remedial rules. On the one hand, old English law created a presumption that specific performance would be available to buyers against breaching sellers when real property was involved, contrary to the strong presumption against equitable remedies for most kinds of agreements (see Chapter 6, Section E).[21] On the other hand, where a buyer of real estate is seeking only money damages against a breaching seller, many jurisdictions still follow a different English rule: holding that buyers can recover only restitution of payments made (rather than expectation damages), unless the seller breached "in bad faith."[22] This rule was apparently grounded on the view that searching land titles had once been quite difficult, and many sellers, acting in good faith, discovered late in the selling process that they could not, in fact, pass on marketable title. A growing number of U.S. jurisdictions are moving to the "American rule," which allows buyers to seek expectation damages against breaching sellers.[23]

E. FRANCHISE AGREEMENTS

Many stores, restaurants, and gasoline stations are operated under franchise agreements.[24] In return for use of the franchise name, certain franchise-linked supplies (whether Shell gasoline or the ingredients for making Dunkin' Donuts), exclusive geographical zones, and centralized marketing, the franchisee usually agrees to follow certain practices and to pay a percentage of sales or profits to the franchisor. Additionally, franchise agreements are usually "at will"; that is, the franchisor has the legal right to terminate the franchise, often with little or no notice, and without needing to have a (good) reason for doing so.

Because "at will" termination – if the franchisee is not sufficiently protected – appears to leave the franchisee vulnerable, there have been a number of cases challenging such clauses as unconscionable or as contrary to state fair-terms

---

[20] For the general rules on disclosure, see Chapter 3, Section E(1). For an example of a statutory duty of disclosure for real estate sales, see *Iowa Code* §§ 558A.1 to 558A.8.

[21] *See also* Farnsworth 2004: § 12.6, at 749–750.

[22] Knapp, Crystal & Prince 2007: 855–856.

[23] Additionally, some jurisdictions, when dealing with sellers breaching contracts to sell property, have applied a mixture of the "English rule" (allowing buyers to recover only restitution for payments made) and the "American rule" (allowing buyers normal, full "benefit of the bargain" recovery, where otherwise appropriate), by normally allowing buyers full benefit of the bargain damages, except in those instances where the seller's breach was based on a title defect of which the seller had earlier not been aware. (The mixed approach is exemplified in the 1975 *Uniform Land Transactions Act* § 2–510, 13 (Part II) U.L.A. 241 (West 2002).)

[24] A failed negotiation for a franchise was the basis of a very important early Section 90 promissory estoppel case, *Hoffman v. Red Owl*, 133 N.W.2d 267 (Wis. 1965). On that case see also Scott 2007, 2010, Whitford & Macaulay 2010. Promissory estoppel is discussed in Chapter 3, Section D.

legislation.[25] There has been some state and federal legislation protecting franchisees. On the other side of the argument, franchisors claim that under regulations that protect franchisees from termination without "good cause," "good cause" may be difficult to prove, even when it is present. This leaves the franchisor with having to maintain bad franchisees that lower the value of the brand for everyone, and it may also discourage the franchisor from "taking a chance" on a potential franchisee with a limited track record.[26]

F. PREMARITAL AGREEMENTS

Premarital agreements (also called "antenuptial" or "prenuptial" agreements) are agreements signed on the verge of marriage, with the intention of modifying the couple's rights and obligations in case of divorce.[27] Until the 1970s, such premarital agreements were generally treated as unenforceable, because contrary to public policy (as they modified the state-imposed terms of marriage and were said to encourage divorce). However, in the course of the 1980s and 1990s, all jurisdictions changed their laws to allow enforcement of premarital agreements in at least some circumstances.[28]

Many states impose procedural and substantive (fairness) requirements on premarital agreements beyond those applicable to conventional commercial contracts. Most jurisdictions require premarital agreements to be in writing and for the party seeking enforcement to have made full disclosure of his or her financial resources prior to the signing of the agreement. Additionally, courts that evaluate enforcement under rubrics of "fairness," "unconscionability," or "voluntariness" will usually consider factors such as how long before the marriage the agreement was discussed and signed, whether both parties had access to independent counsel, the extent to which the agreement explains in clear language what rights are being waived, how the outcome under the agreement would likely differ from outcomes without the agreement, and how one sided the provisions are.[29] Whatever one thinks of these

---

[25] *See* Farnsworth 2004: § 7.17, at 498–499.
[26] Klick, Kobayashi & Ribstein 2009: 358–360. Similar arguments are offered on both sides of "at will" status in employment law.
[27] Most discussions of premarital agreements refer to agreements that affect the parties' rights upon divorce. However, some premarital agreements affect the rights of the parties against a spouse's estate (should the other spouse die first) instead of, or along with, the modification of rights upon divorce. Historically, premarital agreements affecting rights upon death were treated better than comparable agreements affecting rights at divorce, because only the latter raised concerns that the agreement "encouraged divorce." *E.g.*, Bix 1998: 148–149 & n. 13, 153.
[28] Bix 1998: 148–158.
[29] In some states, the courts must consider fairness relative to the time of enforcement, not just relative to the time the agreement was signed. This is also different from conventional unconscionability analysis for conventional agreements, which is relative only to the time the agreement was entered (although the courts doing this fairness inquiry at the time of enforcement often still call their inquiry one of "unconscionability").

restrictions and regulations on premarital agreements, it is important to remember that they developed from a past in which, in nearly all jurisdictions, all premarital agreements (at least all divorce-focused premarital agreements) were unenforceable. The move from never enforceable to enforceable but highly regulated was a move in the direction of greater acceptance. The level of restriction and regulation varies significantly across jurisdictions.[30]

There are restrictions on what can be covered in a premarital agreement.[31] In general, such agreements will be enforced only to the extent that they cover financial matters between the parties, and there are limits even within that category. Financial matters directly related to children (e.g., child support) are unenforceable, at least if there is a colorable claim that the agreement reduces the support that would otherwise be paid. Additionally, a small number of states refuse to enforce provisions waiving the right to alimony.

G. GOVERNMENT CONTRACTS

A number of different rules apply when the U.S. government is a party to a contract buying or selling goods or services. First, contracts with the state and federal governments tend to be heavily regulated. For example, construction contracts with the federal government fall under the Miller Act, which includes a requirement that contractors provide both a performance bond and a bond for payment of their subcontractors and suppliers.[32] Second, although oral modifications are frequently enforced in agreements between private parties (sometimes even in the face of "no oral modification" provisions[33]), courts have held such modifications unenforceable, at least where there are (as there often are) express statutory or regulatory requirements of written authorization for any changes to work for the government.[34]

Third, as discussed earlier (in Chapter 6, Section G), courts are far less likely to allow third-party enforcement in contracts with the government. Part of the concern is with limiting liability to parties who are providing general services (e.g., utility services), and part of the concern is that the decision of whether and how to enforce contracts the government has entered can be a policy choice that should not be disturbed by third parties.[35] And fourth, claims based on contracts with the federal government often need to be brought in a special court, the U.S. Court of Federal Claims.

---

[30] The most enforcement-friendly state is Pennsylvania, with its case of *Simeone v. Simeone*, 581 A.2d 162 (Pa. 1990), which adds to standard contract rules only the requirements that the agreement be in writing and that the party seeking enforcement of the agreement have made full and fair disclosure of his or her financial resources.

[31] To be more precise, parties can put whatever they like into premarital agreements (or any other agreement); the restrictions are on what the courts will enforce.

[32] 40 U.S.C. §§ 3131–3134.

[33] Discussed in passing in Chapter 4, Section D.

[34] *See, e.g., P & D Consultants, Inc. v. City of Carlsbad*, 119 Cal. Rptr. 3d 253 (Cal. App. 2010).

[35] *See generally Restatement (Second) of Contracts* § 313.

H. THEORETICAL IMPLICATIONS

There are a wide variety of transactions that fall under contract law. And within that large range, many transaction types have distinct sets of rules, developed by courts, agencies, or legislators. Theorists have had quite different responses to the factual and legal variety within contract law. For some, the variety just displays the power and flexibility of the basic model, showing how the foundational principles of contract law work equally well in quite distinct contexts.[36] The contrary view is that important policy and moral issues are missed when the factual and legal variety of contract law is deemphasized, either by judges or by law school professors.[37] The argument is connected to one about how much context judges should consider in evaluating the contractual disputes that come before them.[38] This debate is revisited in Chapter 8 and, particularly, in Chapter 9.

A separate point raised, indirectly, by this chapter is the extent to which contractual disputes are now regulated by special legislation or administrative regulations. The centuries-old common law principles of Anglo-American contract law are being supplemented, and to some extent, supplanted, for a wide range of common and important agreements.

SUGGESTED FURTHER READING

Employment Contracts

Mark A. Rothstein & Lance Liebman, *Employment Law Cases and Materials* (7th ed., St. Paul, MN: West Publishing, 2011).

Insurance Contracts

Kenneth S. Abraham, *Insurance Law and Regulation: Cases and Materials* (5th ed., New York: Foundation Press, 2010).
Daniel Schwarcz, "Reevaluating Standardized Insurance Policies," *University of Chicago Law Review*, vol. 78, pp. 1263–1349 (2011).

Landlord-Tenant Law

Robert S. Schoshinski, *American Law of Landlord and Tenant* (St. Paul, MN: West Publishing, 2011).

Real Estate Agreements

Gerald Korngold & Paul Goldstein, *Real Estate Transactions: Cases and Materials on Land Transfer* (5th ed., St. Paul, MN: West Publishing, 2009).

[36] *See, e.g.,* Oman 2005a, 2009. 2010; *see also* Barnhizer 2010.
[37] *See, e.g.,* Bix 2007b, 2008, 2011; *see also* Macaulay 2003.
[38] *E.g., compare* Macaulay 2003 *with* Barnhizer 2010.

Franchise Agreements

W. Michael Garner, *Franchise and Distribution Law and Practice*, 2010–2011 *ed.*, 3 vols. (St. Paul, MN: West Publishing).

Premarital Agreements

Louis I. Parley & Alexander Lindey, *Lindey and Parley on Separation Agreements and Antenuptial Contracts* (2d ed., New York: Matthew Bender, 2011) (loose-leaf, updated twice a year).

Government Contracts

Steven W. Feldman, *Government Contract Handbook* (4th ed., St. Paul, MN: West Publishing, 2010).

8

Modern Contract Law Practices

Questions of Legitimation and Moral Obligation

This chapter deals, first, with the divergence between the way we[1] talk about contract law and actual contract experience. Second, the chapter considers some implications of this divergence, and of current contracting practices, for how we should think about our obligation to keep contracts and how the government should regulate contracts. To some extent, the exploration is one regarding what role theory can and does play and whether our current theories of contract law might be doing more to legitimate unjust practices than to explain the doctrinal area.

A. THE GAP BETWEEN IDEAL AND REALITY

The ideal of freedom of contract (and its corollary, freedom from contract[2]) is that one takes on contractual liability to the extent, and only to the extent, that one has freely chosen to do so. This is an ideal that is not always fully realized, for a variety of reasons, many of them relatively "innocent" and uncontroversial – for example, the move from subjective to objective tests for formation[3] and interpretation,[4] and some grounds for liability that have some but not all the elements of a valid contract (e.g., promissory estoppel, promissory restitution, and unjust enrichment).[5] These modifications have been imposed to serve interests of economic efficiency[6] and/or fairness.[7]

---

[1] "We" used both narrowly to mean legal academics (in the United States) and more broadly to include the general population.

[2] *See* Symposium 2004.

[3] E.g., Farnsworth 2004: §3.6, at 114–117, Rowley 2003.

[4] E.g., Farnsworth 2004: §7.9, at 445–452, Rowley 1999.

[5] Objectivity in formation is discussed in Chapter 3, Section A; objectivity in interpretation in Chapter 4, Section A; and the alternative grounds of liability in Chapter 3, Section D.

[6] With the objective standard making enforceability of contracts much more predictable.

[7] With the equitable claims of promissory estoppel, promissory restitution, and unjust enrichment; there is also an element of fairness in enforcing agreements where one of the parties reasonably understood

At the present time, though, the deviations from the ideal of freedom of contract are not merely minor ones created on the margins to make contract law easier to administer or to protect the most vulnerable. Rather, the deviations from the ideal are pervasive, especially in consumer transactions. It is a commonplace that a relatively small percentage of the contracts most of us enter match the model of face-to-face negotiation of terms that underlies most theories about contract law (both classical and contemporary). It is, therefore, misleading to argue that face-to-face-negotiated agreements are the "paradigm case" of contracts and that the adhesion contracts[8] and other form contracts that dominate commercial life[9] are merely marginal or inferior instantiations.[10] The conventional view – portraying face-to-face-negotiated agreements as the normal or usual contract – has distorted our understanding of contemporary contract law, and perhaps has also legitimized unjust practices.[11]

There are a variety of practices that particularly raise questions regarding contracts – questions that are sometimes posed in terms of consent (whether the consent had been "full," "fully voluntary," or "informed"), and sometimes in terms of fairness or public policy. Along with the now-familiar examples of standard form agreements – and especially "adhesion contracts" – modern contract practice has also given us click-through (i.e., "clickwrap") agreements,[12] agreements based solely on terms posted on an Internet site where use or continued access

---

the other party to be bound, based on the other party's public actions, whatever the other party's private understandings.

[8] Adhesion contracts are standard forms presented to less sophisticated parties with less bargaining power and few alternatives on a take-it-or-leave-it basis. E.g., Slawson 1971, Rakoff 1983. One might reasonably distinguish form contracts presented to consumers in a retail context from the use of standard forms in dealings between merchants.

[9] There is much rhetoric (perhaps in this book as well) that implies that standard forms are a curse and blessing distinctive of modern contracting practice. The fact is that form contracts go back a millennium or so, even if they may be far more prevalent today; *see, e.g.*, Cordes 2005: 62–63 ("As early as the tenth and eleventh centuries, notaries in Genoa and Pisa drew up certain contracts in company law, namely the commenda contracts in a fully standardized form" (footnote omitted)).

[10] There is a rich tradition in theories of social practices of constructing a theory around the most sophisticated, richest, or most developed instances within a category, even if the vast majority of that category's instances are then to be characterized as lesser or marginal. E.g., Finnis 1980: 9–11. This is an approach with which I have some sympathy (particularly in the context of theories about the nature of law generally); however, the approach's theoretical benefits must always be weighed against the potential distorting or legitimating effects.

[11] My point about legitimation is not to be confused with Grant Gilmore's argument that there is distinct lack of fit between the broad proclamations of certain judges and commentators (e.g., Williston) and actual case outcomes. Gilmore 1974: 42–53.

[12] E.g., *I.Lan Systems, Inc. v. Netscout Service Level Corp.*, 183 F. Supp. 2d 328 (D. Mass. 2002) (click-through license terms enforceable); *Mortgage Plus, Inc. v. DocMagic, Inc.*, 2004 WL 2331918 (D. Kan. 2004) (clickwrap agreement enforceable, including forum-selection clause).

would be deemed assent (i.e., "browsewrap"),[13] software licenses,[14] and greater use of mandatory arbitration[15] and forms in the box sent after the purchase.[16] These are cases in which our doubts regarding enforcement of the agreement usually come from a belief that one party's assent was less than fully voluntary, because of either inadequate information or inadequate alternatives.[17] Most obvious, terms are often not read (or expected to be read), and they frequently are not fully understood even when read. However, the questions about modern contracts extend deeper and broader than a concern about notice.

Characterizing the objection as one of inadequate information or inadequate alternatives is common to economic analyses.[18] Some might prefer a more direct reference, at least in some circumstances, to the substantive unfairness of certain terms. The response of those who prefer to speak about information and alternatives, I assume, is that if a party, adult and mentally competent, with full information and adequate alternatives, would choose to accept a particular term, it would be unduly paternalistic for others to object. Nonetheless, there may well still be occasions when reference to (substantive) unfairness seems to get to the heart of our objection more than inadequate information and/or inadequate alternatives. For example, the problem of a mandatory arbitration case in which the firm hired to do First USA's credit card arbitration decided for First USA 99.6 percent of the time[19] does not

[13] *See, e.g., Register.com v. Verio*, 356 F.3d 393 (2d Cir. 2004) (user bound to terms when user repeatedly accessed site where terms were posted).

[14] *E.g., Specht v. Netscape Communications Corp.*, 306 F.3d 17 (2d Cir. 2002) (arbitration terms in software license did not become part of agreement because terms were not brought sufficiently to the attention of the licensees); *cf. ProCD, Inc. v. Zeidenberg*, 86 F.3d 1447 (7th Cir. 1996) (terms inside box of software bind consumers who do not return the software after an opportunity to read the terms).

[15] Under the Federal Arbitration Act (9 U.S.C. §§ 1–16), as construed by Supreme Court decisions, there is a strong general federal policy for enforcing arbitration provisions. *See Buckeye Check Cashing v. Cardegna*, 546 U.S. 440 (2006); *AT&T Mobility LLC v. Concepcion*, 131 S. Ct. 1740 (2011). However, recent federal legislation has also recognized the exploitative potential of mandatory arbitration. *See* John Warner National Defense Authorization Act of 2007, Pub. L. No. 109–364, § 670(a), 120 Stat. 2083 (codified as 10 U.S.C. §§ 987(e)(3), (f)(4)) (making mandatory arbitration provisions in consumer credit agreements with a member of the U.S. military unlawful and unenforceable).

[16] *E.g., Klocek v. Gateway, Inc.*, 104 F. Supp.2d 1332 (D. Kan. 2000) (terms sent in box after oral agreement to purchase do not become part of agreement under UCC § 2–207); *cf. Hill v. Gateway 2000*, 105 F.3d 1147 (7th Cir. 1997) (holding that terms did become part of the agreement through the purchaser's failure to object after receiving the box with the terms).

[17] Again, I want to emphasize that I am focusing primarily on consumer commercial transactions. As will be discussed herein, the concerns may be less (and, at times, different) for other sorts of transactions.

[18] *E.g., Craswell 1993.*

[19] *See* Mayer 2000. The firm, National Arbitration Forum, provided documentation (for litigation) which revealed 87 cases in which the cardholder prevailed, as against 19,618 in which First USA prevailed. National Consumer Law Center 2005: 2, 19. The same arbitration company served the MBNA credit card company; in California cases its arbitrators gave consumers victory in only 781 of 19,294 cases. O'Donnell 2007: 15. A similar claim has been brought against the National Arbitration Forum: that of the 18,075 collection claims brought in the State of California over a four-year period, consumers won only 30 (0.2 percent). Berner & Grow 2008. The firm later

seem to be fully captured by the claim, even if true, that most consumers would choose a different credit card provider if they knew about these figures and could find a provider that did not use the same arbitration service.[20] (Of course, the sort of contracting practices discussed do not always lead to unjust outcomes. Some companies may put one-sided terms in their contracts but then not enforce them, considering other practices (e.g., allowing returns and exchanges of goods even after use) as more likely to create consumer loyalty.[21] Anecdotes of good corporate behavior may match in number the anecdotes of sharp practices, but there are certainly enough of the latter to raise concerns.[22] As regards arbitration, when studies focus on the more reputable arbitrators and arbitration organizations, the indications are that consumers do at least as well in arbitration as they do in court.[23])

The general response of contract law to the complaints grounded on failures to achieve fully voluntary assent – just like the general response of most people (lawyers or otherwise) – is that such complaints are not relevant, as parties should be held to the terms for which they have shown outward consent, through their signature, click-through, or verbal agreement. (This conventional response usually allows for exceptions in extreme cases, and, as discussed elsewhere in this book, courts in fact have a number of doctrinal defenses – such as fraud, economic duress, reasonable expectations, or unconscionability – that they can use to excuse performance in such cases.) The argument goes that contracting parties – at least mentally competent adults who have not been subject to duress or fraud – are able to look after their own interests and, in fact, are better positioned to know and protect their interests than any legislature or court is. Therefore, contracting parties should be bound to what they sign or to which they otherwise assent. If they do not read all the provisions in the standard form or on the scroll-down terms in the software or on the Internet site, so much the worse for them.

This response is grounded in strong intuitions regarding autonomy and responsibility, and it must be taken seriously. At the same time, one may see unexpected exceptions and complications when one tries to translate this general intuition into a more precise theory of moral and legal obligation regarding agreements. Before attempting this, a few words might be helpful regarding theorizing about doctrinal areas of law.

entered an agreement with the Minnesota Attorney General to get out of the business of arbitrating credit card and other consumer collection disputes. Office of Minnesota Attorney General, 2009.
[20] Apparently, National Arbitration Forum was being used by "many other credit-card firms and retailers, such as American Express and Best Buy." Mayer 2000.
[21] Bebchuk & Posner 2006.
[22] And one might wonder at the evidence that companies are over seven times more likely to place a mandatory arbitration provision in their contracts with consumers than they are in their contracts with other businesses. Eisenberg, Miller & Sherwin 2008.
[23] Drahozal & Zyontz 2011.

B. THEORIES OF CONTRACT LAW

Theories about doctrinal areas of law – theories of property or contract or tort – are common and well known.[24] Most such theories sit uneasily between description and prescription and/or evaluation. On the one hand, they purport to fit most of the existing rules and practices; on the other hand, they recharacterize the practices to make them as coherent and/or as morally attractive as possible.[25] This sort of approach to theorizing comes under various titles: rational reconstruction, philosophical foundations of the common law, and constructive interpretation.[26] As both Ronald Dworkin and Michael Moore have argued, there is a strong connection between theories of law understood this way and the way judges and advocates argue about what the law requires in some novel case.[27]

Although this kind of theorizing can be quite valuable – in terms of both explaining an ongoing practice and because of the role such theorizing has in the development (and teaching) of law – one might want to take the theory a step further; one might ask questions of evaluation or justification of the practice, even as reconstructed. Assuming a theory of contract law (or some other area of the law) that broadly fits current rules and practices, and even granting some leeway to recharacterize those rules and practices "charitably," one might ask, "How should we evaluate the area of law as a matter of morality or policy?" In this section, I give a brief overview of some current theories of contract, followed by an initial look at the moral and evaluative side of the question.

Despite the limitations of the freedom-of-contract ideal in current practice, that ideal informs, for many, the justification for the enforcement of agreements. When commentators try to express that ideal in terms that carry theoretical weight while also matching current doctrinal rules, the result is usually an analysis in terms of promise, reliance, or efficiency.[28]

The promise-based or autonomy argument may be the most straightforward[29] and the one that best connects with lay attitudes toward contracts: contracts are promises, and one has a moral obligation – and should have a legal obligation – to

---

[24] E.g., Owen 1995, Weinrib 1995, C. Fried 1981. For a skeptical discussion regarding theories of tort law, see Cane 2007. The topic of theorizing about doctrinal areas of law is discussed at greater length in Chapter 9.

[25] Moore (1990: 124–129) points out that theories of a line of cases or a whole area of doctrine can never be entirely descriptive, for there are an indefinite number of alternative theories that completely fit (or, assuming the possibility of dismissing some cases as mistaken, adequately fit) the relevant cases. To choose among those alternative theories, one must have an evaluative standard.

[26] Dworkin 1986.

[27] Dworkin 1986, Moore 1990: 128–129.

[28] For a useful overview, see Smith 2000.

[29] What has come to be known as the promise or autonomy approach in the United States and the United Kingdom was also developed under the rubric of "will theory," particularly in Continental Europe (where it arose initially from the work of the eighteenth-century French writer Robert Joseph Pothier). E.g., Gordley 1991; *see also* Perillo 2005.

keep one's promises. At a more abstract or more philosophical level, the discussion is often in terms of autonomy. Autonomy is more than just liberty;[30] it is self-guidance or self-rule.[31] The promise or autonomy position is most extensively (and famously) expounded in Charles Fried's *Contract as Promise*.[32] There are well-known difficulties with the "contract as promise" explanation or justification: among the most obvious being that our legal system fails to enforce many promises – the whole doctrine of consideration being aimed at distinguishing enforceable bargains from unenforceable "mere" promises[33] – and that a focus on promise or autonomy fails to explain (and frequently seems inconsistent with) many details of contract law doctrine – in particular the background rules (e.g., remedial and formation rules) and waivable default rules.[34] Contracting parties are often ignorant of these background rules and, in any event, cannot usually be characterized as having actively chosen them.[35]

Modern consent theories of contract law[36] shift the focus away from an act of promising to "a manifest intention to be legally bound."[37] Barnett emphasized that his consent theory of contract law should be viewed in the context of a larger theory of entitlements and the conditions under which entitlement transfers are valid.[38] There is something eminently sensible about a theory of contract law centered on

---

[30] Liberty, as the mere absence of coercion or constraint, narrowly understood, would be too thin a concept to do most of the descriptive or normative work we would want done by a theory of contract law. For example, as Antony Kronman has pointed out, it could not distinguish the sort of advantage taking we consider acceptable in negotiations from the kind we consider unacceptable. Kronman 1980: 474.

[31] Autonomy has a central role in modern moral, political, and legal philosophy, and the concept in its modern form is usually traced back to Immanuel Kant. Schneewind 1998. For a contemporary restatement, see, e.g., Hill 1984.

[32] C. Fried 1981. Fried clarified and modified his views slightly in C. Fried 2007, 2012.

[33] There are equitable doctrines, like promissory estoppel (*Restatement (Second) of Contracts* § 90) and promissory restitution (*Restatement (Second) of Contracts* § 86), which make some nonbargain promises enforceable (these are discussed in Chapter 4, Section D), but the disjunction between the category of promises and the category of enforceable actions remains significant.

[34] E.g., Craswell 1989; Barnett 2012; *cf.* Kraus 2001: 430–436. Fried did not claim otherwise, and he presented his theory as much as an argument for reforming current doctrine as an explanation of or justification for existing law. E.g., Fried 1981: 28–39 (on consideration). For an important partial defense of Fried against Craswell's critique, see Kraus 2002a: 717–732. Smith (2004: 69), following Raz (1982: 937), argues that enforcing contracts on the basis of promises potentially violates "the Harm Principle" – the view, associated with the work of John Stuart Mill (Mill 1974: ch. 1, 68), that government is justified in infringing the liberties of its citizens only for the purpose of preventing harm to others. This claim is critically evaluated in Bix 2012.

[35] As Randy Barnett observes, "contract law is itself one big form contract that goes unread most of the time." Barnett 2002: 644. (I return to this point in the next section.) Additionally, as "Lon Fuller and William Perdue pointed out . . . , the fact that a person has promised to do something does not explain what should happen if he fails to do it." Gordley 2001a: 267 (footnote citing Fuller & Perdue 1936 omitted)

[36] E.g., Barnett 1986, 1992a, 2012.

[37] Barnett 1992a: 1027; *see also* Smith 2000.

[38] Barnett 1986: 270.

consent. For although promise, reliance, or wealth maximization (understanding each of these in a robust rather than diluted or metaphorical sense) is only unevenly present in the various kinds of transactions we associate with contract, some form of assent is basically universally present – and universally required for a valid and enforceable contract. The objections to such theories include, first, that they are basically only promissory theories (with all their strengths and weaknesses) under a different guise,[39] and that consent does little to explain what contract is, which agreements or promises should be enforced, how, and to what extent. What one basically has is "consent to contract"[40] – thus consent does little of the work of determining the nature and scope of contract.[41]

Reliance arguments try to construct a theory of obligation from the idea of reasonable reliance.[42] The well-known difficulty here is that it is not easy to ground the reasonableness of one's reliance without some foundational notion of when someone has an obligation to do what they said they would do, and the analysis of obligation will then usually turn on some other argument, usually of promise and/or efficiency.[43] Thus, reliance arguments seem to be derivative, grounded in another form of argument (promise based or perhaps economic or utilitarian). Additionally, thinking of contractual obligations in terms primarily of reasonable reliance does not seem to match either the way most contracting parties view their interactions or the way that courts and doctrinal commentators discuss contract law.

Property or transfer theories view valid agreements as creating a property right (or something like a property right) in the promisee for the promised performance.[44] Although this approach does a good job of explaining many parts of contract law, it has trouble accounting for the way courts modify the terms of agreements or the remedies available in the service of reasonableness (as in the well-known cases of *Jacob & Youngs v. Kent* and *Peevyhouse v. Garland Coal*).[45]

Law and economics theorists[46] argue that most contract law doctrine can be explained as efforts to maximize the individual and social gains from

---

[39] *See, e.g.*, C. Fried 2012.

[40] Or, more precisely, consent to the transfer of rights or entitlements, or consent to the legal enforcement of such transfers. Barnett 1986: 303–305.

[41] For another critique of consent theory, see Braucher 1990: 703–706.

[42] *See* Gilmore 1974; Atiyah 1979.

[43] The critique is presented in greater detail in Barnett 1986: 274–276.

[44] E.g., Benson 2001b, 2007; Gold 2009b, *cf.* Gold 2011a.

[45] *See, e.g.*, Alces 2008: 543–549; *Jacob & Youngs v. Kent*, 129 N.E. 889 (N.Y. 1921); *Peevyhouse v. Garland Coal*, 382 P.2d 109 (Okla. 1963). The cases are discussed in Chapters 5, Section B, and 6, Section D.

[46] With most law and economics theorists, it is not so much that they have an economic theory of contract law – rather, they have a general theory of law (or, at least, of private law), which they hold to apply to contract law (as well as other areas). E.g., Shavell 2004. There is a growing list of detailed economically based discussions of contract law, including Bolton & Dewatripont 2005, Brousseau & Glachant 2002, Craswell (e.g., 2000a), Edlin & Schwartz 2003, Goetz & Scott (e.g., 1977), Katz (e.g., 2004), Kronman & Posner 1979, E. Posner (e.g., 2005), R. Posner (e.g., 2011: 115–182), Schwartz (e.g., 1992), Schwartz & Scott 2003, and Veljanovski 2007.

trade.[47] This is often phrased in terms of the ability of parties to make a commitment on which another party can rely;[48] allowing parties to authorize or assent to state-enforced awards of expectation damages where performance is defective empowers parties to make such commitments. There are two standard criticisms of economic explanations of common law doctrines that apply to all such theories (the critique may be most common in response to economic theories of tort law) but that are certainly applicable to economic theories of contract law. First, economic theories fail as a matter of fit, in that a maximizing theory leaves out much of the participants' (judges', lawyers', and contracting parties') own understanding of what is going on in contract: that contract law does (or should) reflect foundational moral ideas about promises, duties to perform, and fairness, not just the consequentialist calculation.[49] Second, there is a concern that economic analysis may be too flexible: able to offer a plausible explanation or justification of any doctrine (for any given rule, able to justify the rule and its opposite equally well).[50] One prominent economic theorist, Richard Craswell, argued that economic analysis properly views contract law as being about which rules created the optimal and/or efficient incentives for contracting (or potentially contracting) parties but then listed eight different types of decisions in which the effect of any given rule might affect many at once, in ways that interact or may conflict,[51] thus resulting in overall consequences hard to predict (even under a simplified model).[52]

Relating to the criticisms of poor fit and conflicting incentives, one might consider the parallel to a critique of the economic explanation of tort law. The economic explanation of that area claims that the doctrinal rules create incentives for optimal levels of precaution for both the potential victim (and plaintiff) and the potential injurer (and defendant). However, as a number of theorists have pointed out,[53] the economic approach does not explain – as a corrective justice explanation would – the

---

[47] As Craswell 2001 has pointed out, it is important to understand that economic analysis of contract law has focused on which rules will create the optimal incentives and disincentives, not on when performance would be efficient.

[48] *See, e.g.,* R. Posner 2004.

[49] E.g., Kraus 2002a; Smith 2004: 132–136; *see also* Wilkinson-Ryan & Baron 2009; Wilkinson-Ryan & Hoffman 2010 (describing experiments showing most people's perceptions of breach of contract). Of course, to the extent that economic or efficiency theories are recharacterized as prescriptions for contract law rather than rational reconstructions, descriptions or explanations of (existing) contract law, the "fit" objection would fall away.

[50] *See* Korobkin 2005; *cf.* E. Posner (2003, 2011: 223–232). Some other criticisms of economic approaches are summarized by Benson 1996: 48–50.

[51] Craswell 2001: 26–32.

[52] Craswell lists the following actions or decisions subject to incentives: to perform, to rely on the promised performance, to take interim precautions that will affect the ability to perform, the selection of parties with whom to transact (and at what price), how much time and effort to spend searching for better contracting partners, how carefully to evaluate the proposed transaction before committing to a promise, how much to tell the other party prior to performance, and the effect of enforceability on the allocation of risk. Craswell 2001: 26–32.

[53] E.g., Coleman 2001: 13–40.

bilateral character of tort law: where negligent defendants make payments only to injured plaintiffs, and the amount of compensatory payments is set by the amount of damage proximately caused, rather than being based on the tortfeasor's level of negligence, as one might have expected had the objective been optimal deterrence. A similar critique could be grounded on the bilateral character of contract law:[54] if contract were primarily about proper levels of incentives, it would not be clear why the payments should always go from breaching party to the party that was injured by the breach (rather than, say, to a state fund), and one might raise questions about remedial doctrines like mitigation and certainty, which can significantly affect the level of damages in ways unconnected to the appropriate level of (dis)incentives for defendants.[55]

One could combine the different kinds of general theories in various ways: such as by using an autonomy theory to justify the doctrinal areas and to set its basic parameters while using an economic theory to select the more detailed rules.[56] Of course, the different theories might also be combined in a different sense, if one saw them as having different objectives: such as a purely prescriptive autonomy theory as opposed to an explanatory or justificatory role for an economic theory.[57] (In making such a theory, one would then need a metatheory that explained and justified dividing up contract law in the way indicated.[58])

C. THEORY MEETS PRACTICE

For the commercial (contracting) practices of most modern countries, a simple analysis in terms of the morality of promising or the morality of enforcing fully voluntary

---

[54] This part of the argument was also summarized in Chapter 6, Section D.

[55] *Cf.* Smith 2004: 397–398; Oman 2007, 2012. For a spirited defense of economic explanations against this line of critique, see Kraus 2007. One can make an argument that mitigation is tied to the optimal level of incentives (regarding reliance) for the nonbreaching parties, but that just adds to the general point that a bilateral structure of contract law will inevitably be in tension with trying to create the right level of incentives for both parties, as the optimal amount of damages to be paid by the defendant, to create the right incentives for future defendants, may not be the optimal level of payments to be received by the plaintiff, to create the right incentives for future plaintiffs.

[56] *See* Kraus 2001; Oman 2005a; *cf.* Farber 2000.

[57] *See* Kraus 2002a: 689. Kraus also suggests that theories cannot usefully be compared where one takes doctrinal statements seriously and tries to explain them, whereas another theory focuses primarily on the outcome of cases, ignoring the conceptual distinctions internal to the practice. Kraus 2002a: 689. I would prefer to say that such theories still can be directly compared on a standard of explanatory efficacy, with the ability to incorporate the internal understanding one factor, and perhaps an important factor, but not necessarily conclusive. In analytical legal philosophy, comparable arguments can be found, for example, in the debates between inclusive legal positivism and exclusive legal positivism, and between the will theory of legal rights and the interests theory of legal rights (*see* Bix 2009: 21–22, 48–52, 136–137); in each set of debates, at least one of the theories trades off fit with internal descriptions of the practice for some other metatheoretical value.

[58] *See, e.g.,* Kraus 2001, 2002b.

exchanges is no longer adequate. As other theorists have noted,[59] conventional discussions of "meeting of the minds," "assent," and "freedom of contract" have unclear application (if they have any application at all) when a large proportion of the transactions entered into are based on agreements presented on standardized forms with large amounts of obscure language, and with terms not subject to negotiation, and sometimes involving terms sent in the mail after purchase or placed on a separate Web site. (When software companies that want less regulation of their efforts to impose terms on consumers speak about protecting the freedom of contract, they unintentionally display how far current contracting practices are from true mutual assent.[60])

One commentator has tellingly compared modern contracting practices to promising in advance to do whatever someone else has written in a sealed envelope.[61] In some ways, this raises the problem well: one is offering a broad promise or assent, and like other alleged broad acts of consent, the moral and political question is how much weight a single promise can carry. A similar idea had been raised many decades back by Karl Llewellyn: that a party's acceptance (by action or otherwise) of an offer made on a standard form should be understood as assent to the dickered terms (quantity, price, and perhaps delivery and warranty) and a "blanket assent" to all other not-unreasonable terms.[62]

There are other contexts in which moral and political theorists refer to a statement or action giving broad assent to a wide range of obligations. The most prominent example is the argument that by voting, receiving state benefits, or not leaving the country, one takes on the obligation to obey a country's laws – usually stated more precisely as a prima facie obligation to obey laws from a generally just legal system.[63] One could see this as a parallel to the Llewellyn view: one agrees to abide by not-unreasonable laws (laws from generally just legal systems that are not themselves clearly immoral). The predominant – though by no means universal – view among political and legal theorists is that such actions are not adequate to ground a general moral obligation to obey the law.[64]

One can, of course, press that point even more strongly. Even express promises to obey the law (e.g., the oaths the legal officials frequently must offer) likely have limits in the moral obligations they create. If the law one is asked to uphold or apply is egregiously unjust, there is at least a strong countervailing moral reason not to obey the law, which may override one's moral obligation to keep a promise to obey the law.

---

[59] *E.g.*, Slawson 1971.
[60] And the parallel with the freedom-of-contract analysis of *Lochner v. New York*, 198 U.S. 45 (1905), seems obvious.
[61] Barnett 2002: 635–636
[62] *See* Llewellyn 1960: 362–371; a similar conclusion is reached by Barnett 2002; *cf.* Leff 1970.
[63] *E.g.*, Higgins 2004.
[64] *See, e.g.*, Edmundson 1999, 2004; Higgins 2004.

Some might argue that the example of the obligation to obey the law is too extreme – mostly because Barnett's original image of promising to do everything written in a sealed envelope is itself an (intentional) exaggeration of the situation with form contracts. There is likely to be significant consumer ignorance of the terms in form contracts – because the terms are inaccessible or incomprehensible, or because consumers choose (perhaps rationally[65]) not to read the whole document. However, this level of party ignorance may be little different than the level of party ignorance (or, if one prefers different terminology, asymmetric information) in many other sorts of transactions. As Barnett argues (elsewhere in the same article with the sealed-envelope argument), "contract law is itself one big form contract that goes unread most of the time."[66] That is, most people enter such legal relationships without knowing many (perhaps nearly all) of the important background rules regarding formation, performance, and remedies.[67] In contrast, many people may trust the unknown terms imposed by the state in a way they do not trust the unknown terms offered by large businesses.[68]

All this leads back to the basic questions: To what extent do parties have a moral obligation to comply with all the terms in the agreements to which they have assented in some way? And what consequences should follow for the government's role in regulating agreements?

D. RETHINKING CONTRACT LAW

What happens when the ideal construct at the core of one's theory about a practice diverges so much from the practice that it distorts more than it explains? And what happens when the practice diverges so much from any sort of ideal that one can doubt the moral or policy legitimacy of (at least certain aspects of) the practice? There may come a point when theorists of a practice should no longer be focusing on adjustments or applications at the margin and should return to first principles, to rethink the entire enterprise.[69] And it may be that this point has come (again) for contract law, or at least for some categories of contracting practice. Something approximating a political justification must be offered, at least as a supplementary theory, regarding the enforcement, or selective enforcement, of the agreements for

---

[65] This is sometimes referred to as "rational ignorance": that given the "cost" in time to read through long documents (especially given more valuable potential alternative uses for that time) and the limited probable benefit from doing so, it is usually rational to remain ignorant of the term details.

[66] Barnett 2002: 644.

[67] Similar points have been made about marriage (e.g., L. Baker 1988, 1990) and about the purchase of information goods (Alexander 1993: 936–938).

[68] I am grateful to Daniel Schwarcz for this point.

[69] Compare Lon Fuller's challenge to the great contract theorist and treatise writer Williston: "What may be called the bases of contract liability, notions like consideration, the necessity for offer and acceptance, and the like, are nowhere in his work critically examined in the light of the social interests they serve. These things are accepted on faith." Fuller 1939: 9.

which one cannot speak (except as a legitimating fiction) of informed and voluntary assent to all terms. As Morris Cohen pointed out eighty years ago, contract law is best understood as state resources made available on the basis that enforcing private agreements is generally in the public interest, but it remains open to society to judge that certain types of transactions in fact work against the general good, and therefore state enforcement resources should not be offered for those transactions.[70]

In rethinking this area of law, one likely starting place is to distinguish among agreements, focusing on the nature of the parties and the topic of the agreement. For example, Alan Schwartz and Robert Scott have argued that a different set of rules should apply to commercial contracts entered between large businesses than when the party alignment is different (e.g., where one party is a consumer or small business, or noncommercial agreements between intimates).[71] As Schwartz and Scott point out, many of the factors raising questions about enforcement of agreements (or the moral obligation to comply with agreements) are less present in commercial transactions between large business entities. On the one hand, large business entities are likely less subject both to bounded rationality and to exploitative pressures than are consumers or individuals contracting within intimate relationships. Also, autonomy considerations are absent for businesses, and therefore different sets of rules may be justified for interbusiness transactions compared to transactions involving individuals.[72]

Even as regards consumer agreements, Richard Craswell has warned against a too-quick conclusion that certain contractual agreements or contractual terms should not be enforced because one party's assent was less than fully voluntary.[73] Craswell points out that the regulatory alternatives to enforcing agreements where there has been less than fully voluntary consent (because of inadequate information or insufficient alternatives) are either refusal to enforce the agreement at all or judicial imposition of alternative terms that the court finds to be reasonable. Neither alternative solves the problem of consent or autonomy but at best replaces one set of imposed terms with another. And whether the judicially imposed terms will be better (fairer – or "better" under some other criterion) than the party-imposed, and party-acquiesced, terms will depend on judgments of the relative competence of judges and consumers that may vary across different fact situations.[74]

Also, when one moves to mandatory terms (a likely response or remedy to the problems discussed here, as we will see), there are obvious problems from the

[70] M. Cohen 1933: 585–592
[71] Schwartz & Scott 2003. For an argument that business-to-business agreements in fact warrant the same protections as consumer agreements, see Hesselink 2011.
[72] For an argument rejecting Schwartz and Scott's conclusion that autonomy considerations do not apply to interbusiness transactions, see Oman 2005b.
[73] Craswell 1993.
[74] This would take into account the fact that consumers view the terms ahead of the transaction and judges would review the terms after the fact (and potentially as part of class action litigation).

perspective of the seller, lessor, or more powerful party: first, that it clearly has not assented to those terms; and second, that the reality of the market may make not dealing at all (or dealing less frequently) preferable to dealing on the required terms.

The idea of moving away from a promissory or freedom-of-contract ideal for thinking about contractual obligations is certainly not new. To some extent, all the efforts to understand contract law generally or particular contract law doctrines from within a law and economics perspective are grounded on a broadly consequentialist analysis (whether understood as wealth maximizing, welfare maximizing, or utilitarian).[75] Also noteworthy are the arguments that the line between contract law and tort law has disappeared – or will soon, or should soon;[76] and the analysis that looks at the adhesion contracts of large companies as being (from the perspective of consumers) a kind of private legislation that should accordingly be regulated in some way.[77]

If one were to try to justify something like the status quo in contract law, one would likely offer an argument along the line suggested by law and economics. Under this analysis, the question is whether it will probably maximize social wealth (or welfare or utility) to enforce agreements even where it is likely that at least one of the parties may not have considered or read all of the terms, and even where some of the terms may be harmful or create negative externalities. This is certainly a tenable approach, one that should be considered seriously, especially given the value of predictability for much of commercial discourse.

The issue is how far the consequentialist analysis will go. It is, of course, possible that enforcing all one-sided terms, regardless of how unlikely they are to be read, how unexpected, or how one sided, will in fact maximize social wealth (or welfare or utility). However, it is also possible – and, to many people, more likely – that refusal to enforce at least some of those terms is the rule that would have the better results tested under a consequentialist standard.[78] At the same time, as already discussed, a judge facing a case of not-fully-voluntary assent to terms may not necessarily be able to develop and impose better terms than the parties could themselves (although it may create incentives for better or fairer drafting of standard forms).[79] However, this important caveat still is a far step from assuming that whatever terms a party assents to in some way are the optimal terms to enforce.

[75] *See generally* Kronman & Posner 1979, Shavell 2004: 289–385.
[76] *See* Atiyah 1979; Gilmore 1974.
[77] *See* Slawson 1971; *see also* Kessler 1943.
[78] The problem with consequentialist analyses (utilitarian, welfarist, or wealth maximizing) is that the real-world costs and benefits for most inquiries quickly become so intricate that it usually is pure speculation to claim that the ultimate bottom-line figure is positive or negative. Additionally, the well-known tendencies for people to misjudge badly both the likelihood of an event and its value (*see, e.g.*, Kahneman, Slovic & Tversky 1982) may undermine the normative justification underlying economic prescriptions (that people are in the best position to judge what will be in their own long-term interests).
[79] Craswell 1993; see also Ben-Shahar 2011 (on what terms judges should use to replace terms found to be unconscionable).

E. THE MORAL OBLIGATION TO KEEP CONTRACTS

While there is a lively literature about whether there is a moral obligation to obey the law generally,[80] there is not much discussion about whether we[81] have a moral obligation to keep our contracts.[82] I use the awkward term "keep," because there are doctrinal problems with speaking of an obligation to *perform* one's contracts (even if we confine the discussion to contracts where one does not have a doctrinal justification for not performing – for example, based on misrepresentation, mutual mistake, or duress). As Oliver Wendell Holmes Jr. famously argued, one's (legal) obligation under a valid contract (under American law) is not to perform, but either to perform or to pay damages.[83] There are exceptional circumstances in which a contracting party could obtain an equitable order of specific performance, ordering a breaching party to perform, but these are rare.[84] The fact that parties not only can, but in a sense *should*, breach where they could do better by breaching, paying damages, and taking advantage of an alternative opportunity, is summarized as the

---

[80] *E.g.*, Edmundson 1999, 2004.

[81] Much of the discussion in this section assumes individual (human) contracting parties. The reality of modern contracting, that much of it is done between corporations (and other entities), raises complications. Can one speak of the moral obligations of corporations to keep promises? (Or of respecting the autonomy of corporations?) Nor is it clear that this complication can be resolved simply by shifting the focus to the people who run, or act in the name of, corporations and other entities. See Kraus 2002a: 696 n. 20, Rakoff 1983: 1236.

[82] This has begun to change in just the past few years. *See, e.g.*, Shiffrin 2007, 2009; Shavell 2006a, 2009. The parallel debate about the nature and ground of the moral obligation to keep promises is substantial and largely beyond the scope of this book. One classical source is Hume 1978: book III, section V, at 516–525. Significant recent work includes Kolodny & Wallace 2003; Pratt 2001; Owens 2006, 2007, 2008, 2011; Scanlon 1990, 1998, 2001.

[83] Holmes 1897: 462, Holmes 1963: 236; *see* R. Posner 2009. Holmes here discounts the difference between the primary obligation to perform, and the damages to be paid for failure of performance. To the Holmesian "bad man" (Holmes 1897: 460–461), there may be no such difference, although to those who take their obligation to perform as promised seriously, there will be. (For an argument that Holmes should not be understood as a supporter of "efficient breach," see Perillo 2000a.) Additionally, the Holmes quote needs to be supplemented by the fact that breaching a contract has an important additional consequence of releasing the other party from its obligation to perform. C. Fried 1981: 117–118.

[84] Equitable remedies are discussed in Chapter 6, Section E. Where one is dealing with agreements for which specific performance might be available as a matter of course, such as the purchase of land or the purchase of a unique good (UCC § 2–716(1)), then one might reasonably speak of a legal obligation to perform the agreement (and not just to perform or pay damages), and perhaps, derivatively, a moral obligation to perform. As discussed in Chapter 6, Section E, the whole idea that an equitable order of specific performance should be given only where money damages are inadequate can be traced to the struggles between the common law courts and the chancery courts. Simpson 1975a: 595–598. In modern times, the doctrine can be justified either by the view that the parties would reasonably have understood that the promisor would not be held to perform where an alternative performance was easily available (*e.g.*, Gordley 1996: 17–18) or an efficiency argument that equitable remedies given as a matter of course could too often lead to needless transaction costs, hold-ups and/or economic waste in performance. *E.g.*, R. Posner 2011: 164; Shavell 2004: 312–314.

idea of "efficient breach."[85] The fact that contract law carries a strict liability standard (there are few acceptable excuses for nonperformance and a plaintiff in a breach of contract action does not need to prove that the defendant acted negligently in breaching the contract),[86] and that punitive damages are rarely available for egregious or badly motivated breaches of contracts,[87] echoes and reinforces this attitude of contract law: that it is amoral and focuses only on the compensation of parties' economic losses. In line with the foregoing discussion, Richard Craswell suggests helpfully that one might distinguish between an obligation to perform a promise and an obligation to perform or pay damages, with the second being the one most relevant to discussions of modern (American) contract law.[88]

It may be that one's moral obligation to keep an agreement is affected by the existence of a legal regime of contract enforcement, at least if the legal regime is generally just. For the existence of the working regime may create claims of reasonable reliance that were not present before, and one might have a moral obligation not to act contrary to other parties' reasonable expectations, whatever one's independent obligations to keep one's promises.[89] And the fact that American contract law (and every other comparable regime with which I am familiar[90]) makes some, but not all, promises legally enforceable, adds to the complication. Although I initially focus on the moral obligation that may exist independent of the legal regime of enforcement, the factor of institutional enforcement must eventually be added to the analysis.[91]

For our purposes, the hardest question might be whether or when an obligation to keep contracts or to perform promises is altered by limitations on the parties' knowledge or alternatives. For Thomas Scanlon, who analyzes the question within a general conception of moral obligation known as "contractualism" (only analogically related to contract law, and not to be confused with it), the issue is whether potential

[85] E.g., Goetz & Scott 1977; Craswell 1988; Friedmann 1989; Shavell 2006a. The idea appears to have been introduced by Birmingham 1970, before being popularized by Goetz & Scott. Efficient breach is also discussed in Chapter 6, Section I.

[86] As George Cohen points out, the "strict liability" of contract law is primarily at the level of performance; in questions of formation and remedies, fault remains a significant factor. G. Cohen 2009.

[87] As discussed in Chapter 6, Section B, there is a small category of contracts in which punitive damages are allowed, but these cover a small number (and idiosyncratic selection) of agreements. *Restatement (Second) of Contracts* § 353 & Comment a. For a good overview of the reasons for excluding emotional distress recovery for the vast majority of contracts, see *Erlich v. Menezes*, 21 Cal. 4th 543, 981 P.2d 978, 87 Cal. Rptr. 886 (1999).

[88] Craswell 2001: 27; *cf.* Scanlon 2001: 107.

[89] However, it is also worth noting that research consistently shows that in the real world peoples' perceptions of how parties should act in the performance of agreements tends to deviate significantly from what contract doctrine prescribes (and that peoples' knowledge of contract doctrine tends to be faulty). E.g., Macaulay 1963; Collins 1999: 129–137.

[90] *Cf.* Gordley 2001b.

[91] In a well-known article, Shiffrin (2007) focuses on the different question of whether the rules of contract law undermine the development of moral agency in regards to keeping promises. For responses to Shiffrin, see, e.g., C. Fried 2007; B. Fried 2007; Kraus 2009; Gold 2009a, 2011a.

promisors could reasonably reject a principle that binds them to keep promises or keep contracts despite limitations on alternatives and information.[92] Although the answer seems to be yes, that reasonable people would reject an obligation to be bound, at least in the case of significant limitations on alternatives and information, Scanlon adds that we must then inquire about whether potential promisees could reasonably reject a rule that would allow promisors to void or evade their promises under such circumstances.[93] It seems likely that potential promisors and promisees (especially if they come from relatively distinct groups, like consumers and large businesses) are unlikely to come to consensus on what types of limitations would excuse obligation. (It is also worth noting that, for Scanlon, the reasonableness of objections tends to do a lot of work.[94]) Thus, Scanlon's analysis leaves us somewhat uncertain regarding the moral obligation to keep – or to ignore – our contractual undertakings.

One could imagine a very different sort of contract law system, one that paralleled tort law, in generally imposing obligations not for all damage-causing actions and omissions but only for those that fall below some acceptable standard, and are therefore called faulty. However, that is not the standard that we have. The "strict liability" standard we have is justified on the basis that it serves commercial interests (by increasing the predictability that either performance will be rendered or comparable payments made by way of damages).

Another part of the justification for the current system is that it remains in the parties' hands to set their own standards for full compliance and for actionable conduct.[95] Just as parties can put in their agreements terms excusing nonperformance where the buyer is unable to obtain a mortgage or where the vendor's performance is made extremely difficult by some "act of God," so the parties could insert provisions that would excuse any category of nonfaulty nonperformance they were able to articulate. One should, of course, note that whatever the freedom of contracting the parties have, it remains significant that the baseline or "default" is for strict performance.

Finally, the moral obligation to keep one's contracts is complicated by the uncertainty of what the parties have agreed to or (to the extent that this is different)

---

[92] Scanlon 2001, 111–117.

[93] *Id.*, 115–116.

[94] For example, for Scanlon, it is the basis on which we would refuse a robber's objection to not being paid money promised under physical coercion, but not refuse a physician's objection to not being paid money promised under coercion of circumstances. Scanlon 2001: 115.

[95] This was recognized at least as long ago as the famous case of *Paradine v. Jane*, 82 Eng. Rep. 897 (K.B. 1647), in which the court justified a strict-liability standard by stating: "when the party by his own contract creates a duty or charge upon himself, he is bound to make it good, if he may, notwithstanding any accident or inevitable necessity, because he might have provided against it by his contract." *Id.* at 897–898. One should note, however, that there are some limits on party freedom of contract (e.g., as regards liquidated damages, or agreements to authorize equitable remedies, as discussed in Chapter 6, Section F).

what terms can reasonably be ascribed to their agreement. Commentators as far apart in theoretical terms as the law and economics scholar Steven Shavell and the contract-as-promise theorist Charles Fried seem to agree that contractual promises are incomplete in specifying what the parties' obligations are (under what circumstances one must perform and when one would be excused from performing, and when one has an obligation only to pay some level of damages in lieu of performance); many failures to perform may in fact be consistent with a moral obligation to keep one's promises and one's contracts.[96] When the seller signed a contract to sell five thousand widgets for five thousand dollars, for delivery on June 1, did the parties agree that performance was required (rather than excused performance or payment of damages instead of performance) even if the seller's workers had gone on strike or a war or natural catastrophe had made performance thirty times more expensive, when the buyer, in the meantime, could easily obtain the widgets from another supplier?[97]

F. IMPLICATIONS FOR GOVERNMENT REGULATION

Even if we could ground a fairly skeptical or critical account regarding the moral obligation to comply with agreements, the consequences are not immediately obvious.

First, we must be careful not to (too quickly) equate an analysis of a contracting party's moral obligation with what the state should do regarding contracts. Consider the analogy – suggested earlier – with the moral obligation to obey the law. A number of prominent theorists have argued that there is no general moral obligation to obey the law,[98] but these theorists have not argued that it therefore follows that (morally speaking or otherwise) societies should not set up legal systems. The conclusion that citizens may not have a general or presumptive obligation to obey the laws – even the generally just laws of a generally just legal system – does not entail that governments morally should desist from promulgating laws. Under modern thinking, the questions of what legitimate governments should do, and what citizens should do in response to the actions of those governments, are held to be divergent, if overlapping, questions. Similarly, the question of whether one should (morally speaking) keep all of one's contracts may differ from whether governments ought to enforce them.[99]

---

[96] *See* C. Fried 1981: 57–132; Shavell 2006a, 2009.

[97] One could offer a similar question about the seller's having received a much higher buying price from a third party, the context of "efficient breach." C. Fried 2007: 4–7.

[98] E.g., Raz 1994: 325–338; Kramer 1999: 254–308; Higgins 2004.

[99] To the extent that one accepts a sharp "principle versus policy" distinction, here the governmental "ought" might be thought to be a policy conclusion rather than a purely moral one (i.e., one more of maximizing social welfare rather than, or along with, protecting individual rights or doing what justice requires).

Second, and this is a related point, there are good moral and policy reasons (some of them discussed earlier) for enforcing at least some of the agreements where the contracting parties' consent might be defective. Among the standard arguments here are the importance of predictability of enforcement,[100] the difficulty of proving (or disproving) questions of consent, avoiding incentives to stay ignorant or to lie about one's knowledge, and so on.

Third, as mentioned already, concluding that party assent was less than fully voluntary is only the beginning of the inquiry. There is no reason to believe that, for all cases, refusing enforcement of such agreements is the best outcome (however "best outcome" is understood) or that judges or legislators will always do better than parties – even parties with only limited knowledge and limited alternatives – in choosing terms to govern commercial interactions.[101]

Fourth, it is often far from clear that regulation will solve the underlying problem. Consider the electronic contracting analysis from Chapter 3, Section A: although it may be unreasonable, for example, for licensors of software or sellers of computer hardware not to make contractual terms available ahead of time (e.g., by posting on a Web site) or not to give notice (e.g., during telephone or store transactions) that there will be additional terms "in the box," how much will be achieved by an alternative rule, forcing notice and disclosure? It seems likely that the percentage of consumers who actually read (and understand) the contractual terms will not increase that much, however much legal and moral concerns about "due notice" will be assuaged.[102] In contrast, making terms available ahead of time may facilitate pressure from formal and informal consumer advocates (e.g., *Consumer Reports*, state attorney generals, or even informed bloggers) to create (reputational) pressure for better terms.[103]

Conclusion

An overarching theory of contract law (or even, of American contract law), presented as a rational reconstruction grounded on autonomy, would likely have to be rejected for its failures to explain the detailed rules of contract law and for its poor fit with the enforcement of many far-from-fully-voluntary agreements. However, economic and/or consequentialist theories would likely fare little better, as they do not adequately take into account the doctrinal terms in which parties, judges, and advocates understand contract; also, the claim of these theories to explain the details of contract law results is undermined by doubts about the falsifiability of the efficiency explanations offered.

---

[100] Especially for a market economy in which investments may depend on agreements being both assignable and predictably enforceable.

[101] Craswell 1993, 1995, 2001: 38–39.

[102] E.g., Ben-Shahar & Schneider 2011.

[103] I am grateful to Daniel Schwarcz for this point.

This chapter has also raised issues relating to the divergence between theory and practice. For a large number of contracts, especially those entered by consumers when dealing with large businesses, characterization of the transaction in terms of "a meeting of minds" or freedom of contract so far deviates from what is actually going on as to be unhelpful and distorting. Legal scholars (and other commentators) have known this for a long time, but the consequences have not been fully worked out or worked through. At a minimum, one might suspect that teaching and talking about contracts (both in law school classes and more generally) as if they were normally the result of person-to-person negotiations between parties of comparable sophistication, knowledge, and bargaining power, when that is not the case, might have the effect of giving a level of legitimacy to contracts that some significant subset of them may not deserve. The fact that, at least with consumer contracts, many terms are simultaneously unlikely to be read, are not brought to the attention of the parties, and are substantively one sided may justify government-imposed terms (or at least default terms that can be overcome only with clear evidence of knowing waiver).[104]

These considerations factor both into the practical questions for governments (which agreements to enforce and whether and when to impose mandatory terms) and for individuals (whether and when they have a moral obligation to perform), and also into theoretical questions about the nature of contract law. The theoretical questions are explored further in Chapter 9.

SUGGESTED FURTHER READING

Andrew Robertson, "The Limits of Voluntariness in Contract," *Melbourne University Law Review*, vol. 29, pp. 179–217 (2005).

Hanoch Sheinman (ed.), *Promises and Agreements: Philosophical Essays* (Oxford: Oxford University Press, 2011).

Michael J. Trebilcock, *The Limits of Freedom of Contract* (Cambridge, MA: Harvard University Press, 1993).

---

[104] Korobkin 2003.

9

How Many Contract Laws?

There is an abundance of books and articles offering *the* (or "a") theory of contract law.[1] Theories of contract law commonly discuss a single principle (e.g., promise, consent, reliance, or efficiency) that is said to explain all of contract law, both for this country and for other countries (and perhaps for all time). Rather than add one more general theory to the pile, this book has offered a narrower and more cautious view of contract law, focusing more on the rules of a single time and place, and denying that any single principle can explain the whole field. In the course of the discussion, the text also suggests that there may be more at stake than abstract knowledge claims: that the (often indirect and almost certainly unintended) effect of general theories is to distract attention from the particular difficulties and occasional injustice of types of transactions that depart from the general theory's paradigm.

A. THE HISTORY OF GENERAL THEORY

As discussed in Chapter 2, the idea of contract law as a special category is relatively recent. The idea of a general theory of contract law (or any other area of law) might well derive from the view that law can and should be viewed systematically, or even "scientifically." One finds this approach in England only in the late eighteenth and early nineteenth century, with the earliest legal treatises (and John Austin's development of legal positivist theories of law).[2] The civil law countries had a longer and more established history of treatise writing and other systematic works about areas of law[3] (from which the English treatise writers apparently borrowed

---

[1] E.g., C. Fried 1981, Barnett 1986, Benson 2001b, 2007, Smith 2004.

[2] *See* Simpson 1975b, 1981: 267–268. Ibbetson writes: "Before 1700 the English law of contract had developed without any articulated theory to support it." Ibbetson 1999: 215. On Austin, and the development of systematic thinking about positive law, see Bix 2009: 33–37.

[3] In Germany, much of the important work of thinking systematically, and theoretically, about contract law and other private law areas, occurred in the sixteenth century. E.g., Berman 2003: 158.

liberally⁴), and there is also the natural law tradition, which supported the idea that there might be general principles that did or should underlie the chaos of legal decisions.⁵

B. THE NATURE OF GENERAL THEORY

Where one wants to discuss "a theory of contract law," it seems useful to take a moment to figure out what might be meant by that. Theorizing about social practices and social institutions can be descriptive, prescriptive, or something in between. As it turns out, most discussions of "theories" of areas of law tend mostly to be in that amorphous in-between area, as is discussed in greater detail here. (Theories further along the scale toward pure prescription are certainly possible, although they do not entirely escape the metatheoretical difficulties we find with theories that focus on explanation or justification of existing practices. Whether describing, interpreting, or prescribing, the theorist must face the question of whether the entire complex practice can be explained or reformed in terms of a single principle or value – likely contrary to a good portion of actual current practice; if not, the theorist must find a way to construct an overarching theory that contains some basis for reconciling or balancing multiple values.⁶ This text focuses on theories whose primary purpose is explanation or justification, not prescription.)

I want to consider the nature of "philosophical foundation" explanations, distinguishing them from prescriptive theories and other forms of descriptive theories. "Philosophical Foundations of the Common Law" is an approach exemplified both in courses of that name (including a famous such course at Oxford University), and in books and articles that attempt to elucidate "the basic nature" of a particular common law subject⁷ or an important legal concept common to a number of common law areas.⁸ Philosophical foundation theories are generally similar to the "rational reconstructions" familiar to legal doctrinal writers, in the sense that they mean to give the best justification and recharacterization possible of a given doctrine or area while remaining true to the actual practice and the case results (they could also be considered similar to Dworkin's "constructive interpretation"⁹).

---

⁴ *See* Simpson 1975b, 254–257.
⁵ Simpson 1975b: 255; *see also* Ibbetson 1999: 217–219. For an overview of natural law theory, see, e.g., Bix 2002.
⁶ Kraus 2002a: 687–688 n. 1. Kraus's own suggestion elsewhere (Kraus 2001), in the context of a discussion of rational reconstruction theories, is that different theories might be "vertically integrated" by giving each distinctive "tasks": for example, an autonomy theory might justify the existence and general outline of a contract law system, but particular rules within the area might be chosen on efficiency grounds. A similar suggestion is made by Oman 2005a.
⁷ E.g., in tort law (Owen 1995; Postema 2001), property law (e.g., Penner 1997), criminal law (Moore 1990), and contract law (Benson 2001a).
⁸ E.g., causation (Hart & Honoré 1985).
⁹ Dworkin 1986: 49–53.

In Dworkin's work, the rational reconstruction (i.e., "constructive interpretation") is part of a distinctive theory, in which it is of the nature of law that what it (currently) requires can be determined only by a process like rational reconstruction.[10] For those who do not accept Dworkin's view of law, the motivation for or justification of rational reconstruction (or philosophical foundations) may be a little harder to discern – it certainly is not always made explicit. Within common law countries at least, rational reconstruction might be justified on the ground that it mimics the process of accepted legal and/or judicial reasoning, at least in common law cases.[11]

Whatever the value generally of rational reconstruction at the level of doctrinal development and advocacy, one might question when and whether such reconstructions are useful at a more general or abstract level. Sometimes philosophical foundations theories are presented as being an explanation of individual doctrinal rules or whole areas of doctrine. One needs to keep in mind the different sort of activities that go under the name of "explanation" (while noting that the boundary lines between those activities are often blurred). There can be historical or causal theories of an area of law, descriptive theories, and normative or evaluative theories.[12]

In this context, it is important to keep in mind one form of explanation that is too often ignored or discounted in philosophical foundation discussions: the development of certain common law doctrines may be due primarily to certain historical contingencies rather than reflecting any deep moral or policy justification.[13] In contract law, a historical explanation may well be superior to alternative (morality-based or economics-based) explanations for a number of matters, including the doctrine of consideration and some of the remedies rules. (A point that the historical discussion in Chapter 2 attempted to exemplify.) Here, though, explanation is causal – why we have the doctrines we do – rather than justificatory.

Also, among rational reconstructions, one might distinguish those that put greater emphasis on the explanation (description, plus some element of prediction) from those that place greater emphasis on justification. Jody Kraus has usefully shown how economic theories of contract law tend to fall into the first group, whereas deontic (e.g., autonomy-based or promise-based) theories of contract law tend to fall into the second group.[14]

This section focuses on a (largely undiscussed) problem confronting philosophical foundations: given that different legal systems often have quite different rules (in every relevant area – contract law, tort law, criminal law, property law, and so on), why should we assume, as most discussions in this area do, that we are dealing with

---

[10] Dworkin 1986. Dworkin would apply a similar approach to understanding the meaning of a work of art or the requirements of (many) social practices besides law. *Id.*

[11] Rational reconstruction also mimics the way law tends to be taught, at least in the United States.

[12] Moore 1990: 119–129, Smith 2004: 4–5.

[13] *See, e.g.,* Gordon 2004, *cf.* Simpson 1975a, Stoljar 1975. For a good example of historical explanation (in competition with philosophical explanation), from tort law, see Calabresi 1998: 113–114.

[14] Kraus 2002a.

a single and unitary topic when we talk about (the philosophical foundations of) contract law?

As earlier mentioned, the rules of contract law vary from jurisdiction to jurisdiction at quite basic levels: for example, regarding which promises or exchanges it will enforce and which it will not,[15] with common law legal systems using the doctrine of consideration and some supplementary doctrines to make the primary division between enforceable and unenforceable promises and transactions, and some of the Continental European legal systems using somewhat different criteria, for example, the "cause" of French and German law.[16] Additionally, a basic cleavage is seen between those systems whose doctrinal and remedial rules strongly encourage the performance of contracts (e.g., by general availability of specific performance remedies,[17] or by granting higher compensation for intentional breach of contract) and those systems (e.g., the American system) that generally treat performance and the payment of (purely compensatory) damages as equally acceptable.[18] Even the ability of winning parties to gain their attorney's fees from the losing party – although this may be a rule of private litigation generally rather than a rule of contract law in particular[19] – necessarily affect the nature of contract law (by affecting the ability of parties to be fully compensated for breach on the one hand and by creating strong disincentives to enforcement suits on the other hand).[20]

[15] *See* Chapters 2, Section C, and 3, Section B.
[16] *See, e.g.,* Marsh 1994: 95–111, *cf.* Gordley 2001a.
[17] *But cf.* Lando & Rose 2004, where the authors offer evidence that specific performance is becoming an increasingly rare remedy in Denmark, Germany, and France, and they relate this trend to the administrative costs of running a system where specific performance is an available and attractive alternative remedy.
[18] *See* Chapter 6.
[19] *Cf. Zapata Hermanos Sucesores, S.A. v. Hearthside Baking Company, Inc.,* 313 F.3d 385 (7th Cir. 2002) (refusing to grant attorney's fees as general damages in a CISG action, in part because rules regarding prevailing parties' right to such fees is a general rule rather than a rule of contract law). Smith suggests that we look at contract law only as the rules creating and defining rights, with the remedial rules seen as part of another area of law, probably tort law. Smith 2000: 123, Smith 2004: 103–105; *cf.* Smith 2008, 2009. In *Zapata, supra,* Judge Posner similarly states that "no one would say that French contract law differs from U.S. *because* the winner of a contract suit in France is entitled to be reimbursed by the loser, and in the U.S. not." *Zapata,* 313 F.3d at 388. I respectfully disagree with Prof. Smith and Judge Posner (although I am not disagreeing with the outcome in *Zapata*), preferring the legal realist insight that one cannot understand the nature of a (contractual) right separate from the remedies that are available to protect it.
[20] Even seemingly smaller differences might have significant effects on one's view of a contract law system: for example, whether breaching parties (who did not meet a standard of "substantial performance") should be able to sue for restitutionary compensation, *compare Lancellotti v. Thomas,* 491 A.2d 117 (Pa. Super. Ct. 1985) (applying the *Restatement* standard allowing recovery) *with Mechanical Piping Services, Inc. v. Jayeff Construction Corp.,* 626 N.Y.S.2d 547, 547 (2d Dept. 1995) (following the classical common law rule that no recovery is allowed); whether damages for emotional distress should be available at least in classes of commercial contracts where they are reasonably foreseeable, *compare Erlich v. Menezes,* 21 Cal.4th 543, 981 P.2d 978, 87 Cal. Rptr. 2d 886 (1999) (reaffirming general U.S. rule of no emotional distress damages for breach of contract in a case involving faulty construction of a house) *with Farley v. Skinner,* [2001] 3 W.L.R. 899 (H.L.) (allowing nonpecuniary

The alternative position suggested here is that contract theory should focus on a single legal system at a particular period of time; thus, there should usually be different theories for different countries (although how different each country's theory would be would depend on how divergent the rules and practices are).

To have a theory of contract law assumes that there is a single entity "contract law" to have a theory about. In one sense, this is trivially true: almost every American law school (and many schools outside the United States) has a course called Contract Law;[21] there are a large number of casebooks and treatises purporting to discuss contract law; and the American Law Institute created two different "Restatements" of contract law, the most recent in 1979. The fact that legal materials can be conveniently categorized together for the purpose of teaching a course or writing a textbook may give some evidence of a unity sufficient to ground a general theory. Additionally, one might note that although there are certainly differences in the rules in different jurisdictions, there is also a great deal of similarity, more than one might expect from mere historical accident. This point should not be discounted, and theorists should consider possible sources of convergence. One might look to the influence of particular approaches – the Roman law approach for civil law countries that consciously built from that model and the English approach for countries that once had colonial ties or other significant ties to England. Other arguments explaining convergence might be more functional: contract law converges where it becomes clear that a certain set of rules works best in responding to (common) economic problems and pressures. Nonetheless, although the similarities should be taken into account in any theoretical discussion, this chapter (and this book) concludes that theories focused on the doctrinal rules of particular legal systems are still to be preferred to general, universal, or conceptual theories of contract law.

Michael Moore has suggested that contract law might be thought of as a "functional kind" – a collection of all the rules that have the function of "getting people to keep their promissory obligations, obligations that are distinct from the non-promissory obligations dealt with by criminal law and torts."[22] It might be possible

---

damages for the sale of house case where the object of entire contract was to give pleasure, relaxation, or peace of mind); whether promissory estoppel can ground a cause of action or is only available to prevent enforcement of existing rights, *compare Restatement (Second) of Contracts* § 90(1) (promissory estoppel cause of action) *with Combe v. Combe* [1951] 2 K.B. 215 (under English law, reliance on the promise no basis for enforcing the promise); and whether there is a general common law requirement of good faith and fair dealing (in cases other than the sale of goods cases covered by UCC, art 2), see *Subaru of Am., Inc. v. David McDavid Nissan, Inc.*, 84 S.W.3d 212, 225–26 (Tex. 2002) (Texas is one of the few states to deny that there is an obligation of good faith for non-UCC cases).

21 Though there are also many transactions that look like contracts but tend to be dealt with in courses other than contract law courses (e.g., the treatment of leases and sales of property primarily in property law and real estate transaction courses, the discussion of premarital and separation agreements primarily in family law courses).

22 Moore 1990: 131 (footnote omitted). Moore offers that there are some areas of law (he suggests administrative law as an example) that are neither functional kinds nor natural kinds but arbitrary collections of topics. *Id.* at 132.

to maintain this view of the "functional kind" of contract law while still noting the problems (discussed in Chapter 8) of a promise-based theory of contract law, although some work would need to be done to reconcile the two.

The larger question remains as before: whether focusing on what is common among all these different forms of transactions, while downplaying what is distinct, creates more insight than distortion.

C. GENERAL CONTRACT LAW

One might concede that contract law theory should be focused on a particular legal system (or at least on connected legal systems, like England, the United States, and the Commonwealth countries, whose contract law systems developed from common roots), but still believe that a general contract law theory is appropriate in that particular system or group of systems. Using the example of American contract law, this chapter argues that the diversity in a single contract law system is usually too great to justify a general theory of contract law, in which one or two principles explain or justify the entire doctrinal area.

Contract law discussions too frequently begin from the assumption that there is a single theory or approach that is appropriate for everything that falls under the rubric "contract." (This may in fact be the appropriate conclusion at the end of the day, but it is a dubious point to take for granted.) The basic question is whether different kinds of agreements are subject to different theories of obligation. Are there basic differences, from the perspective of contract law theory, between, for example, commercial transaction between merchants, simple exchanges between individuals, and premarital agreements setting property rights at divorce?[23]

As noted in Chapter 7, in most American jurisdictions, there are areas of contract law, defined by subject matter, which carry distinctive rules (special rules of formation, mandatory terms, performance, or remedies): e.g., landlord-tenant, employment contracts, charitable pledges, construction contracts, franchise agreements, pension promises, and insurance agreements.[24] (While noting the diversity of categories, and the distinctive rules and principles that often go with them, one must, of course, also be aware of a contrary theoretical error, of taking such nominalism

[23] Schwartz & Scott (2003) argue that the set of contract rules that apply to good-sized businesses dealing commercially with one another can and should differ from the contract rules applied in other contexts – for example, when one of the parties is a consumer, or when two individuals are entering a marriage-related agreement (a comparable argument is offered by Farber 2000). The argument is that many of the factors that justify certain protective rules do not apply when discussing the commercial dealings of firms: cognitive biases, protection from overreaching, protection of autonomy interests, and so on.

[24] At least one casebook teaches contract law in a way that emphasizes the different rules for different kinds of agreements. Macaulay, Braucher, Kidwell & Whitford 2011. (I am told that many of the contract law textbooks from a generation or two back were similarly organized.)

too far.[25]) A different sort of division might be suggested, based on the process preceding formation: distinguishing, for example, between agreements that are the result of detailed negotiation and "adhesion contracts."[26]

To some extent, mainstream contract thinking, if not mainstream contract theorizing, recognizes the fact of diversity, for the *Restatement (Second) of Contracts* itself recognizes forms of recovery (promissory estoppel, § 90, and promissory restitution, § 86) other than those based on breach of contract (see Chapter 3, Section D); and most contract law courses include not only those alternative grounds of recovery but also some discussion of unjust enrichment claims arising from contract-like interactions.[27] Recognition of the fact and significance of diversity may also be indicated by the way that, as noted, certain categories of contracts (e.g., insurance policies, landlord-tenant agreements, premarital contracts) are subject to separate regulation (by statute, agency regulation, and/or case law).[28]

One could, of course, argue that forms of action that deviate too much from core contract law examples (however one defines them) simply should be understood as "not contract." Although this is in principle a legitimate move, one must be careful that a theory is not made true simply by exiling all contrary evidence.[29]

Michael Moore has nicely summarized the motivations of theorizing at the level of areas of law: it is in part entailed by the moral requirement that we treat like cases alike; it helps determine the proper outcome in novel cases; and it is entailed by our assumption – or hope – that the law coherently pursues worthy objectives.[30] These are important moral (and psychological) forces pushing us toward having a general theory for an area of law, but it may be that some areas are too various and inconsistent to ground a general theory, despite those reasons for such a theory.[31]

[25] The Supreme Court once notoriously commented: "We deal here with the [constitutional] law of billboards." *Metromedia, Inc. v. City of San Diego*, 453 U.S. 490, 501 (1981), whereas Frank Easterbrook (quoting Gerhard Casper) warns us against the equivalent of looking for "the law of the horse." Easterbrook 1996: 207. We also have Justice Holmes's famous anecdote: "There is a story of a Vermont justice of the peace before whom a suit was brought by one farmer against another for breaking a churn. The justice took time to consider, and then said that he had looked through the statutes and could not find nothing about churns, and gave judgment for the defendant." Holmes 1897: 474–475. In summary, one can easily go too far in focusing on narrow categories rather than general principles.

[26] Adhesion contracts are discussed in Chapter 8, Section A.

[27] E.g., Farnsworth 2004: § 2.20, at 99–106, Knapp, Crystal & Prince 2007: 215–301.

[28] Additionally, some theorists offer arguments that there are categories of law that are usually considered separate from contract law that should be more properly treated as a subset of contract (e.g., corporate law as a nexus of contracts (Easterbrook & Fischel 1989)). Also, negotiable instruments, mortgages, and secured transactions are usually taught in separate courses, although such transactions would seem to be, or to have similarities with, contracts.

[29] *See, e.g.*, Kraus 2002a: 706 n. 38, 716–717 (discussing Fried), Oman 2005a (criticizing Smith).

[30] Moore 1990, 2000.

[31] In Moore 1990, the author discusses considerations regarding a general theory of criminal law. My text does not deny the possibility, value, or persuasiveness of theories of doctrinal law generally – it focuses only on contract law – and I think that there are good reasons to believe that other areas of

D. CONTRACT AND LAW

In some ways, the question of whether one can or should have a theory about contract law generally parallels the question of whether there can and should be a single theory about the nature of law.

As contract law is a subset of law, it is not surprising that a similar analysis might apply to both. For example, both are social products and thus seem less obvious candidates for theories of their nature than natural kinds like "gold."[32] And, for both, there would likely be resistance to a claim that the social practices were instantiations of some Platonic "Idea." It is at least tenable that whatever sorts of arguments ground conceptual arguments or general theories at the level of the nature of law would also ground such theories and arguments at the level of doctrinal areas (and vice versa).[33]

Joseph Raz has argued that law is a part of a community's collective self-understanding.[34] Whatever the merits of that claim, it would seem significantly more tenable than a comparable claim that contract or the doctrines of contract law were an integral part of our communal self-understanding.[35]

The three major challenges to a unitary general theory of law are (1) that conceptual theory has no place to play in jurisprudence (or elsewhere in philosophy) and that it should be replaced by a naturalist and/or empirical analysis;[36] (2) that there is no single "[our] concept of law" sufficiently precise or agreed upon to ground such a theory;[37] and (3) (a somewhat different point) that there are a number of competing alternative theories of law, selection among which requires a moral or political argument.[38] It appears that all three lines of argument might be equally raised against a general theory of contract law.

In raising doubts about general theories of contract law, it is not that anyone questions that there are rules about which agreements and promises will be enforced by official state norms and state institutions. And most would concede that these rules have a certain intellectual coherence (within limits) and some stability over time. Additionally, there are obvious similarities between the rules that are applied to promises and agreements in different states of the United States, and some, if

---

law (perhaps criminal law or perhaps tort law) are better candidates for general theories than contract law is. However, I leave that for others to show.

[32] On natural kinds, see Putnam 1975: 215–271; on the potential application of natural kinds analysis to law, see Bix 1993: 162–171.

[33] Cf. Zipursky 2005, arguing for applying his "pragmatic conceptualism" both to theories of tort law and to general jurisprudence.

[34] Raz 1996, 2005.

[35] There are other important views about conceptual analysis (e.g., Zipursky 2000, 2005), but it is not clear why or how any of them would justify a significantly different response to the challenge presented here – the argument that the variety of practices within and across jurisdictions makes any attempt to create an overarching theory of contract law unlikely to succeed.

[36] See Leiter 2003, 2007.

[37] Cf. Bix 2007a.

[38] Perry 1995, 1998. The contrary view (see Coleman 2001: 197–210, Kramer 1999: 239–253) is that the basis for selection is theoretical and/or explanatory rather than moral and/or political.

frequently weaker, similarities between the rules applied in the United States and in other countries. However, the question is whether these points of convergence are sufficiently numerous and the extent of coherence sufficiently strong to justify a single general theory. Nonetheless, as has been argued in Chapter 8 and this chapter, there remains too much divergence within and among contract law(s) to justify a general and universal theory of contract.[39]

E. CONSEQUENCES

The basic position of this chapter is that there is no general or universal theory of contract law. Assuming that this is correct, what would follow? Michael Moore has pointed out the beneficial role general theories can play in guiding judicial decision making and in making the area of law fairer (in the sense of being more consistent across cases).[40] Some of this may be lost when there is no general theory for all of (American) contract law, but I think the loss would be modest, given that one could (and should) still have theories of areas of or within contract law.

F. NOTE ON PROVING A NEGATIVE

In this chapter, I have argued that there is no single general and universal theory of contract law. In a sense, this involves an assertion of a negative – that a particular truth does not exist, or a particular approach will not work – and it is well known that proving a negative is a difficult task.

In certain unusual sets of circumstances, it might be possible to show that an alternative is conceptually or logically impossible, but there is no reason to believe that contract law theory is one of those unusual sets of circumstances. All that is available is to present the arguments for why a narrower and more particular theory of law will be superior to the likely general and universal theory alternatives.

And one cannot rely simply on asserting that the other side of the argument (here, supporting a general and universal theory of contract law) has the burden of proof and has not met it.[41] One must show that one's own alternative (or class of alternatives) is better than what is being rejected. I hope that this text has at least begun to make that showing.

---

[39] In coming to a similar conclusion, Nigel Simmonds argues that general theories of private law areas are simply efforts to overcome the dissensus and compromises in doctrinal areas by rising to a sufficiently vague and abstract principle. Simmonds argues that this misses the significance of what is going on in the doctrinal areas: "The ability of private law to occupy an area of convergence between diverse moral theories without clearly articulating any one such theory, and without levitating to a plane of abstraction remote from the resolution of concrete disputes, may be the very feature that makes private law a significant element in those structures that make dissensus tolerable." Simmonds 1997: 137.

[40] Moore 1990, 2000.

[41] I recognize that there may be places in the text where such an argument from burden of proof might seems to be implied. I disown any such line of argument and apologize for any place where the text appears to imply it.

G. NOTE ON RIGHTS AND REMEDIES

The issue regarding the relation between rights and remedies is a perennial one.[42] In the early history of Western private law, there arguably were only remedies. Jurists under both Roman law and medieval English law "started life with a list of transactions which were actionable through the procedural forms within which they had to work, rather than with a general principle of accountability."[43] Advocates had to claim whatever peculiar set of facts warranted the remedy they were seeking. Advocates, judges, and commentators in those periods did not speak of anything comparable to a contract law right.[44] Peter Stein has located an important part of the origin of our modern ideas about legal rights in the work of Hugo Donellus (1527–1591).[45] In contrast with the Roman law and old English writ approach of a combination of a fact situation with a specified remedy, Donellus spoke instead in broader, more abstract terms, of the plaintiff having a right that grounded his or her claim to a remedy.

In a sense, my argument here seems a step backward: away from the general rights rubric of modern law and back toward thinking of law as granting specific remedies to a pleaded combination of facts. In advocating this position, I am following a basic lesson of the American legal realists: it is an error to view a legal right completely abstracted from the remedy the legal system will make available for its violation.[46] Under this approach, to say that one has a (contractual) right means different things depending on what kind of remedy one can receive in court for that right: specific performance, full compensation for one's expected benefit, a small fraction of that expectation (as when damages are severely reduced as a result of doctrines like mitigation[47] and certainty[48]), and so on.[49]

---

[42] For a recent contribution, made in the context of discussing contract law, see Friedmann 2005.

[43] Simpson 1975a: 186. He adds: "Indeed for most purposes it was not in the least necessary that they should do more." *Id.* at 187.

[44] *See* Gordley 1990: 371: "Roman law was a law of particular contracts, each with its own rules as to when it became binding." Of course, what was true of Roman law was, if anything, more true of the medieval English writ system: where particular remedies were available tied to a plaintiff's ability to fit the claim within quite specific parameters. *See generally* Simpson 1975.

[45] Stein 1993.

[46] *E.g.*, Llewellyn 1931a: 1244. Llewellyn, in a different article, went further, arguing that one should keep in mind not only the remedy nominally available for the violation of a particular right but also how the practical availability of that remedy is affected, such as by the delays, costs, and uncertainties involved in obtaining the remedy. Llewellyn 1930: 437–438.

[47] Thus, if one has a fixed number of items to sell, and more buyers than items, then a breach of an agreement to purchase may yield only minor, incidental damages. *Cf.* Murray 2011: § 123, at 782–785. *See generally* Chapter 6, Section B.

[48] *See* Chapter 6, Section B. One subcategory of uncertainty or speculation that is in some jurisdictions treated as a per se rule holds that new businesses will not be allowed to claim lost profits; however, some jurisdictions now allow plaintiffs in such cases to at least try to show their lost profits with sufficient certainty. Murray 2011: § 122, at 771–773.

[49] The basic point goes back at least to Holmes: "One of the many evil effects of the confusion between legal and moral ideas . . . is that theory is apt to get the cart before the horse, and to consider the right or the duty as something existing apart from and independent of the consequences of its breach, to

One might point out that the remedy available for a given set of facts is often uncertain prior to court determination (and that there were periods in the history of contract law where the jury's determination of damages was relatively unconstrained by rules or judicial oversight[50]). However, this does not prove any general conclusion, although it is an important point to be incorporated: the nature of a legal right may entail significant uncertainty as to what can be recovered for breach.

One need not deny that, at the level of general moral and legal theory, there is a point to thinking about rights as separate from their associated duties and remedies. Thinking of rights separately from duties and remedies helps emphasize the way that rights can be the justification (in policy discussions or judicial opinions) for new duties and remedies.[51] Additionally, a citizen taking a Hartian "internal point of view" toward the law[52] would want to know her rights and duties (without regard to the remedies attached to them) so as to know what she ought to do.[53]

However, I think that these insights do not foreclose a closer association of right with remedy in one's theorizing about a substantive area of law, like contract law. I would add that the argument in this chapter in no way entails, or relies on, either a strong skepticism about rights or a belief (like that of Alf Ross[54]) that rights are nothing more than shorthand statements of the connection between facts and legal remedies. One need not be a skeptic about rights generally to think that it might be both more accurate and more productive, in the context of thinking about contract law, to believe that analysis should define (contract) rights in terms of what remedies are made available, rather than argue that one starts with (contract) rights and then argue about which remedies should be used to protect those rights.

In law and economics analysis, it is common to speak about how some entitlements are protected by "property rules" (the entitlement cannot be taken without the consent of the entitlement holder) or by "liability rules" (involuntary transfer of the entitlement can occur, but the entitlement holder must be compensated at the entitlement's market value).[55] Under this analysis, one might comment that one can sensibly focus on entitlements and treat how the entitlement is protected as being a secondary matter. In contrast, it makes a great deal of difference, say, to a property owner whether his or her property can be taken away without the owner's consent

---

which certain sanctions are added afterward. But . . . a legal duty so called is nothing but a prediction that if a man does or omits certain things he will be made to suffer in that or that way by judgment of the court; – and so of a legal right." Holmes 1897: 458; for his views specifically on contract law, see *id.*: 462.

50 Simpson 1975: 549–551.
51 E.g.., Raz 1986: 170–171.
52 Hart 1994.
53 I am indebted to Seana Shiffrin for this point.
54 E.g., Ross 1957.
55 Calabresi & Melamed 1972.

(with or without market value compensation – especially as many people value land, homes, or personal effects at far higher than the price the market might put on them).

The current (surface) thinking about legal rights and remedies offers supporting evidence for both sides of the debate under consideration. On the one hand, both legal education and legal practice still often think in broad categories – contract, tort, property, and so on – and those working in comparative law[56] implicitly affirm the application of these broad concepts across jurisdictions, which suggests some unifying essence underlying any differences. As international gatherings on contract law and theory indicate, we can sensibly talk across national boundaries about something common called "contracts" without fearing that we are entirely talking past one another. That does seem to indicate some common ground (whether just the category of enforceable promises, agreements, or transactions).

At the same time, both educators and practitioners are also well aware that one must focus as much on divergences within a doctrinal area as on similarities: for example, within (American) contract law, no practitioner would assume expertise on the law of employment, residential leases, franchise agreements, insurance agreements, or domestic agreements simply because he or she had knowledge of basic contract law principles.[57] There are too many differences in rules, principles, and even basic starting assumptions. For example, as discussed in Chapter 7, American state and federal statutes and regulations frequently impose mandatory terms in employment agreements and insurance agreements (and, in some states, franchise agreements); in many American states, premarital agreements are subject to significant fairness review; and so on. These quite different points about the interpretation and enforcement of these forms of agreement could not be derived from general principles of contract law (or from metaprinciples like autonomy, reliance, and efficiency). The divergence in rules and principles becomes much more pronounced across national boundaries: one's fluency in American contract law rules means relatively little when one is asked about the rules and principles of, say, French or German or Argentine contract law.

Focusing on abstract rights rather than concrete remedies, and overlooking the way that both remedies and rules vary markedly across state borders (and even more markedly across national borders) gives an impression of unity to contract law, an impression that a closer focus on contract practice undermines.

---

[56] E.g., Reimann & Zimmermann 2006.

[57] There remain casebooks more focused on "situation types" than on general principles. E.g., Macaulay, Braucher, Kidwell & Whitford, 2011. This is a modern echo of "Leon Green's groundbreaking 1931 textbook on torts [that] was organized not by the traditional *doctrinal* categories (e.g., negligence, intentional torts, strict liability), but rather by the factual scenarios – the 'situation types' – in which harms occur: for example 'surgical operations,' 'traffic and transportation,' and the like. The premise of this approach was that there was no general law of torts *per se*, but rather predictable patterns of torts decisions for each recurring situation-type that courts encounter." Leiter 2005: 55.

H. ONE OR MANY THEORIES (REVISITED)

1. *Essential and Accidental*

In the terms of classical Western philosophy, someone might argue that I am mistaking accidental properties for essentials.[58] Contract law is contract law everywhere, where the minor differences of rules, procedures, and remedies should not blind one to the shared essence. Of course, the argument would continue, there are small changes in form and procedure as one moves from one system to another: the *stipulatio* of Roman law varies from the wax seal of old English law, and the various forms of action of the old English law differ in obvious ways from the pleading rules used in modern American breach of contract cases. This view would insist, however, that it is dogmatic nominalism to insist on a nongeneral, nonuniversal theory at the first sign of difference.

To this argument I would respond that the differences over time and across jurisdictions for the types of arrangements we call "contracts" are more than trivial deviations of form. Such basic matters as whether and when a ("naked") promise can be enforced, even without consideration or reliance; when a modification of an agreement will be enforceable; and when a wronged party can obtain a court order requiring performance vary considerably from jurisdiction to jurisdiction.[59] I think that there is at least a tenable case that what we are dealing with here are not just trivial variations but differences in essential character.

2. *Deciding between General and Particular Theories*

On what basis – on what criteria – would one judge the question before us: whether legally enforceable agreements are best thought of as a single category, and a proper subject for a general and universal theory, or, instead, are best thought of as a loose cluster, where the best subject for theorizing is the contract law of a particular jurisdiction, or even subtopics within that contract law, at a particular time.[60]

The first focus, I would assert, should be whether more is gained than lost by a particular (type of) theory. Do we explain more (or, alternatively, do we distort more) by downplaying variety or by discounting underlying commonality?[61] My inclination is to say, for example, that an agreement that is enforceable through an

---

[58] *See* Aristotle 1984: 101b11–102b26, at 169–170.

[59] E.g., Gordley 2001b.

[60] This inquiry overlaps, but could be distinct from, the question as to whether contract law rules are best developed in such a way that there are general principles applied to all kinds of agreements, or as largely separate sets of rules for different sorts of transactions. For example, Oman (2009, 2010) argues that maintaining more general principles, rather than separate rules for different sorts of transactions, has the benefit of preventing "capture" by particular interest groups.

[61] I recognize that characterizing the question this way leaves open the possibility that there is no fact of the matter to which the theory must respond; or, alternatively, that even if there is a fact of the

order of specific performance (an order to do what was promised, backed up by the potential judicial order of contempt for noncompliance) is different in kind from a promise in which the only remedy for violation is money damages;[62] I would go further and argue that a promise backed up by full compensation for loss is different in kind from a promise backed up by compensation that inevitably will fall far short of full compensation (as a result of having to pay one's own attorney's fees and the various constraints on recovery). And, under this view, theories that try to put agreements with such different remedies (and different rules) into a single category distort more than they explain.

I realize that these claims may seem to some to be just as puzzling, or just as arbitrary, as the famous American contract law case that held that a fertile cow is essentially different than a sterile cow (even when it is the same identified cow).[63] Are these just bald assertions about which reasonable persons could – and do – have different intuitions? (A barren cow is and/or is not essentially different from a fertile cow; and a promise enforceable by an order of specific performance is and/or is not essentially different from one enforceable by full or partial compensation for losses.) However, I am not sure that the question of whether a theory succeeds at explanation or fails by distorting the underlying subject matter can be tested at anything other than an intuitive (and anecdotal) level.

At the least, one might assert the following as a fallback position. Perhaps universal and/or general theories and local theories each offer partial perspectives, portions of the complex overall truth. Under this view, it is not that general and/or universal theories are entirely false but that they hide aspects of reality. And in a world of private law theory, where general and/or universal theories of contract law dominate, it is important that the arguments for local theories be heard as well.

3. Why Does It Matter?

If there are reasonable arguments both for and against my position (i.e., both for having a general and/or universal theory of contract law and for having local theories), and if the conclusions each way are either grounded on esoteric ontological claims

---

matter, one might intentionally choose a theory inconsistent with the fact of the matter, if that theory otherwise, and overall, had better consequences.

[62] As Horacio Spector comments: "The above difference [between compensation as the usual remedy in Common Law systems for breach of contract and the general availability of specific performance in Civil Law systems] indicates that civilian contract law and Anglo-American contract law are amenable to different sorts of explanations." Spector 2004: 530. Spector goes on to argue that the Common Law approach to contracts should be seen as growing out of a pragmatic approach, and is thus amenable to economic explanation, while the Civil Law approach grew out of an autonomy or promissory approach, and is not amenable to an economic explanation. Spector 2004: 530–532.

[63] This is, of course, *Sherwood v. Walker*, 66 Mich. 568, 33 N.W. 919 (1887), discussed in Chapter 3, Section E. *See also* Murray 2011: § 92, at 501–503.

or perhaps have no grounding at all, someone might understandably wonder why the debate matters at all.

One response is to repeat the claim of Chapter 8: the portrayal of the diverse contract world as exemplifying a single phenomenon frequently may work both to distort the underlying reality and (at least sometimes) to legitimate unjust practices. (I should make clear that I am not accusing any theorist of intentionally distorting or legitimating unjust practices, but I do think that these are sometimes the unintended consequences of such theories.)

I think it is important to realize that the theorizing here is not only a matter of academics talking among themselves. The way contract law (and other areas of law) is understood sometimes filters down (and across): through the discussion of the law in court decisions, legislative debates, and the discussion of legal rights to and among the public. And we all know how far public perceptions of the law – including but hardly limited to contracts and commercial law – vary from the actual legal rules. I would assert that general and/or universal theories of contract law tend to encourage such misunderstandings.[64] For example, courts and commentators in the era of *Lochner v. New York*[65] treated the negotiations between employers and employees as matters of freedom of contract indistinguishable – in policy and morality – from two merchants negotiating at arm's length. And in modern times, just to offer one more example, software manufacturers used the image, ideal, and rhetoric of freedom of contract to support a proposed uniform rule that would have allowed the imposition of one-sided terms on consumers unaware of the terms or the fact that they were entering an agreement.[66]

Conclusion

Skepticism about the tenability of a single general and/or universal theory for contract law is hardly new.[67] However, given the number of prominent theorists who propose or defend general theories of contract law, it is an issue worth revisiting.[68]

Given the significant diversity of rules and approaches, both between different countries (and even, to some extent, among different states of the United States)

---

[64] Though I admit I have mostly anecdotal evidence to support my supposition.

[65] 198 U.S. 45 (1905).

[66] This was the example of the Uniform Computer Information Transactions Act (UCITA). *See* Braucher 2003; Winn & Bix 2006: 180–181.

[67] Recent exponents of similar views include Hillman 1988; Braucher 1990: 701 n. 14; D. Patterson 1991; DiMatteo 1995; Gordley 1996; Simmonds 1997; Oman 2005a; Leib 2005; DiMatteo, Prentice, Morant & Barnhizer 2007; Klass 2008; and Dagan 2011; *cf.* Leff 1970. (It was Justice Holmes who wrote: "Sir James Stephen is not the only writer whose attempts to analyze legal ideas have been confused by striving for a useless quintessence of all systems, instead of an accurate anatomy of one." Holmes 1897: 475.) Randy Barnett (1999) has characterized such skepticism as characteristic of an earlier generation too attached to legal realism.

[68] Of course, it is also important given the nature of the series to which this book is a contribution.

and within a particular jurisdiction between different types of agreements, it seems difficult to believe that a single overarching theory can have explanatory value that outweighs whatever distorting effects it would inevitably have.[69]

Of course, even if it is true that one should not construct general theories about contract law, and that the proper focus is the contract law of a particular legal system (at a particular time), this does not mean that the theory for one legal system's contract law will be of no use in discussing the contract law of different legal systems. Another legal system's contract law theory is particularly likely to be valuable where the two systems have a common historical origin (as with England and the United States), or where the developments in one system are considered influential by officials and commentators in the other (as among the Commonwealth countries).

The focus of this book has been to offer a theory localized to a particular country, the United States,[70] at a particular time (the early years of the twenty-first century), and often localized further, with theories that focused on particular areas of doctrine, or even specific doctrinal rules. However, it is important to discover the extent to which the local focus must be tempered by an understanding of more general principles, general purposes, or general tendencies that may cause different sets of rules and principles to converge.

SUGGESTED FURTHER READING

Peter Alces, *A Theory of Contract Law: Empirical Insights and Moral Psychology* (Oxford: Oxford University Press, 2011).

Peter Benson (ed.), *The Theory of Contract Law: New Essays* (Cambridge: Cambridge University Press, 2001).

Stephen A. Smith, *Contract Theory* (Oxford: Oxford University Press, 2004).

---

[69] This is not to say that the label and category "contract law" cannot continue to serve a purpose in creating a convenient collection of topics of workable size for law school courses, legal treatises, or books like this!

[70] With the possibilities that aspects of this theory would need to be adjusted as one moved between state jurisdictions, to the extent that the state laws varied sufficiently.

Bibliography

Abraham, Kenneth S. (2010), *Insurance Law and Regulation: Cases and Materials*, 5th ed. New York: Foundation Press.

Adler, Barry E. (1999), "The Questionable Ascent of *Hadley v. Baxendale*," *Stanford Law Review*, vol. 51, pp. 1547–1589.

Alces, Peter A. (2007), "The Moral Impossibility of Contract," *William & Mary Law Review*, vol. 48, pp. 1647–1671.

——— (2008), "Unintelligent Design in Contract," *University of Illinois Law Review*, vol. 2008, pp. 505–555.

——— (2011), *A Theory of Contract Law: Empirical Insights and Moral Psychology*. Oxford: Oxford University Press.

Alexander, Larry A. (1993), "Trouble on Track Two: Incidental Regulations of Speech and Free Speech Theory," *Hastings Law Journal*, vol. 44, pp. 921–962.

American Law Institute (2010), *Principles of the Law: Software Contracts*. American Law Institute Publishers.

Anderson, Eugene R. & Fournier, James J. (1998), "Why Courts Enforce Insurance Policyholders' Objectively Reasonable Expectations of Insurance Coverage," *Connecticut Insurance Law Journal*, vol. 5, pp. 335–424.

Angelo, A. P. & Ellinger, E. P. (1992), "Unconscionable Contracts: A Comparative Study of Approaches in England, France, Germany, and the United States," *Loyola of Los Angeles International and Comparative Law Journal*, vol. 14, pp. 455–506.

Aquinas, Thomas (1947), *The Summa Theologica* (Benziger Bros. ed., Fathers of the English Dominican Province, trans.), available at http://www.ccel.org/a/aquinas/summa/.

Aristotle (1984), *The Complete Words of Aristotle*, ed. Jonathan Barnes. Princeton, NJ: Princeton University Press.

Atiyah, P. S. (1978), "Contracts, Promises and the Law of Obligations," *Law Quarterly Review*, vol. 94, pp. 193–223.

——— (1979), *The Rise and Fall of Freedom of Contract*. Oxford, UK: Clarendon Press.

——— (1981), *Promises, Morals, and Law*. Oxford, UK: Clarendon Press.

——— (1986), *Essays on Contract*. Oxford, UK: Clarendon Press.

Ayres, Ian (2003), "Valuing Modern Contract Scholarship," *Yale Law Journal*, vol. 112, pp. 881–901.

———— (2006), "Ya-Huh: There Are and Should Be Penalty Defaults," *Florida State University Law Review*, vol. 33, pp. 589–617.

Ayres, Ian & Gertner, Robert (1989), "Filling Gaps in Incomplete Contracts: An Economic Theory of Default Rules," *Yale Law Journal*, vol. 99, pp. 87–130.

———— (1999), "Majoritarian v. Minoritarian Defaults," *Stanford Law Review*, vol. 51, pp. 1591–1613.

Baker, J. H. (1981), "Origins of the 'Doctrine' of Consideration, 1535–1585," in *On the Laws and Customs of England: Essays in Honor of Samuel E. Thorne* (Morris S. Arnold, Thomas A. Green, Sally A. Scully & Stephen D. White, eds., Chapel Hill: University of North Carolina Press), pp. 336–358.

———— (2002), *An Introduction to English Legal History*, 4th ed. London: Butterworths.

———— (2003), *The Oxford History of the Laws of England. Vol. 6, 1483–1558*. Oxford: Oxford University Press.

Baker, Lynn A. (1988), "'I Think I Do': Another Perspective on Consent and the Law," *Law, Medicine & Health Care*, vol. 16, pp. 256–260.

———— (1990), "Promulgating the Marriage Contract," *Journal of Law Reform*, vol. 23, pp. 217–264.

Bar-Gill, Oren (2008), "The Behavioral Economics of Consumer Contracts," *Minnesota Law Review*, vol. 92, pp. 749–802.

———— (2012), "Competition and Consumer Protection: A Behavioral Economics Account," in Swedish Competition Authority, *The Pros and Cons of Consumer Protection*, available at http://papers.ssrn.com/sol3/papers.cfm?abstract_id=1974499.

Barak, Aharon (2005), *Purposive Interpretation in Law*. Princeton, NJ: Princeton University Press.

Barbour, W. T. (1914), *The History of Contract in Early English Equity*. Oxford, UK: Clarendon Press (reprint; New York: Octagon Books, 1974).

Barnett, Randy E. (1986), "A Consent Theory of Contract," *Columbia Law Review*, vol. 86, pp. 269–321.

———— (1992a), "Some Problems with Contract as Promise," *Cornell Law Review*, vol. 77, pp. 1022–1033.

———— (1992b), "The Sound of Silence: Default Rules and Contractual Consent," *Virginia Law Review*, vol. 78, pp. 821–911.

———— (1999), "The Richness of Contract Theory," *Michigan Law Review*, vol. 97, pp. 1413–1429.

———— (2002), "Consenting to Form Contracts," *Fordham Law Review*, vol. 71, pp. 627–645.

———— (2010), *Contracts*. Oxford: Oxford University Press.

———— (2012), "Contract Is Not Promise; Contract Is Consent," *Suffolk Law Review*, vol. 45, pp. 647–665.

Barnhizer, Daniel D. (2010), "Context as Power: Defining the Field of Battle for Advantage in Contractual Interactions," *Wake Forest Law Review*, vol. 45, pp. 607–640.

Barton, John (1990a), "The Medieval Contract," in John Barton, ed., *Towards a General Law of Contract*. Berlin: Duncker & Humblot, pp. 15–37.

———— (1990b), "The Action on the Case," in John Barton, ed., *Towards a General Law of Contract*. Berlin: Duncker & Humblot, pp. 39–47.

Beatson, Jack & Friedmann, Daniel, eds. (1995), *Good Faith and Fault in Contract Law*. Oxford: Oxford University Press.

Bebchuk, Lucian A. & Posner, Richard A. (2006), "One-Sided Contracts in Competitive Consumer Markets," *Michigan Law Review*, vol. 104, pp. 827–835 (reprinted in Omri

Ben-Shahar, *Boilerplate: The Foundation of Market Contracts.* Cambridge: Cambridge University Press, 2007, pp. 3–11).

Ben-Shahar, Omri (2009), "A Bargaining Theory of Default Rules," *Columbia Law Review*, vol. 109, pp. 396–430.

———— (2011), "Fixing Unfair Contracts," *Stanford Law Review*, vol. 63, pp. 869–906.

Ben-Shahar, Omri & Porat, Ariel, eds. (2010), *Fault in American Contract Law.* Cambridge: Cambridge University Press.

Ben-Shahar, Omri & Schneider, Carl E. (2011), "The Failure of Mandated Disclosure," *University of Pennsylvania Law Review*, vol. 159, pp. 647–749.

Benson, Peter (1989), "Abstract Right and the Possibility of a Nondistributive Conception of Contract: Hegel and Contemporary Contract Theory," *Cardozo Law Review*, vol. 10, pp. 1077–1198.

———— (1995), "The Idea of a Public Basis of Justification for Contract," *Osgoode Hall Law Journal*, vol. 33, pp. 273–336.

———— (1996), "Contract," in Dennis Patterson, ed., *A Companion to Philosophy of Law and Legal Theory.* Oxford: Blackwell, pp. 24–56.

———— ed. (2001a), *The Theory of Contract Law: New Essays.* Cambridge: Cambridge University Press.

———— (2001b), "The Unity of Contract Law," in Peter Benson, ed., *The Theory of Contract Law: New Essays.* Cambridge: Cambridge University Press, pp. 118–205.

———— (2007), "Contract as a Transfer of Ownership," *William & Mary Law Review*, vol. 48, pp. 1673–1731.

———— (2011), "The Idea of Consideration," *University of Toronto Law Journal*, vol. 61, pp. 241–278.

Berman, Harold J. (2003), *Law and Revolution II: The Impact of the Protestant Reformations on the Western Legal Tradition.* Cambridge, MA: Harvard University Press.

———— (2005), "The Historical Foundations of Law," *Emory Law Journal*, vol. 54, pp. 13–24.

———— (2008), "The Christian Sources of General Contract Law," in John Witte Jr. & Frank S. Alexander, eds., *Christianity and Law: An Introduction.* Cambridge: Cambridge University Press, pp. 125–142.

Berner, Robert & Grow, Brian (2008), "Banks vs. Consumers (Guess Who Wins)," *Business Week*, June 5, 2008, pp. 72–79, available at http://www.businessweek.com/magazine/content/08_24/b4088072611398.htm.

Bernstein, Lisa (1996), "Merchant Law in a Merchant Court: Rethinking the Code's Search for Immanent Business Norms," *University of Pennsylvania Law Review*, vol. 144, pp. 1765–1821.

———— (1999), "The Questionable Empirical Basis of Article 2's Incorporation Strategy: A Preliminary Study," *University of Chicago Law Review*, vol. 66, pp. 710–780.

Birmingham, Robert L. (1970), "Breach of Contract, Damages Measures, and Economic Efficiency," *Rutgers Law Review*, vol. 24, pp. 273–292.

———— (1985), "Holmes on Peerless: *Raffles v. Wichelhaus* and the Objective Theory of Contract," *University of Pittsburgh Law Review*, vol. 47, pp. 183–204.

Bix, Brian (1993), *Law, Language, and Legal Determinacy.* Oxford, UK: Clarendon Press.

———— (1998), "Bargaining in the Shadow of Love: The Enforcement of Premarital Agreements and How We Think about Marriage," *William & Mary Law Review*, vol. 40, pp. 145–207.

———— (2002), "Natural Law: The Modern Tradition," in Jules Coleman & Scott Shapiro, eds., *The Oxford Handbook of Jurisprudence and Philosophy of Law.* Oxford: Oxford University Press, pp. 61–103.

_____ (2003), "Raz on Necessity," *Law and Philosophy*, vol. 22, pp. 537–559.

_____ (2005), "Legal Positivism," in Martin P. Golding & William A. Edmundson, eds., *The Blackwell Guide to the Philosophy of Law and Legal Theory*. Oxford, UK: Blackwell, pp. 29–49.

_____ (2007a), "Joseph Raz and Conceptual Analysis," *American Philosophical Association Newsletter on Philosophy and Law*, vol. 06, no. (2), pp. 1–7.

_____ (2007b), "Some Reflections on Contract Law Theory," *Problema*, vol. 1, pp. 143–201.

_____ (2008), "Contract Rights and Remedies, and the Divergence between Law and Morality," *Ratio Juris*, vol. 21, pp. 194–211.

_____ (2009), *Jurisprudence: Theory and Context*, 5th ed. London: Sweet & Maxwell.

_____ (2010), "Contracts," in Franklin G. Miller & Alan Wertheimer, eds., *The Ethics of Consent: Theory and Practice*. Oxford: Oxford University Press, 2010, pp. 251–279.

_____ (2011), "*Mahr* Agreements: Contracting in the Shadow of Family Law (and Religious Law) – A Comment on Oman's Article," *Wake Forest Law Review Online*, vol. 1, pp. 61–68, available at http://wakeforestlawreview.com.

_____ (2012), "Theories of Contract Law and Enforcing Promissory Morality: Comments on Charles Fried," *Suffolk Law Review*, vol. 45, pp. 719–734.

Bolton, Patrick & Dewatripont, Mathias (2005), *Contract Theory*. Cambridge, MA: MIT Press.

Boss, Amelia & Kilian, Wolfgang, eds. (2008), *The United Nations Convention on the Use of Electronic Communications in International Contracts: An In-Depth Guide and Sourcebook*. Alphen aan den Rijn, Netherlands: Wolters Kluwer.

Bouckaert, Boudewijn & De Geest, Gerrit, eds. (1996–2000) *Encyclopedia of Law and Economics*, http:encyclo.findlaw.com (Edward Elgar & University of Ghent).

Boyer, Benjamin F. (1952), "Promissory Estoppel: Principle from Precedents," parts 1 & 2, *Michigan Law Review*, vol. 50, pp. 639–674, 873–898.

Braucher, Jean (1990), "Contract versus Contractarianism: The Regulatory Role of Contract Law," *Washington and Lee Law Review*, vol. 47, pp. 697–739.

_____ (2000), "Delayed Disclosure in Consumer E-Commerce as an Unfair and Deceptive Practice," *Wayne Law Review*, vol. 46, pp. 1805–1867.

_____ (2003), "The Failed Promise of the UCITA Mass-Market Concept and Its Lesson for Policing Standard Form Contracts," *Journal for Small and Emerging Business Law*, vol. 7, pp. 393–423.

_____ (2004), "Amended Article 2 and the Decision to Trust the Courts: The Case against Enforcing Delayed Mass-Market Terms, Especially for Software," *Wisconsin Law Review*, vol. 2004, pp. 753–775.

_____ (2008), "Cowboy Contracts: The Arizona Supreme Court's Grand Tradition of Transactional Fairness," *Arizona Law Review*, vol. 50, pp. 191–226.

_____ (2012), "The Sacred and Profane Contracts Machine: The Complex Morality of Contract Law in Action," *Suffolk Law Review*, vol. 45, pp. 667–693.

Bridge, Michael G. (2003), "Uniformity and Diversity in the Law of International Sale," *Pace International Law Review*, vol. 15, pp. 55–89.

Bridgeman, Curtis (2005), "*Allegheny College* Revisited: Cardozo, Consideration, and Formalism in Context," *U.C. Davis Law Review*, vol. 39, pp. 149–186.

_____ (2007), "Reconciling Strict Liability with Corrective Justice in Contract Law," *Fordham Law Review*, vol. 75, pp. 3013–3040.

_____ (2009), "Contracts as Plans," *University of Illinois Law Review*, vol. 2009, pp. 341–401.

Brousseau, Eric & Glachant, Jean-Michel, eds. (2002), *The Economics of Contracts*. Cambridge: Cambridge University Press.

Brudner, Alan (1993), "Reconstructing Contracts," *University of Toronto Law Journal*, vol. 43, pp. 1–64.

Buckland, W. W. (1945), *Some Reflections on Jurisprudence*. Cambridge: Cambridge University Press.

———— (1963), *A Text-Book of Roman Law from Augustus to Justinian*, 3d ed., revised by Peter Stein. Cambridge: Cambridge University Press.

Buckley, F. H. (2005), *Just Exchange: A Theory of Contract*. New York: Routledge.

Burton, Steven J. (2009), *Elements of Contract Interpretation*. Oxford: Oxford University Press.

Butterfoss, Edwin & Blair, H. Allen (2010), "Where Is Emily Litella When You Need Her? The Unsuccessful Effort to Craft a General Theory of Promise for Benefit Received," *QLR* [*Quinnipiac Law Review*], vol. 28, pp. 385–429.

Calabresi, Guido (1998), "Supereditor or Translator: Comments on Coleman," in Brian Bix, ed., *Analyzing Law*. Oxford: Oxford University Press, pp. 107–115.

Calabresi, Guido & Melamed, A. D. (1972), "Property Rules, Liability Rules, and Inalienability: One View of the Cathedral," *Harvard Law Review*, vol. 85, pp. 1089–1128.

Cane, Peter (2007), "The General/Special Distinction in Criminal Law, Tort Law and Legal Theory," *Law and Philosophy*, vol. 26, pp. 465–500.

Charny, David (1990), "Nonlegal Sanctions in Commercial Relationships," *Harvard Law Review*, vol. 104, pp. 373–467.

———— (1991), "Hypothetical Bargains: The Normative Structure of Contract Interpretation," *Michigan Law Review*, vol. 89, pp. 1815–1879.

Childres, Robert (1970), "Conditions in the Law of Contracts," *New York University Law Review*, vol. 45, pp. 33–58.

CISG Advisory Council (2004), "Opinion No. 3: Parol Evidence Rule, Plain Meaning Rule, Contractual Merger Clause and the CISG," Oct. 22, 2004, available at http://www.cisgac.com.

Cohen, George M. (2009), "The Fault That Lies within Our Contract Law," *Michigan Law Review*, vol. 107, pp. 1445–1460.

Cohen, Morris R. (1933), "The Basis of Contract," *Harvard Law Review*, vol. 46, pp. 553–592.

Coleman, Jules (2001), *The Practice of Principle*. Oxford: Oxford University Press.

Collins, Hugh (1999), *Regulating Contracts*. Oxford: Oxford University Press.

———— ed. (2008), *Standard Contract Terms in Europe: A Basis for and a Challenge to European Contract Law*. Alphen aan den Rijn, Netherlands: Kluwer Law International.

Cooter, Robert (1985), "Unity in Tort, Contract, and Property: The Model of Precaution," *California Law Review*, vol. 73, pp. 1–51.

Cooter, Robert & Eisenberg, Melvin Aron (1985), "Damages for Breach of Contract," *California Law Review*, vol. 73, pp. 1432–1481.

Cordes, Albrecht (2005), "The Search for a Medieval Lex Mercatoria," in Vito Piergiovanni, ed., *From Lex Mercatoria to Commercial Law*. Berlin: Duncker & Humblot, pp. 53–67.

Craswell, Richard (1988), "Contract Remedies, Renegotiation, and the Theory of Efficient Breach," *Southern California Law Review*, vol. 61, pp. 629–670.

———— (1989), "Contract Law, Default Rules, and the Philosophy of Promising," *Michigan Law Review*, vol. 88, pp. 489–529.

———— (1991), "Passing on the Costs of Legal Rules: Efficiency and Distribution in Buyer-Seller Relationships," *Stanford Law Review*, vol. 43, pp. 361–398.

———— (1992), "Efficiency and Rational Bargaining in Contractual Settings," *Harvard Journal of Law and Public Policy*, vol. 15, pp. 805–837.

———— (1993), "Property Rules and Liability Rules in Unconscionability and Related Doctrines," *University of Chicago Law Review*, vol. 60, pp. 1–65.

—— (1995), "Remedies When Contracts Lack Consent: Autonomy and Institutional Competence," *Osgoode Hall Law Journal*, vol. 33, pp. 209–235.

—— (2000a), "Contract Law: General Theories," in Boudewijn Bouckaert & Gerrit De Geest, eds., *Encyclopedia of Law & Economics*. Cheltenham, UK: Edward Elgar, vol. 3, pp. 1–24, available at http://allserv.rug.ac.be/~gdegeest/4000book.pdf.

—— (2000b), "Against Fuller and Perdue," *University of Chicago Law Review*, vol. 67, pp. 99–161.

—— (2001), "Two Economic Theories of Enforcing Promises," in Peter Benson, ed., *The Theory of Contract Law: New Essays*. Cambridge: Cambridge University Press, pp. 19–44.

—— (2003), "In That Case, What Is the Question? Economics and the Demands of Contract Theory," *Yale Law Journal*, vol. 112, pp. 903–924.

—— (2005), "Incomplete Contracts and Precautions," *Case Western Reserve Law Review*, vol. 56, pp. 151–168.

—— (2006), "Taking Information Seriously: Misrepresentation and Nondisclosure in Contract Law and Elsewhere," *Virginia Law Review*, vol. 92, pp. 565–632.

—— (2012), "Promises and Prices," *Suffolk Law Review*, vol. 45, pp. 735–776.

Cunnington, Ralph (2008), "The Measure and Availability of Gain-Based Damages for Breach of Contract," in Djakhongir Saidov & Ralph Cunnington, eds., *Contract Damages: Domestic and International Perspectives*. Oxford, UK: Hart Publishing, pp. 207–242.

Dagan, Hanoch (2011), "Pluralism and Perfectionism in Private Law," available at http://papers.ssrn.com/sol3/papers.cfm?abstract_id=1868198.

Danzig, Richard (1975), "*Hadley v. Baxendale*: A Study in the Industrialization of the Law," *Journal of Legal Studies*, vol. 4, pp. 249–284.

Danzig, Richard & Watson, Geoffrey R. (2004), *The Capability Problem in Contract Law: Further Readings on Well-Known Cases*, 2d ed. New York: Foundation Press.

Dawson, John P. (1937), "Economic Duress and the Fair Exchange in French and German Law," Parts 1 & 2, *Tulane Law Review*, vol. 11, pp. 345–376; vol. 12, pp. 42–73.

—— (1947), "Economic Duress – An Essay in Perspective," *Michigan Law Review*, vol. 45, pp. 253–290.

Decker, Russell (1973), "The Repeal of the Statute of Frauds in England," *American Business Law Journal*, vol. 11, pp. 55–62.

DiMatteo, Larry A. (1995), "The Norms of Contract: The Fairness Inquiry and the 'Law of Satisfaction' – A Nonunified Theory," *Hofstra Law Review*, vol. 24, pp. 349–454.

—— (1997), "The CISG and the Presumption of Enforceability: Unintended Contractual Liability in International Business Dealings," *Yale Journal of International Law*, vol. 22, pp. 111–170.

DiMatteo, Larry A.; Prentice, Robert A.; Morant, Blake D. & Barnhizer, Daniel (2007), *Visions of Contract Theory: Rationality, Bargaining, and Interpretation*. Durham, NC: Carolina Academic Press.

Drahozal, Christopher R. & Zyontz, Samantha (2011), "Creditor Claims in Arbitration and in Court," *Hastings Business Law Journal*, vol. 7, pp. 77–116.

Dworkin, Ronald (1986), *Law's Empire*. Cambridge, MA: Harvard University Press.

Easterbrook, Frank H. (1996), "Cyberspace and the Law of the Horse," *University of Chicago Legal Forum*, vol. 1996, pp. 207–216.

—— (2005), "Contract and Copyright," *Houston Law Review*, vol. 42, pp. 953–973.

Easterbrook, Frank H. & Fischel, Daniel R. (1989), "The Corporate Contract," *Columbia Law Review*, vol. 89, pp. 1416–1448.

Edlin, Aaron S. & Schwartz, Alan (2003), "Optimal Penalties in Contracts," *Chicago-Kent Law Review*, vol. 78, pp. 33–54.

Edmundson, William A., ed. (1999), *The Duty to Obey the Law: Selected Philosophical Readings*. Lanham, MD: Rowman & Littlefield.

―――― (2004), "The Duty to Obey the Law," *Legal Theory*, vol. 10, pp. 215–259.

Eisenberg, Melvin Aron (1979), "Donative Promises," *University of Chicago Law Review*, vol. 47, pp. 1–33.

―――― (1982a), "The Bargain Principle and Its Limits," *Harvard Law Review*, vol. 95, pp. 741–801.

―――― (1982b), "The Principles of Consideration," *Cornell Law Review*, vol. 67, pp. 640–665.

―――― (1992a), "The Principle of *Hadley v. Baxendale*," *California Law Review*, vol. 80, pp. 563–613.

―――― (1992b), "Third-Party Beneficiaries," *Columbia Law Review*, vol. 92, pp. 1358–1430.

―――― (1997), "The World of Contract and the World of Gift," *California Law Review*, vol. 85, pp. 821–866.

―――― (2002), "The Duty to Rescue in Contract Law," *Fordham Law Review*, vol. 71, pp. 647–694.

―――― (2003a), "Disclosure in Contract Law," *California Law Review*, vol. 91, pp. 1645–1691.

―――― (2003b), "Mistake in Contract Law," *California Law Review*, vol. 91, pp. 1573–1643.

―――― (2004), "The Revocation of Offers," *Wisconsin Law Review*, vol. 2004, pp. 271–308.

―――― (2005), "Actual and Virtual Specific Performance, the Theory of Efficient Breach, and the Indifference Principle in Contract Law," *California Law Review*, vol. 93, pp. 975–1050.

―――― (2006), "The Disgorgement Interest in Contract Law," *Michigan Law Review*, vol. 105, pp. 559–602.

―――― (2009), "Impossibility, Impracticability, and Frustration of Purpose," *Journal of Legal Analysis*, vol. 1, pp. 207–261.

Eisenberg, Theodore; Miller, Geoffrey P. & Sherwin, Emily (2008), "Mandatory Arbitration for Customers but Not for Peers," *Judicature*, vol. 92, pp. 118–123.

Endicott, Timothy (2000), "Objectivity, Subjectivity, and Incomplete Agreements," in Jeremy Horder, ed., *Oxford Essays in Jurisprudence*, 4th ser. Oxford: Oxford University Press, pp. 151–171.

Epstein, Richard A. (1975), "Unconscionability: A Critical Reappraisal," *Journal of Law and Economics*, vol. 18, pp. 293–315.

―――― (1989), "Beyond Foreseeability: Consequential Damages in the Law of Contract," *Journal of Legal Studies*, vol. 18, pp. 105–138.

Farber, Daniel A. (2000), "Economic Efficiency and the Ex Ante Perspective," in Jody S. Kraus & Steven D. Walt, eds., *The Jurisprudential Foundations of Corporate and Commercial Law*. Cambridge: Cambridge University Press, pp. 54–86.

Farnsworth, E. Allan (1984), "On Trying to Keep One's Promises: The Duty of Best Efforts in Contract Law," *University of Pittsburgh Law Review*, vol. 46, pp. 1–20.

―――― (1987a), "An International Restatement: The UNIDROIT Principles of International Commercial Contracts," *University of Baltimore Law Review*, vol. 26, pp. 1–7.

―――― (1987b), "Precontractual Liability and Preliminary Agreements: Fair Dealing and Failed Negotiations," *Columbia Law Review*, vol. 87, pp. 217–294.

―――― (2002), "Parables about Promises: Religious Ethics and Contract Enforceability," *Fordham Law Review*, vol. 71, pp. 695–707.

―――― (2004), *Contracts*, 4th ed. New York: Aspen Publishers.

Feinman, Jay M. (2004), "Un-Making Law: The Classical Revival in the Common Law," *Seattle University Law Review*, vol. 28, pp. 1–59.

——— (2010), *Delay Deny Defend: Why Insurance Companies Don't Pay Claims and What You Can Do about It*. New York: Penguin.

Feinman, Jay M. & Brill, Stephen R. (2006), "Is an Advertisement an Offer? Why It Is and Why It Matters," *Hastings Law Journal*, vol. 58, pp. 61–86.

Feldman, Steven W. (2010), *Government Contract Handbook*, 4th ed. St. Paul, MN: West Publishing.

Finnis, John (1980), *Natural Law and Natural Rights*. Oxford, UK: Clarendon Press.

Fried, Barbara H. (2007), "What's Morality Got to Do with It?" *Harvard Law Review Forum*, vol. 120, pp. 53–61.

——— (2012), "The Holmesian Bad Man Flubs His Entrance," *Suffolk Law Review*, vol. 45, pp. 627–646.

Fried, Charles (1981), *Contract as Promise: A Theory of Contractual Obligation*. Cambridge, MA: Harvard University Press.

——— (1987), "Is Liberty Possible?" in Sterling M. McMurrin, ed., *Liberty, Equality, and Law: Selected Tanner Lectures on Moral Philosophy*. Cambridge: Cambridge University Press, pp. 89–135.

——— (2007), "The Convergence of Contract and Promise," *Harvard Law Review Forum*, vol. 120, pp. 1–9, available at http://www.harvardlawreview.org/forum/HLRforum.shtml.

——— (2012), "*Contract as Promise* Thirty Years On," *Suffolk Law Review*, vol. 45, pp. 961–978.

Friedman, Lawrence J. (1965), *Contract Law in America*. Madison: University of Wisconsin Press.

Friedmann, Daniel (1989), "The Efficient Breach Fallacy," *Journal of Legal Studies*, vol. 18, pp. 1–24.

——— (2005), "Rights and Remedies," in Nili Cohen & Ewan McKendrick, eds., *Comparative Remedies for Breach of Contract*. Oxford, UK: Hart Publishing, pp. 3–17.

Fuller, Lon L. (1939), "Williston on Contracts," *North Carolina Law Review*, vol. 18, pp. 1–15.

——— (1941), "Consideration and Form," *Columbia Law Review*, vol. 41, pp. 799–824.

Fuller, Lon L. & Perdue, William R., Jr. (1936), "The Reliance Interest in Contract Damages," Parts 1 & 2, *Yale Law Journal*, vol. 46, pp 52–96, 373–420.

Galanter, Marc (1974), "Why the Haves Come Out Ahead: Speculations on the Limits of Legal Change," *Law and Society Review*, vol. 9, pp. 95–160.

Garner, W. Michael (2010), *Franchise and Distribution Law and Practice, 2010–2011 ed.*, 3 vols. St. Paul, MN: West Publishing.

Gava, John & Greene, Janey (2004), "Do We Need a Hybrid Law of Contract? Why Hugh Collins Is Wrong and Why It Matters," *Cambridge Law Journal*, vol. 63, pp. 605–631.

Giesel, Grace M. (2005), "A Realistic Proposal for the Contract Duress Doctrine," *West Virginia Law Review*, vol. 107, pp. 443–498.

Gillette, Clayton P. (2004), "Rolling Contracts as an Agency Problem," *Wisconsin Law Review*, vol. 2004, pp. 679–722.

Gilmore, Grant (1974), *The Death of Contract*. Columbus: Ohio State University Press.

Gilson, Ronald J.; Sabel, Charles F. & Scott, Robert E. (2010), "Braiding: The Interaction of Formal and Informal Contracting in Theory, Practice, and Doctrine," *Columbia Law Review*, vol. 110, pp. 1377–1447.

Glanvill (1965). *The Treatise on the Laws and Customs of the Realm of England Commonly Called Glanvill*, ed. & trans. G. D. G. Hall. Oxford, UK: Clarendon Press.

Goetz, Charles J. & Scott, Robert E. (1977), "Liquidated Damages, Penalties, and the Just Compensation Principle: Some Notes on an Enforcement Model of Efficient Breach," *Columbia Law Review*, vol. 77, pp. 554–594.

——— (1980), "Enforcing Promises: An Examination of the Basis of Contract," *Yale Law Journal*, vol. 89, pp. 261–322.

Gold, Andrew S. (2009a), "Consideration and the Morality of Promising," in Jason W. Neyers, Richard Bronaugh & Stephen G. A. Pitel, eds., *Exploring Contract Law*. Oxford, UK: Hart Publishing, pp. 115–137.

——— (2009b), "A Property Theory of Contract," *Northwestern University Law Review*, vol. 103, pp. 1–62.

——— (2011a), "A Moral Rights Theory of Private Law," *William & Mary Law Review*, vol. 52, pp. 1873–1931.

——— (2011b), "The Taxonomy of Civil Discourse," *Florida State University Law Review*, vol. 39, pp. 65–83.

Goldberg, Victor (2006), *Framing Contract Law: An Economic Perspective*. Cambridge, MA: Harvard University Press.

——— (2010), "After Frustration: Three Cheers for *Chandler v. Webster*," available at http://ssrn.com/abstract=1703123.

——— (2011), "Traynor (*Drennan*) v. Hand (*Baird*): Much Ado about (Almost) Nothing," available at http://ssrn.com/abstract=1795322.

Gordley, James (1990), "Natural Law Origins of the Common Law of Contract," in John Barton, ed., *Towards a General Law of Contract*. Berlin: Duncker & Humblot, pp. 367–465.

——— (1991), *The Philosophical Origins of Modern Contract Doctrine*. Oxford, UK: Clarendon Press.

——— (1996), "Contract," in Dennis Patterson, ed., *A Companion to Philosophy of Law and Legal Theory*. Oxford, UK: Blackwell, pp. 3–20.

——— (2001a), "Contract Law in the Aristotelian Tradition," in Peter Benson, ed., *The Theory of Contract Law: New Essays*. Cambridge: Cambridge University Press, pp. 265–334.

——— ed. (2001b), *The Enforceability of Promises in European Contract Law*. Cambridge: Cambridge University Press.

——— (2001c), "A Perennial Misstep: From Cajetan to Fuller and Perdue to 'Efficient Breach,'" *Issues in Legal Scholarship: Symposium – Fuller and Perdue*, article 4, available at http://www.bepress.com/ils/iss1/art4/.

——— (2002), "The Moral Foundations of Private Law," *American Journal of Jurisprudence*, vol. 47, pp. 1–23.

——— (2003), "Contract," in Peter Cane & Mark Tushnet, eds., *The Oxford Handbook of Legal Studies*. Oxford: Oxford University Press, pp. 3–20.

——— (2004), "Impossibility and Changed and Unforeseen Circumstances," *American Journal of Comparative Law*, vol. 52, pp. 513–530.

Gordley, James & von Mehren, Arthur Taylor (2006), *An Introduction to the Comparative Study of Private Law*. Cambridge: Cambridge University Press.

Gordon, Robert W. (1984), "Critical Legal Histories," *Stanford Law Review*, vol. 36, pp. 57–125.

——— (2004), "Using History in Teaching Contracts: The Case of *Britton v. Turner*," *Hawai'i Law Review*, vol. 26, pp. 424–434.

Greenawalt, Kent (2010), *Legal Interpretation: Perspectives from Other Disciplines and Private Texts*. Oxford: Oxford University Press.

Greenberg, David I. (1980), "Easy Terms, Hard Times: Complaint Handling in the Ghetto," in Laura Nader, ed., *No Access to Law: Alternatives to the American Judicial System*. New York: Academic Press, pp. 379–415.

Hagerty, James R. (2007), "Getting Hammered" (reviewing Barry B. Lepatner, *Broken Buildings, Busted Budgets*), *Wall Street Journal* (Eastern ed.), Dec. 5, 2007, at D9.

Harrison, Jeffrey L. (2007), *Law and Economics: Positive, Normative and Behavioral Perspectives*, 2d ed. St. Paul, MN: Thomson/West.

Hart, H. L. A. (1994), *The Concept of Law*, 2d ed. Oxford, UK: Clarendon Press.

Hart, H. L. A. & Honoré, Tony (1985), *Causation in the Law*, 2d ed. Oxford, UK: Clarendon Press.

Hegel, G. W. F. (1952), *Hegel's Philosophy of Right*, trans. T. M. Know. Oxford: Oxford University Press (first published 1821).

Helmholz, Richard H. (1975), "Assumpsit and *Fidei Laesio*," *Law Quarterly Review*, vol. 91, pp. 406–432.

——— (1990), "Contracts and the Common Law," in John Barton, ed., *Towards a General Law of Contract*. Berlin: Duncker & Humblot, pp. 49–65.

Hesselink, Martijn W. (2004), "The Concept of Good Faith," in A. S. Hartkamp, E. H. Hondius, C. A. Joustra, C. E. du Perron & M. Veldman, eds., *Towards a European Civil Code*, 3d ed. The Hague: Kluwer Law International, pp. 471–498.

——— (2009), "The Common Frame of Reference as a Source of European Private Law," *Tulane Law Review*, vol. 83, pp. 919–971.

——— (2011), "Unfair Terms in Contracts between Businesses," available at http://papers.ssrn.com/sol3/papers.cfm?abstract_id=1871130.

Higgins, Ruth C. A. (2004), *The Moral Limits of Law: Obedience, Respect, and Legitimacy*. Oxford: Oxford University Press.

Hill, Thomas E. (1984), "Autonomy and Benevolent Lies," *Journal of Value Inquiry*, vol. 18, pp. 251–267.

Hillman, Robert A. (1988), "The Crisis in Modern Contract Theory," *Texas Law Review*, vol. 67, pp. 103–136.

——— (1998), "Questioning the 'New Consensus' on Promissory Estoppel: An Empirical and Theoretical Study," *Columbia Law Review*, vol. 98, pp. 580–619.

——— (2006), "Online Boilerplate: Would Mandatory Website Disclosure of E-Standard Terms Backfire?" *Michigan Law Review*, vol. 104, pp. 837–856.

Hillman, Robert A. & O'Rourke, Maureen A. (2010), "Principles of the Law of Software Contracts: Some Highlights," *Tulane Law Review*, vol. 84, pp. 1519–1540.

Hillman, Robert A. & Rachlinski, Jeffrey J. (2002), "Standard-Form Contracting in the Electronic Age," *New York University Law Review*, vol. 77, pp. 429–495.

Holdsworth, W. S. (1920), "The History of the Treatment of *Choses* in Action by the Common Law," *Harvard Law Review*, vol. 33, pp. 997–1030.

Holmes, Oliver Wendell, Jr. (1897), "The Path of the Law," *Harvard Law Review*, vol. 10, pp. 457–478.

——— (1899), "The Theory of Legal Interpretation," *Harvard Law Review*, vol. 12, pp. 417–420.

——— (1941), Letter to Frederick Pollock, Dec. 11, 1928, in Mark DeWolfe Howe, ed., *Holmes-Pollock Letters*, vol. 2, pp. 233–234.

——— (1963), *The Common Law*, ed. Mark DeWolfe Howe. Boston: Little, Brown.

Horwitz, Morton J. (1977), *The Transformation of American Law, 1780–1860*. Cambridge, MA: Harvard University Press.

Howarth, David (2005), "Against *Lumley v. Gye*," *Modern Law Review*, vol. 68, pp. 195–232.

Hume, David (1978), A *Treatise of Human Nature*, 2d ed., ed. L. A. Selby-Bigge & P. H. Nidditch. Oxford, UK: Clarendon Press (originally published 1739).

Hyland, Richard (1994), "*Pacta Sunt Servanda*: A Meditation," *Virginia Journal of International Law*, vol. 34, pp. 405–433.

Hyman, David A.; Black, Bernard & Silver, Charles (2010), "Settlement at Policy Limits and the Duty to Settle: Evidence from Texas," *Journal of Empirical Legal Studies*, vol. 8, pp. 48–54.

Ibbetson, David J. (1990), "Consideration and the Theory of Contract in Sixteenth Century Common Law," in John Barton, ed., *Towards a General Law of Contract*. Berlin: Duncker & Humblot, pp. 67–123.

––––––– (1999), A *Historical Introduction to the Law of Obligations*. Oxford: Oxford University Press.

Imwinkelreid, Edward J. (2009), "The Implied Obligation of Good Faith in Contract Law: Is It Time to Write Its Obituary?" *Texas Tech Law Review*, vol. 42, pp. 1–21.

Johnston, David (1999), *Roman Law in Context*. Cambridge: Cambridge University Press.

Kahneman, Daniel (2011), *Thinking, Fast and Slow*. New York: Farrar, Straus & Giroux.

Kahneman, Daniel; Slovic, Paul & Tversky, Amos, eds. (1982), *Judgment under Uncertainty: Heuristics and Biases*. Cambridge: Cambridge University Press.

Kar, Robin (2009), "Contractualism about Contract Law," available at http://papers.ssrn.com/sol3/papers.cfm?abstract_id=993809.

Kaser, Max (1980), *Roman Private Law*, 3d ed., trans. Rolf Dannenbring. Pretoria: University of South Africa.

Katz, Avery Wiener (2004), "The Economics of Form and Substance in Contract Interpretation," *Columbia Law Review*, vol. 104, pp. 496–538.

––––––– (2012), "Virtue Ethics and Efficient Breach," *Suffolk Law Review*, vol. 45, pp. 777–798.

Keeton, Robert E. (1970), "Insurance Law Rights at Variance with Policy Provisions," *Harvard Law Review*, vol. 83, pp. 961–985.

Kelman, Mark (1987), A *Guide to Critical Legal Studies*. Cambridge, MA: Harvard University Press.

Kennedy, Duncan (1982), "Distributive and Paternalist Motives in Contract and Tort Law, with Special Reference to Compulsory Terms and Unequal Bargaining Power," *Maryland Law Review*, vol. 41, pp. 563–658.

––––––– (2000), "From the Will Theory to the Principle of Private Autonomy: Lon Fuller's 'Consideration and Form,'" *Columbia Law Review*, vol. 100, pp. 94–175.

Kesan, Jay P. & Hayes, Carol M. (2012), "The Law and Policy of Non-Compete Clauses in the United States and Their Implications," in Marilyn Pittard et al., eds., *Comparative Business Innovation: A Legal Balancing Act*. Cheltenham, UK: Edward Elgar, available at ssrn.com/abstract=1948593.

Kessler, Friedrich (1943), "Contracts of Adhesion – Some Thoughts about Freedom of Contract," *Columbia Law Review*, vol. 43, pp. 629–642.

Kidwell, John (2000), "Ruminations on Teaching the Statute of Frauds," *St. Louis University Law Journal*, vol. 44, pp. 1147–1462.

Kimball, Bruce A. (2007), "Langdell on Contracts and Legal Reasoning: Correcting the Holmesian Caricature," *Law and History Review*, vol. 25, pp. 345–399.

Kimel, Dori (2003), *From Promise to Contract: Towards a Liberal Theory of Contract*. Oxford, UK: Hart Publishing.

Klass, Gregory (2008), "Three Pictures of Contract: Duty, Power, and Compound Rule," *New York University Law Review*, vol. 83, pp. 1726–1783.

––––––– (2009), "Intent to Contract," *Virginia Law Review*, vol. 95, pp. 1437–1501.

Klick, Jonathan; Kobayashi, Bruce & Ribstein, Larry (2009), "Federalism, Variation, and State Regulation of Franchise Termination," *Entrepreneurial Business Law Journal*, vol. 3, pp. 355–379.

Knapp, Charles L. (1969), "Enforcing the Contract to Bargain," *New York University Law Review*, vol. 44, pp. 673–728.

———— (1998), "Rescuing Reliance: The Perils of Promissory Estoppel," *Hastings Law Review*, vol. 49, pp. 1191–1335.

Knapp, Charles L.; Crystal, Nathan M. & Prince, Harry G. (2007), *Problems in Contract Law: Cases and Materials*, 6th ed. New York: Aspen Publishers.

Kniffin, Margaret N. (2009), "Conflating and Confusing Contract Interpretation and The Parol Evidence Rule: Is the Emperor Wearing Someone Else's Clothes?" *Rutgers Law Review*, vol. 62, pp. 75–129.

Kolodny, Niko & Wallace, R. Jay (2003), "Promises and Practices Revisited," *Philosophy & Public Affairs*, vol. 31, pp. 119–154.

Korngold, Gerald & Goldstein, Paul (2009), *Real Estate Transactions: Cases and Materials on Land Transfer*, 5th ed. St. Paul, MN: West Publishing.

Korobkin, Russell (2000), "Behavioral Economics, Contract Formation, and Contract Law," in Cass R. Sunstein, ed., *Behavioral Law and Economics*. Cambridge: Cambridge University Press, pp. 116–143.

———— (2003), "Bounded Rationality, Standard Form Contracts, and Unconscionability," *University of Chicago Law Review*, vol. 70, pp. 1203–1295.

———— (2005), "Possibility and Plausibility in Law and Economics," *Florida State University Law Review*, vol. 32, pp. 781–795.

Kramer, Matthew (1999), *In Defense of Legal Positivism*. Oxford: Oxford University Press.

Kraus, Jody S. (2001), "Reconciling Autonomy and Efficiency in Contract Law: The Vertical Integration Strategy," in Ernest Sosa & Enrique Villanueva, eds., *Philosophical Issues, 11: Social, Political, and Legal Philosophy*. Boston: Blackwell Publishers, pp. 420–441.

———— (2002a), "Philosophy of Contract Law," in Jules Coleman & Scott Shapiro, eds., *The Oxford Handbook of Jurisprudence and Philosophy of Law*. Oxford: Oxford University Press, pp. 687–751.

———— (2002b), "Legal Theory and Contract Law: Groundwork for the Reconciliation of Autonomy and Efficiency," in Enrique Villanueva, ed., *Legal and Political Philosophy: Social, Political, & Legal Philosophy, Volume 1*. Amsterdam: Rodopi, pp. 385–445.

———— (2007), "Transparency and Determinacy in Common Law Adjudication: A Philosophical Defense of Explanatory Economic Analysis," *Virginia Law Review*, vol. 93, pp. 287–359.

———— (2009), "The Correspondence of Contract and Promise," *Columbia Law Review*, vol. 109, pp. 1603–1649.

Kraus, Jody S. & Walt, Steven D., eds. (2000), *The Jurisprudential Foundations of Corporate and Commercial Law*. Cambridge: Cambridge University Press.

Kreitner, Roy (2001), "The Gift beyond the Grave: Revisiting the Question of Consideration," *Columbia Law Review*, vol. 101, pp. 1876–1957.

———— (2012), "On the New Pluralism in Contract Theory," *Suffolk Law Review*, vol. 45, pp. 915–933.

Kröll, Stefan; Mistelis, Loukas & Viscasillas, Pilar Perales, eds. (2011), *UN Convention on Contracts for the International Sales of Goods (CISG)*. Oxford, UK: Hart Publishing.

Kronman, Anthony T. (1978), "Mistake, Disclosure, Information, and the Law of Contracts," *Journal of Legal Studies*, vol. 7, pp. 1–34.

—— (1980), "Contract Law and Distributive Justice," *Yale Law Journal*, vol. 89, pp. 472–511.

—— (1983), "Paternalism and the Law of Contracts," *Yale Law Journal*, vol. 92, pp. 763–798.

Kronman, Anthony T. & Posner, Richard A., eds. (1979), *The Economics of Contract Law*. Boston: Little, Brown.

Laithier, Yves-Marie (2005), "Comparative Reflections on the French Law of Remedies for Breach of Contract," in Nili Cohen & Ewan McKendrick, eds., *Comparative Remedies for Breach of Contract*. Oxford, UK: Hart Publishing, pp. 104–133.

Lando, Henrik & Rose, Caspar (2004), "On the Enforcement of Specific Performance in Civil Law Countries," *International Review of Law and Economics*, vol. 24, pp. 473–487.

Lando, Ole & Beale, Hugh, eds. (2000), *Principles of European Contract Law, Parts I and II*. The Hague: Kluwer Law International.

Lando, Ole; Clive, Eric; Prüm, André & Zimmermann, Reinhard (2003), *Principles of European Contract Law, Part III*. The Hague: Kluwer Law International.

Law Commission and the Scottish Law Commission (2005), *Unfair Terms in Contracts*. London and Edinburgh: The Law Commission and Scottish Law Commission.

Laycock, Douglas (1993), "The Triumph of Equity," *Law and Contemporary Problems*, vol. 56, pp. 53–82.

Lawrence, William H. (2004), "Rolling Contracts Rolling over Contract Law," *San Diego Law Review*, vol. 41, pp. 1099–1122.

Leff, Arthur Allen (1967), "Unconscionability and the Code – The Emperor's New Clauses," *University of Pennsylvania Law Review*, vol. 115, pp. 485–559.

—— (1970), "Contract as Thing," *American University Law Review*, vol. 19, pp. 131–157.

—— (1974), "Economic Analysis of Law: Some Realism about Nominalism," *Virginia Law Review*, vol. 60, pp. 451–482.

Leib, Ethan J. (2005), "On Collaboration, Organizations, and Conciliation in the General Theory of Contract Law," *Quinnipiac Law Review*, vol. 24, pp. 1–23.

Leiter, Brian (2003), "Beyond the Hart/Dworkin Debate: The Methodology Problem in Jurisprudence," *American Journal of Jurisprudence*, vol. 48, pp. 17–51.

—— (2005), "American Legal Realism," in Martin P. Golding & William A. Edmundson, eds., *The Blackwell Guide to the Philosophy of Law and Legal Theory*. Oxford, UK: Blackwell, pp. 50–66.

—— (2007), *Naturalizing Jurisprudence: Essays on American Legal Realism and Naturalism in Legal Philosophy*. Oxford: Oxford University Press.

Lemley, Mark A. (2006), "Terms of Use," *Minnesota Law Review*, vol. 91, pp. 459–483.

Llewellyn, Karl N. (1930), "A Realistic Jurisprudence – The Next Step," *Columbia Law Review*, vol. 30, pp. 431–465.

—— (1931a), "Some Realism about Realism – Responding to Dean Pound," *Harvard Law Review*, vol. 44, pp. 1222–1264.

—— (1931b), "What Price Contract? – An Essay in Perspective," *Yale Law Journal*, vol. 40, pp. 704–751.

—— (1938–1939), "On Our Case-Law of Contract: Offer and Acceptance," Parts 1 & 2, *Yale Law Journal*, vol. 48, pp. 1–36, 779–818.

—— (1950), "Remarks on the Theory of Appellate Decision and the Rules or Canons about How Statutes Are to Be Construed," *Vanderbilt Law Review*, vol. 3, pp. 395–406.

—— (1960), *The Common Law Tradition: Deciding Appeals*. Boston: Little, Brown.

Lookofsky, Joseph (2008), *Understanding the CISG*, 3d ed. New York: Wolters Kluwer Aspen.

Lucy, William (2004), "Philosophy and Contract Law," *University of Toronto Law Journal*, vol. 54, pp. 75–108.

Macaulay, Stewart (1963), "Non-Contractual Relations in Business: A Preliminary Study," *American Sociology Review*, vol. 28, pp. 55–67.

———— (1966), "Private Legislation and the Duty to Read – Business by IBM Machine, the Law of Contracts and Credit Cards," *Vanderbilt Law Review*, vol. 19, pp. 1051–1121.

———— (1985), "An Empirical View of Contract," *Wisconsin Law Review*, vol. 1985, pp. 465–482.

———— (1989), "Bambi Meets Godzilla: Reflections on Contracts Scholarship and Teaching vs. State Unfair and Deceptive Trade Practices and Consumer Protection Statutes," *Houston Law Review*, vol. 26, pp. 575–601.

———— (2000), "Relational Contracts Floating on a Sea of Custom? Thoughts about the Ideas of Ian Macneil and Lisa Bernstein," *Northwestern Law Review*, vol. 94, pp. 775–804.

———— (2003), "The Real and the Paper Deal: Empirical Pictures of Relationships, Complexity and the Urge for Transparent Simple Rules," *Modern Law Review*, vol. 66, pp. 44–79.

———— (2004), "Freedom from Contract: Solutions in Search of a Problem?" *Wisconsin Law Review*, vol. 2004, pp. 777–820.

———— (2011), "The Death of Contract: Dodos and Unicorns or Sleeping Rattlesnakes?" in Robert W. Gordon & Morton J. Horwitz, eds., *Law, Society, and History: Themes in the Legal Sociology and Legal History of Lawrence Friedman.* Cambridge: Cambridge University Press, pp. 193–208.

Macaulay, Stewart; Braucher, Jean; Kidwell, John & Whitford, William (2011), *Contracts: Law in Action*, 3d ed., vols. 1 & 2. Newark, NJ: LexisNexis.

Macneil, Ian (1974), "The Many Futures of Contract," *Southern California Law Review*, vol. 47, pp. 691–816.

———— (1978), "Adjustment of Long-Term Economic Relations under Classical, Neoclassical, and Relational Contract Law," *Northwestern University Law Review*, vol. 72, pp. 854–905.

———— (1982), "Efficient Breach of Contract: Circles in the Sky," *Virginia Law Review*, vol. 68, pp. 947–969.

———— (2001), *The Relational Theory of Contract: Selected Works of Ian Macneil*, ed. David Campbell. London: Sweet & Maxwell.

Maine, Henry Sumner (1986), *Ancient Law*. Tucson: University of Arizona Press (first published in 1861).

Markovits, Daniel (2004), "Contract and Collaboration," *Yale Law Journal*, vol. 113, pp. 1417–1518.

———— (2006), "Making and Keeping Contracts," *Virginia Law Review*, vol. 92, pp. 1325–1374.

Markovits, Daniel & Schwartz, Alan (2011), "The Myth of Efficient Breach: New Defenses of the Expectation Interest," *Virginia Law Review*. vol. 97, pp. 1939–2008.

Marotta-Wurgler, Florencia (2007), "What's in a Standard Form Contract? An Empirical Analysis of Software License Agreements," *Journal of Empirical Legal Studies*, vol. 4, pp. 677–713.

———— (2008), "Competition and the Quality of Standard Form Contract: The Case of Software License Agreements," *Journal of Empirical Legal Studies*, vol. 5, pp. 447–475.

———— (2009), "Are 'Pay Now, Terms Later' Contracts Worse for Buyers? Evidence from Software License Agreements," *Journal of Legal Studies*, vol. 38, pp. 309–343.

———— (2011), "Will Increased Disclosure Help? Evaluating the Recommendations of the ALI's 'Principles of the Law of Software Contracts,'" *University of Chicago Law Review*, vol. 78, pp. 165–178.

Marsh, P. D. V. (1994), *Comparative Contract Law, England, France, Germany*. Aldershot, UK: Gower.

Martin, Charles H. (2005), "The UNCITRAL Electronic Contracts Convention: Will It Be Used or Avoided?" *Pace International Law Review*, vol. 17, pp. 261–300.

Maute, Judith L. (2007), "The Unearthed Facts of *Peevyhouse v. Garland Coal & Mining Co.*," in Douglas G. Baird, ed., *Contracts Stories* (New York: Foundation Press), pp. 265–303.

Mayer, Caroline E. (2000), "Win Some, Lose Rarely? Arbitration Forum's Rulings Called One-Sided," *Washington Post*, Mar. 1, 2000.

McGovern, William M., Jr. (1968), "Contract in Medieval England: Wager of Law and the Effect of Death," *Iowa Law Review*, vol. 54, pp. 19–62.

——— (1978), "Dependent Promises in the History of Leases and Other Contracts," *Tulane Law Review*, vol. 52, pp. 659–705.

Medina, J. Michael (1988), "The Take-or-Pay Wars: A Further Status Report," *Oklahoma Law Review*, vol. 41, pp. 381–416.

Metzger, Michael B. & Phillips, Michael J. (1983), "The Emergence of Promissory Estoppel as an Independent Theory of Recovery," *Rutgers Law Review*, vol. 35, pp. 472–557.

Mill, John Stuart (1974), *On Liberty*. Harmondsworth, UK: Penguin Books (first published in 1859).

Miller, Lucinda (2007), "Specific Performance in the Common and Civil Law: Some Lessons for Harmonisation," in Paula Giliker, ed., *Re-examining Contract and Unjust Enrichment: Anglo-Canadian Perspectives*. Leiden: Martinus Nijhoff Publishers, pp. 281–310.

Milsom, S. F. C. (2003), *A Natural History of the Common Law*. New York: Columbia University Press.

Mitchell, Catherine (2003), "Leading a Life of Its Own? The Roles of Reasonable Expectation in Contract Law," *Oxford Journal of Legal Studies*, vol. 23, pp. 639–665.

Mooney, Ralph James (1995), "The New Conceptualism in Contract Law," *Oregon Law Review*, vol. 74, pp. 1131–1207.

Moore, Michael S. (1990), "A Theory of Criminal Law Theories," *Tel Aviv University Studies in Law*, vol. 10, pp. 115–185.

——— (2000), "Theories of Areas of Law," *San Diego Law Review*, vol. 37, pp. 731–741.

——— (2009), *Causation and Responsibility*. Oxford: Oxford University Press.

Murray, John Edward, Jr. (2011), *Murray on Contracts*, 5th ed. New Providence, NJ: LexisNexis.

National Conference of Commissioners on Uniform State Laws (1988), "Uniform Electric Transactions Act, Task Force on State Law Exclusions, Report, September 21, 1998."

National Consumer Law Center (2005), Press release: "New Trap Door for Consumers: Card Issuers Use Rubber–Stamp Arbitration to Rush Debts into Default Judgments," Feb. 17, 2005, available athttp://www.consumerlaw.org/initiatives/model/content/ArbitrationNAF.pdf.

Niglia, Leone (2003), *The Transformation of Contract in Europe*. The Hague: Kluwer.

Note (1948), "The Status of Infancy as a Defense to Contracts," *Virginia Law Review*, vol. 34, pp. 829–834.

O'Donnell, John (2007), *The Arbitration Trap: How Credit Companies Trap Consumers*. Washington, DC: Public Citizen.

Office of Minnesota Attorney General (2009), Press release: "National Arbitration Forum Barred from Credit Card and Consumer Arbitrations under Agreement with Attorney General Swanson," July 20, 2009, available at http://www.ag.state.mn.us/consumer/pressrelease/090720nationalarbitrationagremnt.asp.

O'Hara, Erin Ann (2000), "Opting Out of Regulation: A Public Choice Analysis of Contractual Choice of Law," *Vanderbilt Law Review*, vol. 53, pp. 1551–1604.

Oman, Nathan (2005a), "Unity and Pluralism in Contract Law," *Michigan Law Review*, vol. 103, pp. 1483–1506.

——— (2005b), "Corporations and Autonomy Theories of Contract: A Critique of the New *Lex Mercatoria*," *Denver University Law Review*, vol. 83, pp. 101–145.

——— (2007), "The Failure of Economic Interpretations of the Law of Contract Damages," *Washington and Lee Law Review*, vol. 64, pp. 829–875.

——— (2009), "A Pragmatic Defense of Contract Law," *Georgetown Law Journal*, pp. 77–116.

——— (2010), "Bargaining in the Shadow of God's Law: Islamic *Mahr* Contracts and the Perils of Legal Specialization," *Wake Forest Law Review*, vol. 45, pp. 579–606.

——— (2011), "Consent to Retaliation: A Civil Recourse Theory of Contractual Liability," *Iowa Law Review*, vol. 96, pp. 529–579.

——— (2012), "Promise and Private Law," *Suffolk Law Review*, vol. 45, pp. 935–960.

Owen, David, ed. (1995), *Philosophical Foundations of Tort Law*. Oxford, UK: Clarendon Press.

Owens, David (2006), "A Simple Theory of Promising," *Philosophical Review*, vol. 115, pp. 51–77.

——— (2007), "Duress, Deception, and the Validity of a Promise," *Mind*, vol. 116, pp. 293–315.

——— (2008), "Promising without Intending," *Journal of Philosophy*, vol. 105, pp. 737–755.

——— (2011), "The Problem with Promising," in Hanoch Sheinman, ed., *Promises and Agreements: Philosophical Essays*. Oxford: Oxford University Press, pp. 58–79.

Parley, Louis I & Lindey, Alexander (2011), *Lindey and Parley on Separation Agreements and Antenuptial Contracts*, 2d ed. New York: Matthew Bender (loose-leaf, updated twice a year).

Patterson, Dennis M. (1991), "An Open Letter to Professor James Gordley," *Wisconsin Law Review*, vol. 1991, pp. 1432–1436.

Patterson, Edwin W. (1942), "Constructive Conditions in Contracts," *Columbia Law Review*, vol. 42, pp. 903–954.

——— (1958), "An Apology for Consideration," *Columbia Law Review*, vol. 58, pp. 929–963.

——— (1964), "The Interpretation and Construction of Contracts," *Columbia Law Review*, vol. 64, pp. 833–865.

Peel, Edwin (2007), *Treitel: The Law of Contract*, 12th ed. London: Sweet & Maxwell.

Penner, J. E. (1997), *The Idea of Property in Law*. Oxford, UK: Clarendon Press.

Perillo, Joseph M. (2000a), "Misreading Oliver Wendell Holmes on Efficient Breach and Tortious Interference," *Fordham Law Review*, vol. 68, pp. 1085–1106.

——— (2000b), "The Origins of the Objective Theory of Contract Formation and Interpretation," *Fordham Law* Review, vol. 69, pp 427–477.

——— (2003), *Calamari and Perillo on Contracts*, 5th ed. St. Paul, MN: West Publishing.

——— (2005), "Robert J. Pothier's Influence on the Common Law of Contract," *Texas Wesleyan Law Review*, vol. 11, pp. 267–290.

Perry, Stephen R. (1995), "Interpretation and Methodology in Legal Theory," in Andrei Marmor, ed., *Law and Interpretation*. Oxford, UK: Clarendon Press, pp. 97–135.

——— (1998), "Hart's Methodological Positivism," *Legal Theory*, vol. 4, pp. 427–467.

Pettit, Mark, Jr., (1983), "Modern Unilateral Contracts," *Boston University Law Review*, vol. 63, pp. 551–596.

Philippe, Julie M. (2005), "French and American Approaches to Contract Formation and Enforceability: A Comparative Perspective," *Tulsa Journal of Comparative and International Law*, vol. 12, pp. 357–399.

Pollock, Frederick (1893), "Contracts in Early English Law," *Harvard Law Review*, vol. 6, pp. 389–404.

Pollock, Frederick & Maitland, Frederic William (1895), *History of English Law before the Time of Edward I*. Cambridge: Cambridge University Press.

Posner, Eric (1996), "The Regulation of Groups: The Influence of Legal and Nonlegal Sanctions on Collective Action," *University of Chicago Law Review*, vol. 63, pp. 133–197.

———— (1998), "The Parol Evidence Rule, the Plain Meaning Rule, and the Principles of Contractual Interpretation," *University of Pennsylvania Law Review*, vol. 146, pp. 533–577.

———— (2003), "Economic Analysis of Contract Law after Three Decades: Success or Failure?" *Yale Law Journal*, vol. 112, pp. 829–880.

———— (2005), "Contract Theory," in Martin P. Golding & William A. Edmundson, eds., *The Blackwell Guide to the Philosophy of Law and Legal Theory*. Oxford, UK: Blackwell Publishing, pp. 138–147.

———— (2006), "There Are No Penalty Default Rules in Contract Law," *Florida State University Law Review*, vol. 33, pp. 563–587.

———— (2010), "*ProCD v. Zeidenberg* and Cognitive Overload in Contractual Bargaining," *University of Chicago Law Review*, vol. 77, pp. 1181–1194.

———— (2011), *Contract Law and Theory*. New York: Wolter Kluwer Aspen.

Posner, Richard A. (1977), "Gratuitous Promises in Economics and Law," *Journal of Legal Studies*, vol. 6, p. 411–426.

———— (1981), "The Concept of Corrective Justice in Recent Theories of Tort Law," *Journal of Legal Studies*, vol. 10, pp. 187–206.

———— (2004), "Law and Economics – Contracts," *IVR Encyclopaedia of Jurisprudence, Legal Theory, and Philosophy of Law*, available at http://encyclopedia.ivr2003.net.

———— (2005), "The Law and Economics of Contract Interpretation," *Texas Law Review*, vol. 83, pp. 1581–1614.

———— (2009), "Let Us Never Blame a Contract Breaker," *Michigan Law Review*, vol. 107, pp. 1349–1363.

———— (2011), *Economic Analysis of Law*, 8th ed. New York: Wolter Kluwer Aspen.

Posner, Richard A. & Rosenfeld, Andrew M. (1977), "Impossibility and Related Doctrines in Contract Law: An Economic Analysis," *Journal of Legal Studies*, vol. 6, pp. 83–118.

Postema, Gerald J., ed. (2001), *Philosophy and the Law of Torts*. Cambridge: Cambridge University Press.

Pratt, Michael G. (2001), "Scanlon on Promising," *Canadian Journal of Law and Jurisprudence*, vol. 14, pp. 143–154.

———— (2003), "Promises and Perlocutions," in Matt Matravers, ed., *Scanlon and Contractualism*. London: Frank Cass, pp. 93–119.

———— (2007), "Promises, Contracts and Voluntary Obligations," *Law and Philosophy*, vol. 26, pp. 531–574.

———— (2008), "Contract: Not Promise," *Florida State University Law Review*, vol. 35, pp. 801–816.

Preston, Cheryl B. & Crowther, Brandon T. (2012), "Infancy Doctrine Inquiries," *Santa Clara Law Review*, vol. 52, pp. 47–80.

Pryor, C. Scott & Hoshauer, Glenn M. (2005), "Puritan Revolution and the Law of Contracts," *Texas-Wesleyan Law Review*, vol. 11, pp. 291–360.

Putnam, Hilary (1975), *Mind, Language and Reality: Philosophical Papers, Volume 2*. Cambridge: Cambridge University Press.

Radin, Margaret Jane (2012), *Boilerplate*. Princeton, NJ: Princeton University Press.

Rakoff, Todd D. (1983), "Contracts of Adhesion: An Essay in Reconstruction," *Harvard Law Review*, vol. 96, pp. 1173–1284.

_____ (2007), "Good Faith in Contract Performance: *Market Street Associates Ltd. Partnership v. Frey*," *Harvard Law Review*, vol. 120, pp. 1187–1198.

Raz, Joseph (1977), "Promises and Obligations," in P. M. S. Hacker & J. Raz, eds., *Law, Morality and Society*. Oxford, UK: Clarendon Press, pp. 210–228.

_____ (1982), "Promises in Morality and Law" (book review), *Harvard Law Review*, vol. 95, pp. 916–938.

_____ (1986), *The Morality of Freedom*. Oxford, UK: Clarendon Press.

_____ (1994), *Ethics in the Public Domain*. Oxford, UK: Clarendon Press.

_____ (1996), "On the Nature of Law," *Archiv für Rechts- und Sozialphilosophie*, vol. 82, pp. 1–25.

_____ (2005), "Can There Be a Theory of Law?" in Martin P. Golding & William A. Edmundson, eds., *The Blackwell Guide to the Philosophy of Law and Legal Theory*. Oxford, UK: Blackwell Publishing, pp. 324–342.

Reimann, Mathias & Zimmermann, Reinhard (2006), *The Oxford Handbook of Comparative Law*. Oxford: Oxford University Press.

Richman, Barak D. (2007), "The King of Rockingham County and the Original Bridge to Nowhere," in Douglas G. Baird, ed., *Contracts Stories*. New York: Foundation Press, pp. 304–334.

Richman, Barak D. & Schmelzer, Dennis (2011), "When Money Grew on Trees: The Untold Story of *Lucy v. Zehmer*," available at http://papers.ssrn.com/sol3/papers.cfm?abstract_id=1754780.

Ricks, Val D. (1999), "In Defense of Mutuality of Obligation: Why 'Both Should Be Bound, or Neither,'" *Nebraska Law Review*, vol. 78, pp. 491–549.

_____ (2000), "The Sophisticated Doctrine of Consideration," *George Mason Law Review*, vol. 9, pp. 99–143.

_____ (2004), "The Death of Offers," *Indiana Law Journal*, vol. 79, pp. 667–709.

Ripstein, Arthur (2011), "Civil Recourse and Separation of Wrongs and Remedies," *Florida State University Law Review*, vol. 39, pp. 163–207.

Robertson, Andrew (2005), "The Limits of Voluntariness in Contract," *Melbourne University Law Review*, vol. 29, pp. 179–217.

Robertson, R. J., Jr. (1988–1980), "The Right to Demand Adequate Assurance of Due Performance: Uniform Commercial Code Section 2–609 and Restatement (Second) of Contracts Section 251," *Drake Law Review*, vol. 38, pp. 305–353.

Rogers, James Steven (1995), *The Early History of the Law of Bills and Notes*. Cambridge: Cambridge University Press.

de Roover, Raymond (1958), "The Concept of Just Price: Theory and Economic Policy," *Journal of Economic History*, vol. 18, pp. 418–434.

Ross, Alf (1957), "Tû-Tû," *Harvard Law Review*, vol. 70, pp. 812–825.

Rothstein, Mark A. & Liebman, Lance (2011), *Employment Law Cases and Materials*, 7th ed. St. Paul, MN: West Publishing.

Rowley, Keith A. (1999), "Contract Construction and Interpretation: From the 'Four Corners' to Parol Evidence (and Everything in Between)," *Mississippi Law Journal*, vol. 69, pp. 73–344.

_____ (2001), "A Brief History of Anticipatory Repudiation in American Contract Law," *University of Cincinnati Law Review*, vol. 69, pp. 565–639.

_____ (2003), "You Asked for It, You Got It . . . Toy Yoda: Practical Jokes, Prizes, and Contract Law," *Nevada Law Journal*, vol. 3, pp. 526–559.

Saidov, Djakhongir & Cunnington, Ralph, eds. (2008), *Contract Damages: Domestic and International Perspectives*. Oxford, UK: Hart Publishing.

St. Germain, Christopher (1874), *The Doctor and Student, or Dialogues between a Doctor of Divinity and a Student in the Laws of England*, ed. William Muchall. Cincinnati: Robert Clarke & Co. (first published in 1580).

Sayre, Francis Bowe (1923), "Inducing Breach of Contract," *Harvard Law Review*, vol. 36, pp. 663–703.

Scanlon, Thomas M. (1990), "Promises and Practices," *Philosophy and Public Affairs*, vol. 19, pp. 199–226.

—— (1998), "Promising," in E. Craig, ed., *Routledge Encyclopedia of Philosophy*. London: Routledge, available at http://www.rep.routledge.com/article/L118.

—— (2001), "Promises and Contracts," in Peter Benson, ed., *The Theory of Contract Law: New Essays*. Cambridge: Cambridge University Press, pp. 86–117.

Schauer, Frederick (1987), "Precedent," *Stanford Law Review*, vol. 39, pp. 571–605.

Schneewind, J. B. (1998), *The Invention of Autonomy: A History of Modern Moral Philosophy*. Cambridge: Cambridge University Press.

Schoshinski, Robert S. (2011), *American Law of Landlord and Tenant*. St. Paul, MN: West Publishing.

Schwarcz, Daniel (2007), "A Products Liability Theory for the Judicial Regulation of Insurance Policies," *William & Mary Law Review*, vol. 48, pp. 1389–1463.

—— (2011), "Reevaluating Standardized Insurance Policies," *University of Chicago Law Review*, vol. 78, pp. 1263–1349.

Schwartz, Alan (1979), "The Case for Specific Performance," *Yale Law Journal*, vol. 89, pp. 271–306.

—— (1992), "Relational Contracts in the Courts: An Analysis of Incomplete Agreements and Judicial Strategies," *Journal of Legal Studies*, vol. 21, pp. 271–318.

Schwartz, Alan & Scott, Robert E. (2003), "Contract Theory and the Limits of Contract Law," *Yale Law Journal*, vol. 113, pp. 541–619.

—— (2007), "Precontractual Liability and Preliminary Agreements," *Harvard Law Review*, vol. 120, pp. 661–707.

—— (2008), "Market Damages, Efficient Contracting and the Economic Waste Fallacy," *Columbia Law Review*, vol. 108, pp. 1610–1669.

Schwartz, Alan & Wilde, Louis L. (1983), "Imperfect Information in Markets for Contract Terms: The Example of Warranties and Security Interests," *Virginia Law Review*, vol. 69, pp. 1387–1485.

Scott, Robert E. (2007), "*Hoffman v. Red Owl Stores* and the Myth of Precontractual Reliance," *Ohio State Law Journal*, vol. 68, pp. 71–101.

—— (2010), "*Hoffman v. Red Owl Stores* and the Limits of Legal Method," *Hastings Law Journal*, vol. 61, pp. 859–880.

Scott, Robert E. & Triantis, George C. (2004), "Embedded Options and the Case against Compensation in Contract Law," *Columbia Law Review*, vol. 104, pp. 1428–1491.

Shavell, Steven (2004), *Foundations of Economic Analysis of Law*. Cambridge, MA: Harvard University Press.

—— (2006a), "Is Breach of Contract Immoral?" *Emory Law Journal*, vol. 56, pp. 439–460.

—— (2006b), "Specific Performance versus Damages for Breach of Contract: An Economic Analysis," *Texas Law Review*, vol. 84, pp. 831–876.

—— (2009), "Why Breach of Contract May Not Be Immoral Given the Incompleteness of Contracts," *Michigan Law Review*, vol. 107, pp. 1569–1581.

Sheinman, Hanoch (2000), "Contractual Liability and Voluntary Undertakings," *Oxford Journal of Legal Studies*, vol. 20, pp. 205–220.

———— (2004), "Are Normal Contracts Normal Promises?" *Oxford Journal of Legal Studies*, vol. 24, pp. 517–537.

————, ed. (2011), *Promises and Agreements: Philosophical Essays*. Oxford: Oxford University Press.

Shiffrin, Seana Valentine (2000), "Paternalism, Unconscionability Doctrine, and Accommodation," *Philosophy and Public Affairs*, vol. 29, pp. 205–250.

———— (2007), "The Divergence of Contract and Promise," *Harvard Law Review*, vol. 120, pp. 708–753.

———— (2008), "Promising, Intimate Relationships, and Conventionalism," *Philosophical Review*, vol. 117, pp. 481–524.

———— (2009), "*Could* Breach of Contract Be Immoral?" *Michigan Law Review*, vol. 107, pp. 1551–1568.

Simmonds, N. E. (1997), "The Possibility of Private Law," in John Tasioulas, ed., *Law, Values and Social Practices*. Aldershot, UK: Dartmouth. pp. 129–164.

———— (2001), "Contract Law, Theories Of," in E. Craig, ed., *Routledge Encyclopedia of Philosophy* (online), available at http://www.rep.routledge.com/article/T065.

Simpson, A. W. B. (1975a), *A History of the Common Law of Contract*. Oxford, UK: Clarendon Press.

———— (1975b), "Innovation in Nineteenth Century Contract Law," *Law Quarterly Review*, vol. 91, pp. 247–278.

———— (1979), "The Horwitz Thesis and the History of Contracts," *University of Chicago Law Review*, vol. 46, pp. 533–601.

———— (1981), "Contract: The Twitching Corpse," *Oxford Journal of Legal Studies*, vol. 1, pp. 265–277.

Slawson, W. David (1971), "Standard Form Contracts and Democratic Control of Lawmaking Power," *Harvard Law Review*, vol. 84, pp. 529–566.

Smith, Stephen A. (1997), "Contracts for the Benefit of Third Parties: In Defense of the Third-Party Rule," *Oxford Journal of Legal Studies*, vol. 17, pp. 643–663.

———— (2000), "Towards a Theory of Contract," in Jeremy Horder, ed., *Oxford Essays in Jurisprudence*, 4th ser. Oxford: Oxford University Press, pp. 107–129.

———— (2004), *Introduction to Contract Theory*. Oxford, UK: Clarendon Law Series.

———— (2008), "The Law of Damages: Rules for Citizens or Rules for Courts?" in Djakhongir Saidov & Ralph Cunnington, eds., *Contract Damages: Domestic and International Perspectives*. Oxford, UK: Hart Publishing, pp. 33–63.

———— (2009), "The Limits of Contract," in Jason W. Neyers, Richard Bronaugh & Stephen G. A. Pitel, eds., *Exploring Contract Law*. Oxford, UK: Hart Publishing, pp. 1–24.

Spector, Horacio (2004), "The Future of Legal Science in Civil Law Jurisdictions," *Louisiana Law Review*, vol. 65, pp. 255–269.

Speidel, Richard E. (2007), *Contracts in Crises: Excuse Doctrine and Retrospective Government Acts*. Durham, NC: Carolina Academic Press.

Spence, Muriel Morisey (1993–1994), "Teaching *Williams v. Walker-Thomas Furniture Co.*," *Temple Political & Civil Rights Law Review*, vol. 3, pp. 89–104.

Stein, Peter (1988), *The Character and Influence of Roman Civil Law: Historical Essays*. London: Hambledon Press.

———— (1993), "Donellus and the Origins of the Modern Civil Law," in J. A. Ankum, F. Feenstra, J. E. Spruit, C. A. Cannata, Y. Le Roy & P. Weimar, eds., *Mélanges Felix Wubbe*. Fribourg, Switzerland: University Press Fribourg, pp. 439–452.

Stein, Peter & Shand, John (1974), *Legal Values in Western Society*. Edinburgh: Edinburgh University Press.

Stoljar, S. J. (1975), *A History of Contract at Common Law*. Canberra: Australian National University Press.

Suchmann, Mark C. (2003), "The Contract as Social Artifact," *Law and Society Review*, vol. 37, pp. 91–141.

Summers, Robert S. (1968), "'Good Faith' in General Contract Law and the Sales Provisions of the Uniform Commercial Code," *Virginia Law Review*, vol. 54, pp. 195–267.

———— (1982), "The General Duty of Good Faith – Its Recognition and Conceptualization," *Cornell Law Review*, vol. 67, pp. 810–840.

Sunstein, Cass R. (1997), "The Behavioral Analysis of Law," *University of Chicago Law Review*, vol. 64, pp. 1175–1195.

Super, David A. (2011), "The Rise and Fall of the Implied Warranty of Habitability," *California Law Review*, vol. 99, pp. 389–463.

Symposium (2004), "Freedom *from* Contract," *Wisconsin Law Review*, vol. 2004, pp. 261–836.

Thayer, James B. (1893), "The 'Parol Evidence' Rule," *Harvard Law Review*, vol. 6, pp. 325–348.

Threedy, Debora (2000), "A Fish Story: *Alaska Packers' Association v. Domenico*," *Utah Law Review*, vol. 2000, pp. 185–221.

Trebilcock, Michael J. (1994), *The Limits of Freedom of Contract*. Cambridge, MA: Harvard University Press.

Treitel, G. H. (1988), *Remedies for Breach of Contract: A Comparative Account*. Oxford, UK: Clarendon Press.

———— (2004), *An Outline of The Law of Contract*, 6th ed. Oxford: Oxford University Press.

Unger, Roberto Mangabeira (1983), "The Critical Legal Studies Movement," *Harvard University Press*, vol. 96, pp. 561–675.

———— (1986), *The Critical Legal Studies Movement*. Cambridge, MA: Harvard University Press.

Valsan, Remus (2009), "*Causa Fidei Laesionis* in the English Courts and Its Influence on the Court of Chancery," unpublished abstract, available at http://www.law.ox.ac.uk/event=2840.

Veljanovski, Cento (2007), *Economic Principles of Law*. Cambridge: Cambridge University Press.

Vogenauer, Stefan & Kleinheisterkamp, Jan, eds. (2009), *Commentary on the UNIDROIT Principles of International Commercial Contracts (PICC)*. Oxford: Oxford University Press.

Waters, Anthony John (1985), "The Property in the Promise: A Study of the Third-Party Beneficiary Rule," *Harvard Law Review*, vol. 98, pp. 1109–1210.

Watson, Alan (1984), "The Evolution of Law: The Roman System of Contracts," *Law and History Review*, vol. 2, pp. 1–20.

Weinrib, Ernest J. (1995), *The Idea of Private Law*. Cambridge, MA: Harvard University Press.

———— (2003), "Punishment and Disgorgement as Contract Remedies," *Chicago-Kent Law Review*, vol. 78, pp. 55–103.

Weintraub, Russell J. (2010), *Commentary on the Conflict of Laws*, 6th ed. New York: Foundation Press.

Wertheimer, Alan (1996), *Exploitation*. Princeton, NJ: Princeton University Press.

Wessman, Mark B. (1993), "Should We Fire the Gatekeeper? An Examination of the Doctrine of Consideration," *University of Miami Law Review*, vol. 48, pp. 45–117.

———— (1996), "Retraining the Gatekeeper: Further Reflections on the Doctrine of Consideration," *Loyola of Los Angeles Law Review*, vol. 29, pp. 713–845.

———— (2008), "Recent Defenses of Consideration: Commodification and Collaboration," *Indiana Law Review*, vol. 41, pp. 9–53.

White, James J. (2000), "Autistic Contracts," *Wayne Law Review*, vol. 45, pp. 1693–1731.

———— (2004), "Contracting under Amended 2–207," *Wisconsin Law Review*, vol. 2004, pp. 723–751.

White, James J. & Summers, Robert S. (2010), *Uniform Commercial Code*, 6th ed. St. Paul, MN: West Publishing.

Whitford, William & Macaulay, Stewart (2010), "*Hoffman v. Red Owl Stores*: The Rest of the Story," *Hastings Law Journal*, vol. 61, pp. 801–857.

Wilkinson-Ryan, Tess & Baron, Jonathan (2009), "Moral Judgment and Moral Heuristics in Breach of Contract," *Journal of Empirical Legal Studies*, vol. 6, pp. 405–423.

Wilkinson-Ryan, Tess & Hoffman, David A. (2010), "Breach Is for Suckers," *Vanderbilt Law Review*, vol. 63, pp. 1001–1045.

Williston, Samuel (1901), "Repudiation of Contracts, Part II," *Harvard Law Review*, vol. 14, pp. 421–441.

———— (1920–1924), *The Law of Contracts*, 5 vols. New York: Baker, Voorhis and Co.

———— (1921), "Freedom of Contract," *Cornell Law Quarterly*, vol. 6, pp. 365–380.

Winn, Jane K. & Bix, Brian H. (2006), "Diverging Perspectives on Electronic Contracting in the U.S. and EU," *Cleveland State Law Review*, vol. 54, pp. 175–190.

Wright, Lord (1936), "Ought the Doctrine of Consideration Be Abolished from the Common Law?" *Harvard Law Review*, vol. 49, pp. 1225–1253.

Yorio, Edward (1989), *Contract Enforcement: Specific Performance and Injunctions*. New York: Aspen Law & Business.

Zeller, Bruno (2009), *Damages under the Convention on Contracts for the International Sale of Goods*, 2d ed. Oxford: Oxford University Press.

Zimmermann, Reinhard (1996), *The Law of Obligations: Roman Foundations of the Civilian Tradition*. Oxford: Oxford University Press.

———— (2001), *Roman Law, Contemporary Law, European Law: The Civilian Tradition Today*. Oxford: Oxford University Press.

———— (2005), *The New German Law of Obligations: Historical and Comparative Perspectives*. Oxford: Oxford University Press.

———— (2006), "The UNIDROIT Principles of International Commercial Contracts 2004 in Comparative Perspective," *Tulane European & Civil Law Forum*, vol. 21, pp. 1–33.

Zipursky, Benjamin C. (2000), "Pragmatic Conceptualism," *Legal Theory*, vol. 6, pp. 457–485.

———— (2005), "Pragmatic Conceptualism in Jurisprudence," unpublished manuscript.

Table of Cases

Statutes and Restatements

Index